Dear Mama

23th Spt

I am having a lovely time here. I play foot ball every day here. The beads have no springs. Will you send my album, and quite a lot of swops. masters are very nice. I've my clothes ~~now~~, and a belt, and a ~~school~~ school Jersey.

love from

Boy

Love
from
BOY

Also by Donald Sturrock

Storyteller: The Life of Roald Dahl *(HarperCollins, 2010)*

Love from BOY

Roald Dahl's letters to his mother

Edited by

DONALD STURROCK

JOHN MURRAY

First published in Great Britain in 2016 by John Murray (Publishers)
An Hachette UK company

1

Copyright © 2016 Roald Dahl Nominee Limited
Introduction, essays, selection and compilation –
Copyright © 2016 Donald Sturrock

A CIP catalogue record for this title is available from the British Library.

ISBN 978-1-444-78627-9
Trade paperback ISBN 978-1-473-63602-6
Ebook ISBN 978-1-444-78626-2

Typeset in Bembo by Hewer Text UK Ltd, Edinburgh

Printed and bound by Clays Ltd, St Ives plc

John Murray policy is to use papers that are natural, renewable and
recyclable products and made from wood grown in sustainable forests.
The logging and manufacturing processes are expected to conform
to the environmental regulations of the country of origin.

John Murray (Publishers)
Carmelite House
50 Victoria Embankment
London EC4Y 0DZ

www.johnmurray.co.uk

For extraordinary mothers, everywhere.

CONTENTS

Index of Locations   ix

Map: Roald Dahl,
The International Letter Writer, 1925–1965   x

Introduction   xv

A Note on Spelling and Punctuation   xxv

1. 1925–1929 'Send me some conkers'   I

2. 1930–1934 'Graggers on your eggs'   33

3. 1935–1939 'Another iced lager'   91

4. 1939–1940 'Thoroughly good
   for the soul'   147

   Map: Roald Dahl's War, 1939–1941   148

5. 1940–1942 'Don't worry'   181

6. 1942–1943 'Teeth like piano keys'   213

7. 1943–1945 'A good time
   was had by all '   243

Epilogue, 1946–1965
'I won't write often'   277

Acknowledgements   295

Sources and Illustration Credits   297

Notes   299

INDEX OF LOCATIONS

St Peter's School, Weston-super-Mare

Repton School, Derby

RMS *Nova Scotia*

Norway

Newfoundland, Canada

SS *Mantola*

Dar es Salaam, Tanganyika

Nairobi, Kenya

Habbaniya, Iraq

Gen. Hospital, Middle East Command, Egypt

Ismailia, Egypt

Washington

Los Angeles, USA

Texas, USA

New York, USA

Roald's writing hut, Buckinghamshire

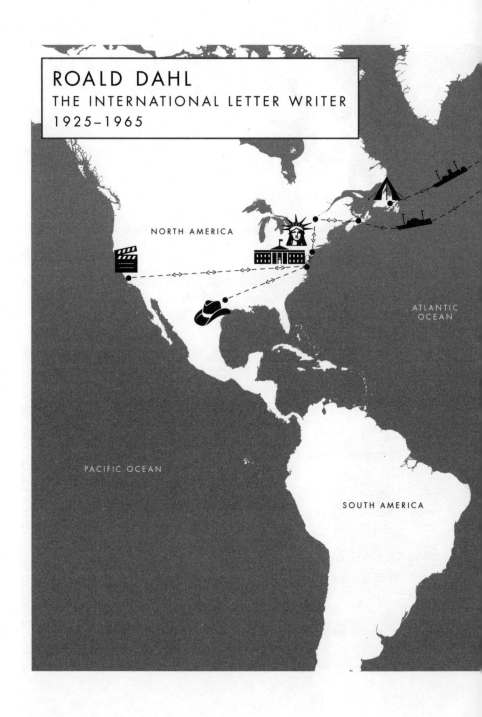

ROALD DAHL
THE INTERNATIONAL LETTER WRITER
1925–1965

NORTH AMERICA

ATLANTIC OCEAN

PACIFIC OCEAN

SOUTH AMERICA

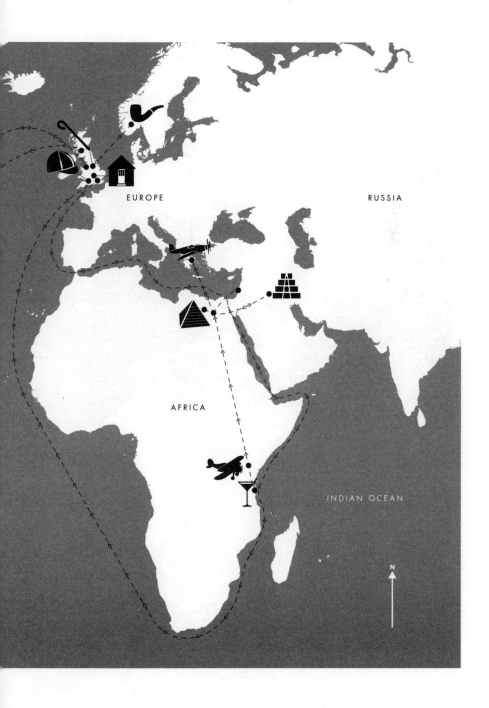

EUROPE

RUSSIA

AFRICA

INDIAN OCEAN

N

Love
from
BOY

Dear Mama   23th Spt
    I am having a lovely time here.
& We play foot ball every day here. The beds
to beds have no springs. Will you send my
stamp album, and quite a lot of swops.
The masters are very nice. I've
got all my clothes now, & and a belt,
and, tie, and a school Jersy.
            love from
                Boy

Roald's first letter home, written in 1925. 'In order to please
the dangerous Headmaster who was leaning over our shoulder,'
he later wrote, 'we would say splendid things about the
school and go on about how lovely the masters were'

INTRODUCTION

Roald Dahl is widely acknowledged as one of the very greatest children's writers. Yet he was a strangely reluctant traveller on the road to that destiny. It was only when he was in his forties that he attempted to write a book for children. And, for many years before that, he appeared to have no aspirations to become a writer at all. He ascribed this sudden change of gear to a 'monumental bash on the head' he had sustained as a wartime fighter pilot in 1940. Crashing his plane in the Libyan desert, he believed, had not only given him something to write about, but the resultant head injuries had also changed his personality, liberating his desire to write. The observation was perhaps disingenuous. For, while Roald did indeed show little interest in writing as a way of earning his living until 1942, he had, since childhood, been practising his craft in another context: writing letters to his mother, Sofie Magdalene.

These letters are remarkable. More than 600 in total, they span a forty-year period, beginning in 1925 when, as a nine-year-old, Roald was sent away to boarding school and ending in 1965, two years before his mother's death. Sofie Magdalene carefully kept each one, and most of their envelopes, holding on to them despite wartime bombings and many subsequent house moves. In his memoir of childhood, *Boy*, Roald movingly described how he discovered them:

My mother . . . kept every one of these letters, binding them carefully in neat bundles with green tape, but this was her own secret. She never told me she was doing it. In 1967, when she knew she was dying, I was in hospital, in Oxford, having a serious operation on my spine and I was unable to write to her, so she had a telephone specially installed beside my bed in order that she might have one last conversation with me. She didn't tell me she was dying nor did anyone else for that matter because I was in a fairly serious condition myself at the time. She simply asked me how I was and hoped I would get better soon and sent me her love. I had no idea she would die the next day, but *she* knew all right and she wanted to reach out and speak to me for one last time. When I recovered and went home, I was given this vast collection of my letters . . .[1]

Roald was given the cache of letters he had written to his mother after her death in 1967. They cover a period of forty years between 1925 and 1965

The larger part of them – and the most intriguing – were written before 1946, when Roald's first collection of short stories was published and he returned home from the USA to live with Sofie Magdalene in rural Buckinghamshire. They are of considerable biographical interest as they provide a comprehensive and fascinating account of Roald's schooldays in the 1920s and 1930s, of his time in Tanganyika just before the outbreak of war, of his training as a fighter pilot in Iraq and Egypt, and of how he saw action in Greece and Palestine. They chronicle his time as a diplomat in Washington too, and his foray into intelligence work in New York, as well as recording in fresh detail how his career as a writer began.

All the letters share the intimate perspective of only son to single mother. And though Roald's personality comes across in bold colours, Sofie Magdalene's is more mysterious. For her side of the correspondence is entirely missing.

She was born in Oslo in 1884 to solid middle-class parents. Her father, Karl Laurits Hesselberg, trained as a scientist, then studied law and eventually went to work as an administrator in the Norwegian Public Service Pension Fund. He rose to become its treasurer. Her mother, Ellen Wallace, was a descendant of the medieval Scottish rebel, William Wallace, whose family had fled to Norway after the English crushed the rebellion.

Karl Laurits and Ellen – the 'Bestepeople' as Roald sometimes affectionately called them – were controlling parents and by Sofie Magdalene's mid-twenties neither she, her brother Alf, nor her two sisters were married. Then in 1911, while visiting friends in Denmark, she met a wealthy Norwegian widower, more than twenty years her senior. His name was Harald Dahl. He was on holiday from Cardiff, where he was joint owner of a successful shipbroking business. Within a matter of weeks, Sofie Magdalene and Harald were engaged.

She was twenty-six years old, sturdy, strong-willed and eager to break the tie with her parents. They reluctantly consented to the wedding, though they disapproved of their daughter marrying a man old enough to be her father and of her abandoning Oslo to live in Cardiff. Perhaps Sofie Magdalene foresaw the fate that would befall her two younger sisters, Roald's aunts, Tante Ellen and Tante Astrid? They failed to escape their father's thrall and were destined to live out their entire lives in the parental home in Josefinegate, like forlorn characters in an Ibsen play. Other members of Roald's family remembered them with a mixture of amusement and curiosity, either drunk or drugged, methodically picking maggots out of raspberries with a pin.[2]

Roald with his elder sister Alfhild and younger sisters Else and Asta on holiday in Norway, probably in 1925. 'We all spoke Norwegian and all our relations lived over there,' he would write in Boy. *'So, in a way, going to Norway every summer was like going home'*

Sofie Magdalene arrived in Cardiff after a short honeymoon in Paris and immediately took charge of her new home. Harald had two children, Ellen and Louis, from his first marriage to his Parisian wife, Marie. Since her death they had been cared for by Marie's mother, Ganou. Sofie Magdalene acted swiftly, summarily kicking Ganou out, and hiring a Norwegian nanny, Birgit, to look after the children. French was banned. From now on only Norwegian and English were permitted in the house.

Within five years Sofie Magdalene had given birth to four children of her own: Astri (1912), Alfhild (1914), Roald (1916) and Else (1917). Asta, a fifth and the youngest, was born after Harald's death in 1920. Roald was named after the Norwegian explorer Amundsen, who had successfully reached the South Pole in 1911, and whose nephew, Jens, worked briefly for Harald's firm, Aadnesen and Dahl, during the First World War.[3] He was his mother's 'pride and joy', her only boy, and therefore treated with special care. His siblings affectionately dubbed him 'the apple of the eye'.[4]

The First World War meant registration cards for Harald and Sofie Magdalene, as both were still Norwegian nationals, but it did no harm to Harald's business and, in 1917, he bought a large Victorian farmhouse at nearby Radyr. It had 150 acres of land, its own electricity generator, a laundry and a collection of farm outbuildings that included a working piggery. Roald later recalled with nostalgia its grand lawns and terraces, its numerous servants, and the surrounding fields filled with shire-horses, hay wagons, pigs, chickens and milking-cows. But Harald was not the easiest of husbands. He could be withdrawn and undemonstrative, sometimes almost cold. Years later, Sofie Magdalene wrote to Roald's friend, Claudia Marsh, confiding that her husband could be 'difficult if the babies made a noise to disturb his work'.[5] She even told her granddaughter, Lou Pearl, that at times she felt frightened of him.[6]

At the beginning of February 1920 Astri, the eldest daughter, was diagnosed with acute appendicitis. The doctor operated at home, on the scrubbed nursery table, but it was too late. The appendix had burst and Astri contracted peritonitis. About a week later she died from the infection. She was seven years old. Harald never recovered from the blow. 'Astri was far and away my father's favourite,' Roald wrote in *Boy*. 'He adored her beyond measure, and her sudden death left him literally speechless for days afterwards. He was so overwhelmed with grief that when he himself went down with pneumonia a month or so afterwards, he did not much care whether he lived or died.'[7] Writing those words, Roald knew only too well what his father was feeling, for some forty years later, he too was to lose his own eldest daughter – also aged seven. 'My father refused to fight,' he concluded. 'He was thinking, I am quite sure, of his beloved daughter, and he was wanting to join her in heaven. So he died. He was fifty-seven years old.'[8]

Sofie Magdalene, his widow, was thirty-six years old. But she was independent and determined. She was also something of a spiritualist and mystic, believing that fate had determined a role for her. And she bravely seized her destiny, single-handedly raising Roald and his sisters and decisively shaping their attitudes. 'Practical and fearless',[9] was how her youngest daughter described her. 'Dauntless'[10] was the adjective Roald used in *Boy*. He admired her toughness, her lack of sentiment, her buccaneering spirit and her laissez-faire attitude towards her offspring, describing her as 'undoubtedly the primary influence on my own life',[11] and singling out her 'crystal clear intellect'[12] and her 'deep interest in almost everything under the sun'[13] as two of her most admirable qualities. He acknowledged her as the source for his own interest in horticulture, cooking, wine, paintings, furniture and animals. She was the 'mater familias', his constant reference-point and guide.

Sofie Magdalene never remarried. 'She devoted herself entirely to the children and the home,' recalled her daughter

*Roald's mother, Sofie Magdalene Hesselberg, before her
marriage to Roald's father, Harald. Roald would later describe
her as 'undoubtedly the primary influence on my own life'*

Alfhild, adding that her mother 'was very like Roald . . . a bit
secret, a bit private'.[14] Soon after Harald's death she sold the
farmhouse in Radyr and moved to Cumberland Lodge, a town
house in nearby Llandaff. Though considerably smaller, the
house had several acres of grounds and was staffed by two
maids and a full-time gardener. In 1927, when Roald was
eleven, the family moved to a rambling house in Bexley, some
twenty miles south of London, where they lived in similar
style until wartime bombing raids forced them to evacuate to
rural Buckinghamshire.

Sadly, not one of Sofie Magdalene's letters to Roald has escaped
the vicissitudes of time. From the handful of her own letters to

other people that have survived, one can see that she writes in a clear, lucid, elegant style, much like her son, though it is sometimes evident that English was not her first language. Yet even so, her powerful, pragmatic, unshockable personality emerges strongly, if only by inference, through her son's correspondence.

Sofie Magdalene was a remarkable mother. She was calm. She stayed behind the scenes. She sought no public acknowledgement of the sacrifices she made for her family. Indeed it was not until Roald was an old man that he wrote about her directly – in *Boy* (1984) and in *Memories with Food at Gipsy House* (1991). But from the beginning of Roald's writing career to the end, she was present in his fiction: whether as the anxious mother desperately identifying herself with her bomber pilot son in *Only This* (1942), or as the wise, imperturbable grandmother in *The Witches* (1983). She was a catalyst too – in ways she probably did not fully appreciate. As a young boy, Roald had been fired by her tales of Norse mystery and magic and by her gossipy love of human frailty and weakness. As he grew into adulthood, he sought to return the compliment, entertaining her with his own stories and observations. Sofie Magdalene was Roald's first audience, but she was also his unacknowledged inspiration to become a writer. One might say Roald's own career as a storyteller begins in these letters.

The idea of publishing some of the letters was first discussed in the early 1980s, when Roald was working on his own autobiographical reminiscences, *Boy*. His editor at Jonathan Cape, Valerie Kettley, was so fascinated by them, she sent an internal memo to her boss, Tom Maschler. 'I read every one of the boyhood letters and enjoyed doing so enormously,' she told him, 'and the more I think about them the more I think it would be a pity to disperse them in *Boy*. They would, of course, be amusing, but their real value and impact to my mind would be dissipated, because I'm doubtful that the younger end of the readership for this book would appreciate them

Roald and his elder sister Alfhild

to the full. They really deserve to be read in sequence (selected of course) when they give a wonderful picture of an emerging personality and growth in every direction . . . Has Roald considered this, do you know . . . ?'[15]

Stephen Roxburgh, Roald's editor in New York, agreed. Roxburgh had been the first person, other than Roald, to look through the letters since Sofie Magdalene's death, and thought they told an amazing story. 'I hope some day something can be done with the letters,' he commented. 'They constitute a remarkable archive chronicling Roald's growth as a person and a writer, and give a vivid portrait of a period and place. Perhaps you can think of a way to use them some time in the future?'[16]

Now, more than thirty years later, in his centenary year, that prospect has at last become a reality. Now we too can revisit the experiences that formed Roald – whether at school, in Africa, as a fighter pilot in the Middle East or a diplomat in Washington.

Stepping into Sofie Magdalene's shoes, we can experience his adventures, recounted in his own unique voice: a delightful and sometimes disconcerting mixture of honesty, humour, earthiness and fantasy. And, as we do so, we will be aware of something she was not; that we are watching the world's favourite storyteller emerge as a writer.

A NOTE ON SPELLING AND PUNCTUATION

In a public letter Roald wrote to schoolchildren in 1984, shortly before *Boy* was published, he talked about his childhood letters and the fact that some of them would appear in his new book. 'They are so badly written and badly spelled they will make you laugh,' he told his audience.[17] Roald's poor spelling continued right through his life – as did his misuse of the apostrophe – and, after hours of careful transcription of these errors, I have taken the decision to correct his spelling. At least for the adult letters. I did this because while, in small doses, his spelling mistakes can be amusing, over the span of a long book such as this, they can become irritating too. I imagined Roald looking over my shoulder as I worked – a bit like Mr. Francis, his fearsome headmaster at St Peter's – and as I did so, I felt sure this is what he would have wanted.

For the record, an ellipsis within the body of an individual letter almost always indicates an internal cut.

CHAPTER 1

'Send me some conkers'

1925–1929

School, on the whole, was not a happy experience for Roald. In the summer of 1925 Sofie Magdalene removed her eight-year-old son from the Cathedral School in Llandaff, Cardiff, because the headmaster had savagely beaten him. Perversely, she then dispatched him to an even more Spartan educational establishment across the Bristol Channel, in Somerset. She told Roald that she was doing this because she had promised her dying husband that she would not return to Norway until she had given all their children an English boarding-school education.

Roald would later vividly recreate his life at St Peter's School, in the run-down seaside resort of Weston-super-Mare (or Weston-super-Mud as he often described it), in his memoir of childhood, *Boy*. He would also use the experience in a more fantastical light in his final children's novel, *Matilda*. Though a glorious piece of exaggerated invention, Crunchem Hall – whose terrifying headmistress, Miss Trunchbull, dominates the book – bears some striking similarities to St Peter's, both in appearance and in the rules of its scary headmaster, Mr Alban J. Francis, which foreshadowed those of the Trunchbull. *Never argue. Never answer back. Always do as I say.*

St Peter's had been founded in 1900 and was housed in a three-storey gabled building, constructed largely out of local stone and blanketed in Virginia creeper. It was surrounded by playing fields, allotments and tennis courts. Around eighty boys, aged between eight and thirteen, were billeted there. Classrooms were

St Peter's, Weston-super-Mare, the boarding school where Roald
was educated between the ages of nine and thirteen. There were
about eighty boys. In hindsight he would describe it as 'a purely
money-making business owned and operated by the headmaster'

on the ground floor, below bleak, uncomfortable dormitories.
Apart from the matron – who ruled the dormitory floor and
prowled the corridor 'like a panther'[18] – the staff was entirely male.
Roald would later describe the school as 'rather like a private luna-
tic asylum'.[19]

The headmaster was the asylum's chief villain, with his gold-
rimmed front tooth, shark-like grin and hair slicked down with so
much pomade that it 'glistened like butter'.[20] Roald's best friend at
school, Douglas Highton, recalled him as 'absolutely brutal . . .
a beastly cane-happy monster', who 'seemed to enjoy beating little
boys on the slightest pretext'.[21] And it was at St Peter's, watched
over by the sharp eyes of its headmaster, that Roald wrote his very
first letter home.

As Roald was eager to remind his young readers, these 'epistles' were written in an atmosphere of censorship. 'If we thought the food was lousy or if we hated a certain master or if we had been thrashed for something we did not do, we never dared say so in our letters,' he explained. 'In fact we often went the other way. In order to please the dangerous Headmaster who was leaning over our shoulders and reading what we had written, we would say splendid things about the school and go on about how lovely the masters were.'[22]

Initially he was profoundly homesick. In *Boy*, he maintained he was so unhappy that he accurately feigned the symptoms of appendicitis and was sent home to Cardiff, where his local doctor quickly discovered his ruse and sent him back to school. But there is no evidence of this melancholy in his letters to his mother. Nor is there any mention of the beatings that he would later describe there. Instead his reports are generally upbeat and filled with curious and comic detail. One senses, right from the outset, that Roald is trying primarily to entertain.

He wrote home to his mother at least once a week, first to Cardiff and then later to Bexley. Many of his early letters touch fondly on the domestic life he had left behind him, though the welfare of the family pets – Mike, Buzz, Barney, Jack and others – often seems of more concern to him than that of his sisters Alfhild, Else and Asta, or 'Baby'. Sofie Magdalene encouraged Roald's love of invention, of natural history, and of collecting. As with several of his schoolteachers, she even indulged in that quintessential schoolboy activity, stamp-collecting. Roald wrote to her about swapping stamps and imperfect Penny Blacks almost as if she was his contemporary – only at a different school. He wrote regularly too to his godfather 'Parrain' – Ludvig Aadnesen, his late father's business partner – as well as to his maternal grandparents, Bestemama and Bestepapa, and his two spinster aunts, Astrid and Ellen in Oslo.

Duckworth Butterflies house photograph, St Peter's, 1925, with
Mr Corrado. 'They were tough, those masters,' Roald would
write in Boy, *'and if you wanted to survive, you had to become*
pretty tough too.' Roald is in the front row, fourth from the right

These early letters already reveal a pleasure in the art of story-telling. Roald's enthusiasm for yarns from the world of nature, his fascination with flying, protagonists who get their just deserts, tales with unexpected endings, and his delight in the triumph of the underdog emerge even in his very first 'story-telling' letter, about bird legends, written as a nine-year-old. Many of the other incidents in these letters – such as the making of fire-balloons, or the Chinese doctor's potion recipe – are antecedents of tales that would later reappear in some form or another in his fiction. Poignantly, the thrill and drama of flying on the back of a bird would feature in his very last children's story, *The Minpins*.

The letters too are interesting for what they do not say. They seldom convey self-pity or unhappiness. This was of course partly due to the critical eyes of the headmaster peering over Roald's shoulder, but it was also the result of a prevailing mental-ity that would continue at British boarding schools for another fifty years. In that situation, admitting vulnerability was treated with scorn and derision. This attitude was held by both masters and children alike. Parents too believed in the values of uncomplaining stoicism and usually took the side of the teacher in any dispute with the child.

Roald addressed this value system in *Matilda* and articulated it through the character of 'a rugged ten-year-old with a boil on her nose', called Hortensia. She has suffered all the tortures that the school can offer, including the dreaded prison punishment cell, the 'chokey'. She is a survivor and she speaks to Matilda, 'with the air of an old warrior who has been in so many battles that bravery has become commonplace'.[23] Matilda quickly perceives that school life is 'like a war'.[24]

Hortensia is a role model for Matilda and, of course, for Roald. She is an outsider, a subversive. She does not complain. She is fearless. She pours golden syrup on to the headmistress's chair and puts itching-powder in her gym knickers. She is an object of reverence: 'somebody who had brought the art of skulduggery to the highest point of perfection.' Her spirit of obstinate resistance informs most of Roald's childhood letters home from St Peter's and helps explain why he never complains. In a conflict like this, there is no point in protesting. It simply makes things worse. Even the kindest parents are of no assistance. 'How can she get away with it?' Matilda's friend Lavender complains, speculating that if she told her father about some of Miss Trunchbull's cruelties, he would surely do something about it. '"No he wouldn't," Matilda responds quietly. "He simply wouldn't believe you."'[25]

October 11th 1925   St Peter's
                                                Weston-super-Mare

Dear Mama

I am sorry I have not writting before. ~~We~~ there was a foot-ball
match yestarday, ~~so I a~~ agenst clarence, and the first eleven lost by
2 goals, the score was 3 goals to 2, but the second eleven won by 5
goals the score was 5 nill. We playd Brien house* on Wedensday,
and the score was 1 all. I hope none of you have got coalds. It is
quite a nice day to-day, I am just going to church. I hope mike is
quite all right now, and Buzz. Major Cottam is going to recite
something caled 'as you like it' to night. Plese could you send me
some conkers as quick as you can, but ~~doant~~ don't send to meny,
~~the~~ just send them in a tin and wrap it up in paper
    Love from
    BOY

 November 8th 1925   St Peter's
                                                Weston-super-Mare

Dear Mama

Thank you for your letter. We had a lovely time on Thursday,
that S.2 Mount Vesuvius was the prettiest. At first it made a gold
fountain and then a silver one, and we had big bonfire with a guy
on top, and another of the prettiest of my fireworks was the snow
storm, it lit up the whole place . . . once I was holding a squib
and I did not know it was going off bang in my hand, and it
made me jump like anything, we had some lovely rockets, they
were going up all the time, there was quite a lot of people

---

* Brean House School was another preparatory school in Weston-
super-Mare.

watching them from the road behind the school; if we had
enough fireworks left over we had to throw them in the bonfire,
on Friday morning the bonfire was still alight. The field was full
of used fireworks in the morning, and we found quite a lot
unused as well.

We played Brien House yesterday but they beet us 4 goals to
none, but they had such a tall goal keeper that his head could
touch the top bar of the goal and he must have been about
fifteen years old, I expect it was because we beat them last time
we played them.

A man called Mr. Nicholl gave us a fine lecture last night on
birds, he told us how owls eat mice. They eat the whole mouse,
skin and all, and then all the skin and bones goes into a sort of
little parcel inside him and he puts it on the ground, and those
are called pellets, and he showed us some pictures of some
which he has found, and of a lot of other Birds. We have got a
new master called Mr Bryant he took us for a walk to a place
called anchor head and we went along a sort of concrete pier
and there was a little island and a few of us jumped on to it and
I was jumping back and I went in up to my knees, it was lucky
I did not go further. We have had quite fine weather but it is a
bit cold today. I hope you are alright. I think this is the longest
letter I've ever written to you. I had a letter from tante-astrid
and I have sent her one back.

Love from
Boy

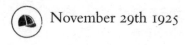 November 29th 1925 St Peter's
Weston-super-Mare

Dear Mama

... We had a lecture last night on bird legends, it was fine, he told us that the wren was the king of birds, he said because the birds were going to have a test, and the one which could fly the highest would be king, and so they started, and the Eagle flew up and up until he could not go any further, nearly all the other birds had dropped out, just then the wren dropped out of the Eagle's feathers and managed to fly a few yards higher, so he was the [King of the] Birds.

Another good legend he told us was how the Blackbird got black. Well he was sitting on the branch of a tree when he saw a magpie hopping about on the tree next to him, and he went over to see what he was doing, and he saw he was hiding some jewels in a hole of a tree. The Blackbird asked him where he got them, the magpie said, just over there, there is a cave, and in this cave ... there are lots of precious jewels, and the prince of riches lives there, but you must not touch anything until you have asked him, and he will let you have as much as you can carry, so the Blackbird found the cave, and he went in and the first room he came to, was full of silver, but he would not touch it until he has asked the prince of riches, the second room he came to was full of gold, still nicer, the Blackbird could not stand it any longer, so he dug his beak in to the thing which looked so nice, and just then the prince of riches came flying through the door, and was spitting fire and smoke at the Blackbird. The Blackbird just escaped, and the smoke made the Blackbird black, and the gold made his beak yellow, but of course that is only a legend. And he showed us all the names the people use to call birds, the Irish used to think the wren was unlucky so they called it the devil Bird.

Love from
Boy

Roald aged ten on a school outing to the beach at Weston-super-Mare

 December 13th 1925   St Peter's
                                          Weston-super-Mare

Dear Mama

Thank you for the letter you sent me.

We had a kind of lecture Friday night, it was really a kind of story, it was on the Pickwick papers, told by a very funny and very nice man called Mr Moss, first he told us a little about the man who wrote it his name was Charles Dickins I expect you have herd of him and the Pickwick papers, well he told us the story it was very funny, once Mr Pickwick was staying at a hotel and in the middle of the night he found he had forgotten his gold watch, so he went down to look for it when he got down there he found it, but how was he to find his bedroom, when he got up the stairs, he went in to a bedroom which he thought was his, when he had got his waistcoat off he put his night cap on he went to the other side of the room and to his seprise he saw some certains drawen across the room, he peeped in and he saw a lady ~~ww~~ with yellow cerl papers on her head, he told us lots of funy things about Pickwick papers.

PTO I will be coming home by the 1.36 I will arive at Cardiff at 4 o'clock on the 17th Thursday please meet me on the station, this is the last letter I am sending you.

Love from
<u>B</u>oy

 March 17th 1926   St Peter's
                                                Weston-super-Mare

Dear Alfhild

Thank you very much for the letter you sent me. The barber is a very funny man, his name is Mr Lundy, when I went to have my haircut last Monday, a lot of spiders came out from under a kind of cupboard and he stepped on them and there was a nasty squashey mess on the floor. In the Drill Display we have a Pyramid, there are a lot of boys standing in the shape of a star fish and some boys in the middle, and a boy standing on one of the boys shoulders with his hands out, it looks very nice.

Love from
Boy

P.S. Dear Mama could you find out the value of a $5 yellow and black and let me know. it is a picture of a kangaroo.
It is from Australia from Boy

The stamp is like this

Nov. 29th 1926.

Dear Mama,

This is my order:-

French = 7m.
Geometry = 3rd
Div. = 3rd.
History = 8m.
Gram & comp = 5m.
Latin = 2nd.
G.P. = 1st.
Geog = 3rd.
Arith = 1st.
Algebra = 1st.

I have gone down in Divinity because a boy told me the wrong preperation and I did not know much about it.

Love from

Roald

Roald's subject class positions for November 1926. He was young for his year and academically bright, but his school reports described him as 'slow' and 'overgrown'

Nov 14th 1926.

St. Peter's
Weston-super-mare.

Dear Mama

I am glad you got home all wright. I ~~last night~~ am writing this letter in the sick-room, I am lying down in a kind of a chair, because I have sprained my ankle, I have also got a cut in my and it is inflaymed, but both of them will soon be all right. We had a paper chase last tuesday it was a topping one, we got awfuly dirty, Another boy called Tilley and me had quite a job finding our way back, in the woods, ~~but~~ and we stoped for about 5 munits because we found a chest nut tree and we got a lot of chest nuts, ~~it~~ and I think it was on that paper chase that I sprained my ankle. On Wednesday we had a House match, we beat Crawford 2 goals to ~~no~~ we had quite a good game. We have been having a lot of heavy showers, but the weather has been quite good. I hope you recieved my order, which wasn't bad, I am now sending you my half term report, which ~~I~~ think is also quite good, and the School Magazine which I think you would like to read. Last Friday I had a letter from Berts papa, he tried to write in

A letter to his mother at Cumberland Lodge, Llandaff,
written from the sick bay. The school was an unhealthy
place. Roald was often ill and at least one boy died in
his four years there. Mike was the family dog

it was very funny, but I think it was quite good for him, he
sent me a lot of swaps, some of them I had not got myself.
I have already swapped a lot, will you send me his <u>adress</u>.
There is not much to say this week, I will send you my order to-morrow
We are having a lecture this afternoon. How is the garden getting
on, and my date & orange tree and how is Jones. Have we got
many apples.

       Love from

      Roald.

HOW IS MIKE.

P.S. have you heard from Louis yet?

November 21st 1926   St Peter's
                                                   Weston-super-Mare

Dear Mama

    Thank you very much for the letter you sent me. My foot is
all right now, and the cut in my finger is much better. I had a
post card from Parrain, he did not say much, it was a picture of
his island and house I think. Is the grave looking nice now? Is
that beautiful yellow Chrysanthemum out yet? That one we had
in the porch last year . . .*

    I am glad you have swopped a lot of rare stamps with Mr
Baker. I am longing to see them. What a pity you can't find the
two yellow stamps Bestepapa gave me. I don't think I want any of
those annuals . . .

    We had a section match on Friday we played the Crawford
Buterflies, they won 4 goals to 2. I have got another quarter-star
this week for Geography from Mr Corrado.

    How is Jack and Pallot
    I will send you my order tomorrow.
    Love from
    Roald

 [postmarked January 20th 1927]

Dear Mama

    I have arrived here all right. I have not eaten any of what you
gave me accept one little chocolate, and on Bristol Station

---

* The grave is that of Roald's father Harald and elder sister Astri in the churchyard of St Peter's, Radyr. Constructed out of pink granite and decorated with
an elaborate Celtic cross, it is by far the largest monument in the cemetary.

Hoggart was sick, and when I looked at it I was sick but now I am quite all right.

Love from

Roald

P.S. Remember <u>not</u> to send *Bubbles* but *Children's Newspaper.**

 January 30th 1927   St Peter's

                                                                         Weston-super-Mare

Dear Mama

. . . I am in bed with flu. Thank you very much for the lovely grapes you sent me they were lovely and the meat juice. What a pity the Red House was no good. What happened to Louis when he was late for school again. Marshali† is lucky to get the brush of the fox.

I am glad Asta is better, but I hope Else will not get it, Alfhild never gets it when we've got it. Did the Bestemama's feel the Earthquake? Once my temperature was 100 and then it suddenly went right down to 97, I have still got one. We have three doses a day of some horribly medicine called quinine, I expect you've tasted it. The doctor has been to see me twice, he has given me some medicine to take now, it is yellow, not very nice. There have been 22 boys in bed and one master has got it. My first two days up here I was starved with only a little jelly in two days. I have been in since last Monday morning. Last Sunday (Jan 23rd) Matron told me to ask you in this letter to send me that birch stuff you put on my hair in the holidays for scurf in a bottle, can you send it as

---

* *The Children's Newspaper* in 1919 with the aim of keeping young children abreast with the latest in world news and science. At its peak it sold half a million copies each week. *Bubbles* was a similar, but less practical, weekly journal for kids.

† Adventurous friend of the Dahl family who hunted, travelled and lived near Radyr.

soon as you can, please. I don't know when I am going to get up, a few days, perhaps. I don't want you to send me raisins for a little time now because I wont be able to have them. I can't write well lying in bed (with a pencil). Give my love to every body.

Love from
Roald

 February 27th 1927   St Peter's
                                                                Weston-super-Mare

Dear Mama

. . . Yesterday we had a topping lecture on cave dwellers, and Prehistoric animals from Mr. Savory, he gives us one every term.

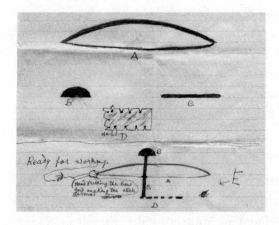

The most interesting thing of all, how they made fire, I have shown you more or less the things required, a bow with some strong cord in it as in A, then a piece of wood (cedar is the best) with notches in the side, and where the notch ends a small hole is to be made as in D, then you get a bit Holly wood as in C rounded at both ends so that one can fit in one of the notches in D, then a solid piece of wood as in B with a

18

notch underneath it which fits into one of the rounded off end of C.
Now how it works! – Place an end of C into one of the notches of D,
C is now standing upright, then twist the cord of the bow round the
stick (C) You know there is a notch in the bottom of the buffer, place
this on top of C, you will have to make it fit nicely, and make it smooth
so that it can go round, then you pull the bow, and you will find that
the stick (C), will go round, and then it gets very hot at the bottom. By
the way you put a flat bit of tin under the notch which you are using,
and after a minute pulling you will see a little heap of dust from the
stick, then you will see the thing smoking like Hell, and then you will
stop and fan the little heap a little, and you will see it go red, if you get
some thin wood shaving and put it on the heap it will flare up.

I have swopped a black penny and an imperf blue penny, the
black penny is of course was imperf, they are both perfect
specimens, I could not get a black penny for you I am sorry,
because he would not swop any more.

Love from Roald

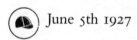 June 5th 1927   St Peter's
                                                 Weston-super-Mare

Dear Mama

Thank you for your letter . . .

How much are the monkeys at Harrods? It would be rather
nice to have one. Last Sunday I sailed my submarine, but it did
not dive at all, and did not go fast, then we took off the front
fins, it went just the same along the surface, only much faster.

Did Harrods say that it dived? But I like it nearly as much as it
is now . . .

I am sending you the school mag.

Love from

Roald

12/7/27

Dear Mama.

I'VE WON THE
SWIMMING CHAMPIONSHIP
CUP UNDER ELEVEN this afternoon.

love from

Roald

One of many letters Roald wrote telling his mother of
his sporting successes. He was tall for his age and boxed
as well as playing cricket, football and rugby

October 2nd 1927 St Peter's
Weston-super-Mare

Dear Mama

Thanks for your letter. You haven't sent my watch yet, isn't it ready? I am going to write to Parrain as soon as I have finished this letter, but if I'd written to him before I would have saved a penny-halfpenny.

You know there were two warts on my feet which he didn't get out properly, well, matron scraped them out easily, I didn't feel anything, they were quite dead.

Ask Alf, Else and Asta to collect all the conkers they can when they get to Bexley. There's a good conker tree there, I want to keep them for next year, I got quite a lot here off the conker trees.

By the way, I've got the highest conker in the school, 273, its last years.

I've just had a bad cold, but it's nearly gone now . . .
Love from
Roald

 October 16th 1927 St Peter's
Weston-super-Mare

Dear Mama

. . . I recieved my watch alright on Thursday, it's going splendidly now, it was a bit fast at first so I regulated it.

All my five warts have disappeared, you couldn't tell there'd been any there at all now.

Mr. Corrado has got bronchial pneumonia, and will be away for about a month, so we've got a new master called Mr. Millington, he's very nice, he has got a long hanging ginger moustache, and is quite fat. I hope you haven't forgotten my

Chrysalis which I found in Norway, I left it in a small pot, just where Alfhild & co. had the Garden of Eden.

I hope you'll like Bexley, especially the woods . . .

Love from

Roald

 October 22nd

Don't be surprised if you don't receive my letter on Monday. I'm going out with Mrs. Highton on Sunday, so I will write to you at the first opportunity, probably Monday.

Love from

Roald

J'esperè que Tu comprenez Ce letter. D.H.

P.S. Yeg har vegt ent meg Highton i aftens*

Comprenez–Vous

---

* This letter, composed by both Dahl and Douglas Highton in four languages, shows Highton attempting to write 'Love from Roald' in Greek script and a less successful attempt by Roald to write 'I am going out with Highton for dinner' in Norwegian. Sofie Magdalene must have been amused when Highton asked her in French whether she understood their game.

January 22nd 1928   St Peter's
                                                      Weston–super–Mare
Dear Mama

   Being the first Sunday there isn't much news worthy to be related.
   We arrived here at four-ten and went up by Charabanc, and
the driver stopped so that we could visit Woolworths, etc. I went
to Smiths to get a fountain pen clip.
   We started doing prep yesterday (Saturday) having had all the
extra books we needed doled out on the previous morning.
   By the way I've been moved up into the fifth form this term.
   We've got a new matron called Miss Farmer in place of Miss
Turner who left last term, one night in the washing room, having
inspected a boy called Ford she KISSED HIM.
   We have four new boys this term, only one border, Ragg II
from Petergate, Braithwaite, Curby, and Dickenson are the day
boys. Ragg II, a rogue I think, is unfortunately in our section . . .
   Love from
   Roald

P.S. Please send my riding breeches as soon as possible.
Also a pot of Marmite please. RD

 February 12th 1928   St Peter's
                                                      Weston–super–Mare
Dear Mama

   Thanks for your letter. There are exactly 23!!!!!!! boys with the
measles! and all the other schools (boys) in Weston have got it. Hope
Louis hasn't had anything else wrong with him at the doctor. By the
way, what a Salamander? You said the Kesslers had put one in the
garden; Pears' Dictionary sais it a kind of Lizard, uncombustable to fire!!

... Yesterday we 'made fire'!! with a stick and some wood, you know, I tried to show you once at Glentworth Hall. We've got four nurses (including matron) now, one is a night nurse.

The French Play is on the 17th of March, do come and see it, Highton is acting, and on the following Sunday there is a kind of recital of some poem by Shakespeare; oh! Of course, you always go on in the afternoon don't you.

Highton is taking a Scholarship exam to a school called Oakham in Rutlandshire on the thirteenth of March; hope he gets it.

Not much news this week.

Love from

Roald

 February 25th 1928   St Peter's
                                                     Weston-super-Mare

Dear Mama

Thanks for your letter. Most of the measles boys are down, except about two ... Ford is still very bad, he got better on Friday, but has again got very ill.

I rode on Friday morning, and Hill's horse cantered on in front, I was going to catch him up when he suddenly started off at full speed. My horse, Dilerish got very peeved at this and tried to catch Hill's horse up, we both went an terrific lick, and nearly came off.

Angel has just received a marvellous motor canoe, which is paddled by a man, all his joints move just like real, and if you set a thing at 20 yards it will go twenty yards turn and come back to you, or if you like it will right turn or quarter turn, its furthest is 35 yards which in all is 70 because it comes back and its least is 5 yds. We are going to try it in the boat pond today.

Love from

Roald

P.S. We have just been informed that poor little Ford died early this morning.

 March 18th 1928   St Peter's
                                            Weston-super-Mare

Dear Mama

. . . When I come home, wouldn't it be best for you, when you had met Alfhild, to stay in town and do your shopping etc. have dinner there and then come and meet me. It would save you from going backwards and forwards from Bexley. Yesterday we played St. Dunstans, and got beaten in both elevens, this was proved by two donkeys first, when (I went as linesman) when we go there we always pass a field with two donkeys in it, and when they are facing us we loose and when they've got there backs to us we win; it always comes true.

By the way, HIGHTON has got a SCHOLARSHIP to Oakham, it's jolly good because they get a half holiday. It the first scholarship to Oakham from this school!!!! He won't be leaving till September, thank goodness!

Love from
Roald

P.S. Have you heard from Louis, yet? This is a marvellous contraption of an X-ray, which I sent up for, and paid only 1s in stamps, you look through the little holes at some writing on the other side, then place a coin or something in between, you can still see, I'll show you at home.

Roald

Duckworth Butterflies house photograph, 1928.
Roald is in the middle row, first on the left

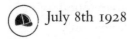 July 8th 1928

St Peter's
Weston-super-Mare

Dear Mama

. . . Last Friday we went down to the station and saw the
Duke and Duchess of York who came to Weston to open a
Hospital (didn't you see it in the Paper), we had to wait three
quarters of an hour before they came, you see they came by the
ordinary 1.15 from Paddington, except that they had a whole 1st
class coach for themselves, we got quite a good view but not a
long one, they were driving at about ten miles an hour.

As the train was passing Yatton, just outside Weston, it ran
over a man and killed him! And as they were driving through the
streets of Weston, the iron monger, 'Dover' who's a bit mad, fired

6 shots of a blank cartridge, and the Duke thought he was going to be assassinated, and nearly fainted!!!

. . . At present I'm reading quite a decent library book, because I've finished From the East to the Moon*. You know, it didn't say anything about finding dwarfs there, perhaps it is a shorter edition.

Love from
Roald

 February 17th 1929   St Peter's
                                               Weston-super-Mare

Dear Mama

Thank you for your letter. Have you had a lot of snow? We have! But, in spite of the cold, our water supply hasn't frozen, like yours did . . .

On Friday, it snowed again so that in the end the snow was about six inches deep. Yesterday we had a really topping time . . . we all went to Uphil by Charabanc and we found a topping slope there, something like the one at Bexley only longer, and quite as steep, we went at least 35m.p.h.; you see, Ragg lay on top of me.

On the side of this was a very steep slope, which I tried three times but each time I came off. We got very wet but that didn't matter at all because we were in our footer clothes . . .

By the way you haven't yet told me what kind my bike is, although you've told me all about it.

Love from
Roald

---

* Probably *East of the Sun and West of the Moon*, an old Norse fairy tale.

P.S. (i) I'm quite warm enough thanks, I don't think I want a scarf or a Pullover.

Roald

P.S. (ii) Please enclose a bulb for my Nonox torch when you send my watch, as my mine has bust.

Roald

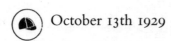 October 13th 1929   St Peter's
                                                    Weston-super-Mare

Dear Mama

Thanks awfully for the Roller skates, they are topphole. Were they the largest pair? At full stretch they fit toppingly, but if my feet grow much more they won't fit. We skate on the yard; we had a fine time last night after tea; You see, the chaps who haven't got pairs, pull you. At one time I had eight chaps pulling me with a long rope, at a terrific lick, and I sat down in the middle of it; my bottom is all blue now! We also have 'trains'; you get about ten chaps to pull, and with a long rope, and all the roller-skaters hang on to each other, and go around; but if one chap falls all the ones behind him come on top of him! The yard is getting quite smooth now . . .

By the way, I had a birthday present from Marshali yesterday. It was a thing called a 'Yoo Yah' which runs up and down on a string, but is very hard to work.

It is very fascinating, but she confessed that it was bought at Woolworths; and she said that it was the craze there. I show you when I get home . . .

Love from

Roald

November 3rd 1929

St Peter's
Weston-super-Mare
Somerset

Dear Mama

Thanks awfully for my pen and the chocs. The nib is not functioning properly yet, but I hope that is only because it is new; otherwise it is fine.

Roller-skating is going toppingly, and the whole school, with the exception of about five is now on wheels!

I am glad you did'nt get me another pair of gymshoes; you know, the ones I bought in Bexley and you said they smelt like a cats crap. Well, they fit wonderfully on to my roller-skates, (or, rather, the other way around), and on Friday when we box, we are allowed to skate, and no one else is able to, much, because roller-skates wont fit onto other gymshoes. Oh dash, I've just dropped my pen onto the letter, and there isn't time to write it out again. Incidentally, the pen thought it necessary to make a blotch over a certain word [CRAP], but it did not quite succeed in covering it up!!

P.T.O.

Last Sunday we had a cinematograph, about the Navy it was jolly good.

Isn't Alfhild a lucky dog getting two pounds from Parrain, I must write to him!

Love from
Roald

29

November 10th 1929   St Peter's
                                                        Weston-super-Mare

Dear Mama

Thanks for your letter; my pen nib is topping now, and is just right. So glad the balloons and fire-works went well, where did you have the bonfire?

. . . I had a letter from Ashley the other day, and he told me about the fire-balloons, but he didn't mention the maroon. He must be having a fine time now; he said he sits down and smokes, and watches bugs through his microscope.*

. . . We also had our fire-works on Wednesday, as it rained on Tuesday. The bonfire was enormous, with a topping Guy on the top, and when it had been covered with petrol it was set alight; you can imagine that there was a blaze. And we each had our fire works, and it was great fun.

Yesterday we had a lecture on China, it was jolly good, and the person described a Chinese Doctor, and said their prescriptions for flu' was generally as follows:

A Rats tail.
A snake.
Chickens legs.
Grass.
Ashes of paper.
Tiger bone-tea.
And the shavings of a Rhinoceros Horn.

I think that that would beat any of Ashley's!
Love from
Roald

---

* Ashley Miles was a young pathologist, later a distinguished immunologist, who got engaged to Roald's half-sister Ellen in 1929. They married the following year.

December 1st 1929   St Peter's
                                                  Weston-super-Mare
                                                  Somersetshire

Dear Mama

Thanks awfully for your letter, and Else's. I think you are quite right about the presents for the masters. Only don't get books which they have read, for instance, they have all read 'All Quiet on the Western Front'. I expect one of the animal books will do for Capt. Lancaster, because he is especially interested in animals.* Then you will get Mr. and Mrs. Francis something in the way of a flower vase or something like that; but please don't forget to address it to me.

Just now, I asked Mr. Francis what they meant by having to wear 'tail-coats', so he took me up and dressed me in his, they are horrid things, coming right down at the back.†

Yesterday we played Walton Lodge at Clifton, but as their field was flooded, we played in another big field, where there was another navvy game in progress; it was very amusing; they argued with the referee, saying things such as this: 'He's no more off side than I am'

'Garn, stop yer gob, ref, or I'll come along and clump you over the ear' . . .

You must excuse my writing going rather bad at the end, but as Mr. Francis put that coat on me! I hadn't much time left. The coat looked awfully funny.

Love from

Roald

---

* Captain Lancaster was the model for Captain Hardcastle in *Boy*.
† These were the tailcoats Roald would have to wear at his next school, Repton.

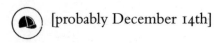 [probably December 14th]
St Peter's
Weston–super–Mare
Somersetshire

Dear Mama

I am writing to tell you that this afternoon I received quite safe and sound the vase in an enormous box. There is no chip or anything, and it is topping, and at the moment, not knowing where to put it, I have left it in the charge of Miss Farmer, the Matron, for that is where some other chaps have left their leaving presents. And I think it will be quite safe there . . .

I suppose you know I am coming home on FRIDAY 20th by the 8.20 train (in the morning) I believe it arrives at about 11.30, but you better look it up. As I said in my last epistle, I can easily come home alone, if you don't want to come up. Let me know.

Please excuse this bad writing, but I am writing it in Prep, under rather a bad conditions, also, and an excuse is that someone is singing downstairs and the noise closely resembles that of a fly's kneecap, rattled about in a billious buttercup, both having kidney trouble and lumbago!

Love from

Roald

CHAPTER 2

—

'Graggers on your eggs'

1930–1934

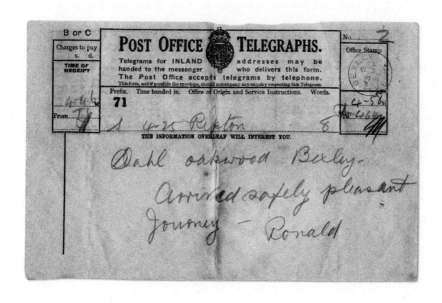

POST OFFICE TELEGRAPHS.

Telegrams for INLAND addresses may be handed to the messenger who delivers this form. The Post Office accepts telegrams by telephone.

This form, and if possible the envelope, should accompany any enquiry respecting this Telegram.

THE INFORMATION OVERLEAF WILL INTEREST YOU.

Dahl oakwood Bexley.
Arrived safely pleasant
Journey — Ronald

Roald arrived at Repton in January 1930. Originally a sixteenth-century foundation, the school had been revitalised by Victorian energy in the nineteenth century and was now an archetypal British public school, located in a strip of rolling English countryside not far from Derby. Roald was placed in the Priory – one of nine boarding houses that were scattered around the town. Each was a community of its own: around fifty boys, roughly twelve from each academic year. It was where Roald ate, slept and studied; where he made friends and enemies; and where, dressed in the regulation school uniform of pinstripe trousers, starched butterfly collars and long black tailcoats, he would write home once a week to his mother about his adventures and experiences.

Charles Pringle was a couple of years junior to Roald in the Priory and, even at the age of eighty-eight, could still vividly recall its complex routines. Each new boy, he remembered, was assigned a study – occupied by around five others and run by a senior boy, a 'studyholder' – as well as a bedroom dormitory or 'bedder'. The studies were small. 'Each person had a little desk, in which they kept their books . . . Prep [preparation for the next day's classes] was done communally for the first two years, then in the study.' Bedders were also shared by between five and seven boys of all ages and there were similarly strict rules of seniority. 'Each boy moved bedder every term, moving up the room as you got more senior. There were communal washing facilities, and communal loos, with no doors on the loos. These were out in the open by the yard near the fives courts opposite the boot room.'[26]

The school practised the custom of 'fagging', in which younger boys were treated by older boys almost as if they were their personal servants. Tim Fisher, another ex-student and the son of Dahl's first headmaster, Geoffrey Fisher, explained the system to me. 'The new boy was the "bim fag", the junior fag, then there was the "tip fag", the senior fag who would show him the ropes and [help him] discover how the place worked.' The fag's tasks included cleaning the study, supplying it with coal for the fire, keeping the fire lit, and polishing the studyholder's shoes, buttons, badges and buckles.[27] The studyholder might also have been a school prefect or 'boazer' and these – at least according to Roald – were the most dangerous and feared characters in the school. If they did not exactly have 'the power of life and death' over younger boys, they certainly had the capacity to inflict mental pain on them, as well as physically punishing them.[28]

Roald was profoundly unhappy at Repton. The first draft of *Boy* paints a picture of a young man for whom the pleasures of childhood had been stifled by an unfair system, devoid of affection and feeling, which had forced him into the role of outsider. 'Four years is a long time to be in prison,' he writes. 'It seemed as if we were groping through an almost limitless black tunnel at the end of which there glimmered a small bright light, and if we ever reached it we would be eighteen years old.'[29]

In that early draft of *Boy*, Roald describes being bullied by several senior boys, including one incident where he was left 'half-drowned' in the house lavatories.[30] But these same tormentors adopt a different guise in his letters home. The abusive and supercilious Middleton, for instance, whose 'cold, rather close eyes', Roald villainously recreated in his short story 'Galloping Foxley', comes across in the letters as nothing more threatening than a connoisseur of wild irises. Flowers act as camouflage too for W.W. Wilson – the ringleader of those responsible for the bog-holing – who emerges instead as something of a dandy, obsessed with exotic breeds of chrysanthemum. Roald was creating a diversionary illusion. And, at least for his mother, these fictions were largely effective. She had no idea of her son's sufferings when she came up for the school's Speech Day in the summer of 1930. Writing shortly afterwards to her daughter Else, she noted that she was 'very pleased' with Repton. 'It is much nicer than I expected it to be . . . Roald's study was absolutely crammed with flowers.'[31]

Roald was not an academic high flier. He was a misfit. A Norwegian. As a thirteen-year-old, he had size eleven feet and was taller than most of the teachers. Nor did he care to toe anyone else's line. Charles Pringle summed him up in one adjective: 'unconventional'.[32] He was always ill at ease with Repton's authoritarian hierarchy. His school reports accuse him of 'idleness', 'apathy' and 'stupidity' and he is described by turns as 'lethargic', 'languid' and 'too pleased with himself'. He never became a boazer. He was however good at sports, including boxing, which doubtless helped ease some of his torments. 'You had to be good at games,' Nancy Deuchar, his housemaster's daughter explained to me, with a knowing grin. 'If you weren't good at games, life could be *really* hard.'[33]

His friendships too were unpredictable. Roald respected his housemaster, S.S. Jenkyns or 'Binks', and liked his wife, 'Ma' Binks, and their daughters, 'the Binklets', but his closest friendship was with an older boy. Michael Arnold was some two years his senior and similarly self-reliant. Roald hailed him to his mother as 'the cleverest boy in England'[34] and later insisted she call him by his first name, which was unusual in a world where everyone was referred to by their surnames. Roald's unabashed delight in smoking may surprise some younger readers, unfamiliar with its prevalence in 1930s Britain. From the age of sixteen, Roald was allowed to smoke at home and his mother thought nothing of buying him a special meerschaum pipe to use while on holiday in Norway. The habit was even tolerated at school.

Repton, like St Peter's, was not a healthy place. 'Roald caught everything there,'[35] recalled his elder sister Alfhild. He had a heart murmur. He got mumps. He suffered from headaches and constipation. He was often injured and always desperately trying to avoid the latest bouts of cold and flu. His letters from this period brim over with medical information and sometimes his requests read like a lexicon of contemporary medicines. Food also features strongly. The boys received regular rations from home in the post – including eggs, which often broke on the journey – to supplement what the school provided and several times a week the fags cooked meals for the other members of their study on portable paraffin primus stoves.

Roald's love of wildlife and the countryside is much in evidence and he spends a lot of his spare time at school walking and bird-watching in the surrounding fields and dales. It was a passion he shared with his mother and sisters. The family home in Bexley was a dizzying menagerie of dogs, cats, mice, tortoises, rabbits and canaries which, like the cardinal birds – imported from the Americas – were allowed to fly free through some parts of the house. His mother's letters were filled with the antics of her domestic menagerie and Roald's involvement in them is delightfully expressed in a comic letter, written to the cardinals themselves and expressed in Repton vernacular.

The letters abound with the classical adjectives of the moment. 'Topping', 'decent' and 'graggers' – Repton slang for 'Congratulations' – pepper many of the letters. Yet through the schoolboy slang, the Repton letters show Roald practising as a humorist and growing into a dextrous narrator, able to make sharp, comic observations about the adults around him. His relish for the joys of youth is also striking. Whether tobogganing down a hill, rioting on a train, chucking powder around his dormitory, or climbing illicitly up the tower of Repton Church, the letters convey an exuberant and infectious delight in the adventures of childhood, and a sense that these simple, unsophisticated pleasures can put misery and adversity to flight.

The world outside school hardly seems to exist. There is barely a mention of politics, while a sense of the Great Depression appears only when it is rumoured that, because of economic cutbacks, the school's fancy tailcoats might be replaced by regular, more inexpensive suits. Fortunately for the Dahls, the children's trust funds seem to have seen them through these bumpy times. The regular 'field days' and activity in Corps, however, are a reminder that outside the dales of Derbyshire, Europe was moving steadily towards armed conflict. Roald, though, is more interested in plotting holidays in Cornwall, Tenby and Norway than he is in the fate of the National Government in Britain or the rise of Nazism in Germany.

In Roald's penultimate year at Repton, Michael Arnold was expelled for having sexual relations with younger boys in the Priory. Both Roald and his mother appear to have been very forgiving of Michael and the two boys remained close, going on holiday together to Norway and the Côte d'Azur after Michael's expulsion. The incident once again reveals how much Roald sanitised the more disagreeable aspects of school life for his mother and how eager he was to create a reassuringly carefree fiction. When the truth emerged, Roald was forced to admit to his mother that he had lied. His housemaster also felt compelled to write to her and explain what had happened.

The tone of his letters to his mother changes subtly after this incident, which possibly marked a rite of passage into adulthood for young Roald. I have included a letter from Roald's housemaster S.S. Jenkyns to Sofie Magdalene in this chapter, not only because it reflects the prevailing attitudes to teenagers and sex in schools at the time, but also because it is so revealing of Roald's psychology and his desire not to worry his mother with bad news. It is interesting that she kept it with Roald's own letters.

For a family that appeared to be so open about many things, it is curious that the subject of Roald's own sexual life is strictly off limits. It always would be. At the end of his time at Repton, his sister Alfhild's Norwegian friend Kari became the object of Roald's desire, but although some boys were known to have 'wives' in the local village, Roald was not one of these.[36] Indeed, later in his life he would argue that the world had got too casual about sex and that adolescents would do well to return to the values that marked his own teenage years.

> I am very glad I did not have to go through the horrors of promiscuity that torture today's children. In this benighted age, girls and boys treat the sexual act rather as rabbits do, or cattle . . . Some of you may not believe this, but I promise you that a young man in the 1930s would have to court a girl for six months before he got anywhere near the mattress. He would have to ply her with flowers, give her meals he could ill-afford and behave generally with immense circumspection. If he tried anything too early, he got the boot.[37]

In his remaining time at Repton, Roald indulged his passions, both for invention and photography. One senses that his darkroom gave him a creative hinterland, as well as a refuge from some of the unpleasantness of school life. Then, in 1932, after months of persuasion, his mother bought him a motorcycle for Christmas. The machine was chosen by his half-brother Louis. Roald hid it in the barn of a local farm and revelled in driving it through town, muffled up to the eyeballs so no one could recognise him. His final weeks at Repton were also spent building gigantic fire-balloons, which he and his friends constructed out of tissue paper, wire and paraffin. They launched them with glee into the night sky. Roald claimed the biggest was eighteen feet high.[38]

Before he left Repton in the summer of 1934, Roald had already decided university was not for him. He wanted something more adventurous. He was finished with education and with hierarchies and so he set off on a walking expedition to map uncharted areas of Newfoundland. He left his schooldays behind him with no regrets whatsoever.

January 18th 1929 [*sic*]*   The Priory House
                                                                Repton

Dear Mama

I don't suppose that you will get my postcard before this letter, it is Sunday tomorrow.

It's topping here, I don't have to fag for the first fortnight, and I have a desk in a very decent chap's study, K Mendl. I am in Lower four, B, Mr. Carter's form, and I believe by a fluke I'm top of it in Maths; All the chaps here are very decent, both Mr. and Mrs. Jenkins, being exceedingly decent; (Mr. Jenkins is always called Biggs.)† The dormitories are called 'Bedders' and the school shop sells everything from an unsophisticated piece of bacon fat, to the school blazer. That reminds me, I have got all my footer things, and straw hat; my house colour is black and blue, the hat-band being something like this:

The white stripes are really blue, and the bit filled in is black.

I think Priory is easily the nicest house of the whole 9. All the houses being totally separate buildings, and a good way apart from each other . . .

The best bit of it is we are allowed to go anywhere we like when nothing is happening. This afternoon I went for a walk over the fields and over a stream called the 'Stinker.' Tonight we are cooking our own supper, sausages etc.

---

* The year was actually 1930.
† Jenkyns was actually known as 'Binks', not 'Biggs'. Dahl gets this right in future letters.

Our study is called the Gramophone Study and has a large gramophone and heaps of records. It is jolly good; it's singing away just behind me now.

Please tell Else and Asta not to forget to feed my mice.

I don't at present want a cake, but I'll let you know when I do.

Love from

Roald

P.S. I forgot to tell you, I sleep in a comparatively small bedder; seven chaps in it.

R.D.

The arch through which all boys entered the main buildings of Repton School. Originally built for Repton Priory, which was dissolved in 1538, it was moved to its current position in 1906 Roald's 'house' on a neighbouring site was called the Priory

January 25th 1930

Priory House
Repton
Derby

Dear Mama

Thanks awfully for the tablets. I took some a few times and the indigestion has stopped now, they are jolly good. I have just got the diary, it's a topping one, thanks awfully; I was just going to ask you for one. Oh! Before I forget it, will you send me a new tooth-brush, and a tube of Euthymol;* my tooth-brush is getting soft, and I am running out of tooth-paste. Please don't forget to send it.

We have half-holidays on Tuesdays, Thursdays and Saturdays, and the latter day we have no prep, at least I don't because I have joined the 'Mussoc,' or Musical Society! It's jolly good fun; to begin with you get off prep, and sing instead; you see when you come first, you have to go to Dr. Stocks to have your voice tested, and he may ask you if you with to join the 'mussoc', and you say 'yes', and he puts your name down, and on Saturday evenings, instead of doing prep we go and practice, for an exhibition at the end of the term; there are about a hundred chaps, but we practise in sets. They try to make me sing Alto! At any rate its much better than prep, in fact its jolly good sport, and rather funny.

I am in form, 'Four, two, B,' or 'Lower Four B', I am top of it in maths, and fourth in French. The work is comparatively easy, and at present it is easier than the St. Peter's. The form master is Mr. Jack Carter, a jolly good chap. Mr Jenkyns provides supper on ordinary days but on the three half-holidays, we get same thing for ourselves at the Grubber.† The Grubber is a very worthy man who keeps the school shop, and he has in stock

---

* Dahl's favourite brand of antiseptic toothpaste was characterised by its pink colour and medicinal taste.
† Dahl would later recreate the Grubber in his children's story *The Giraffe, The Pelly and Me* (1985).

every conceivable kind of sweets, chocolate, or anything like
Force* or tinned fruit and even sardines and biscuits. He also sells
everything to do with sports-clothes and sport. For supper I
generally have tinned fruit or force. Next term, I'll bring a
Primus and have baked beans, tomato soup, asparagus, or eggs
and bacon, and having fires in our studies, we have toast.

. . . The chap who takes us in maths; Major Strickland
(Stricker), who is chief of the O.T.C. is terrifically humorous.
For instance, he will suddenly turn to you and say 'Are you a
slug, do you leave a long slimy track behind you?' The chap says
'no' and he then says, 'Well you're a fungus, in fact you're wet!'
And perhaps he'll make a statement: 'Do you understand,' and
then he will repeat it about six times, either getting louder and
louder, or softer and softer, in the end developing into a
concentrated mumble. He doesn't mind being answered back,
but rather likes it; he is also very funny when arguing. For
instance, if he can't think of an answer, he'll say 'Well you're . . .'
then after the 'you're' he will start mumbling, gradually getting
louder and louder, and in the end developing into a low pitched
groan. I believe he's half-baked! He's a short man with a face like
a field elderberry, and a moustache which closely resembles the
African jungle. A voice like a frog, no chest and a pot-belly, no
doubt a species of Rumble-hound.

Please don't forget the toothpaste and brush.

Love from

Roald

---

* An American cereal, popular in the UK from 1903 until it ceased production
in 2013. It was promoted using a popular cartoon figure called Sunny Jim.

March 2nd 1930   Priory House
                                                    Repton
                                                    Derbyshire

Dear Mama

. . . You seem to have been doing a lot of painting; but when
you paint the lav. don't paint the seat, leaving it wet and sticky, or
some unfortunate person who has not noticed it, will adhere to
it, and unless his bottom is cut off, or unless he chooses to go
about with the seat sticking behind him always, he will be
doomed to stay where he is and do nothing but shit for the rest
of his life. But no doubt an excellent cure for constipation, as the
person, having nothing else to do but to 'rear', will consequently
be trying to rear the whole time!

The school boxing competition was held last week
(damn I can't write straight, I'm sorry). We all
watched it, one chap was knocked out from half past
eleven, and came round at half past one. It was just a
lucky shot, the other boy got him just on the side of his face, just
above the eye.

I don't think that I've told you what we do every day, sort of
thing: the First bell goes at quarter-past seven, and the fag who is
on water in each bedder, gets up and fills the cans with hot water,
and closes the windows. Then, if he wants to, gets into bed again.
The second bell goes at half past seven, and everyone must be
down for prayers by quarter to eight. Then we have a cup of
cocoa and biscuits, and go out to an hour of work. On arriving
back we have breakfast, then there is about half an hour in which
you may do what you like. Then you have prep in the house
then go out for the rest of morning's school.

The house wireless is now working toppingly,

Love from

Roald

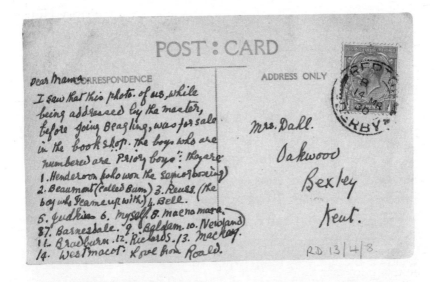

*Roald (no. 6) joins fellow schoolboys beagling, March 8th
1930. 'Yesterday,' he told his mother, 'there was a meet of the
Burton Beagles, and half the school went Beagling (you know,
they have a pack of small hounds, and a master, and several
other men called whips). The thing is to catch a hare'*

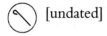 [undated]

The Priory House
Repton
Derby

Dear Mama

Thanks awfully for your letter, and the eggs and cake, of which none were broken. The cake is topping.

Do you know what Turton & I had yesterday for supper? Stewed Gooseberries. You see Turton had some sent him, amongst other things, by an ex-cook of his living in Norfolk! At any rate we stewed them & put sugar in and they were fine.

I mustn't forget to tell you all about Field Day. It was lovely weather, though very foggy when we paraded on the paddock at half past seven, (in uniform, of course.) Then we received our rations, including two apples, and stuffed it all in our packs then we marched to Willington, which is about 20 minutes march.

Then we assembled in houses on the platform, and got into the train. There was heaps of room, and they were jolly good carriages, each lot of seats had a table, you know the kind. The journey took about an hour and a half.

When we got to Kettering we fell in again in our platoons, and marched through the town, (which is quite large, at least it took about 20 minute to get to the other end of it.)

Then we marched 4 miles out into the country, where we split up into companies of about 8 people. By the way there was no time to eat our lunch, so we ate it on the march. The boy commanding my company was called Yates, a school boazer and Head of New House. He is jolly nice.

The enemy had got into a wood called Geddington Chase, quite a big one, and we had to attack them.

However Yates thought he would do something rather cunning, so he took us (10 boys including myself) round the side of the wood and to avoid being seen we often had to crawl about on our bellies in the long grass, and over fields. Then we got to the part of the wood which the enemy were not occupying, and marched right through it at a colossal pace, (it was about 4 miles wide!) Two boys could not keep it up so they were left behind. When we got to the other side, we marched to the left so that we were directly behind the enemy. As a matter of fact it was rather a cunning thing to do, on Yates' part.

Then we moved towards them, but we were spotted just below the wood, and very soon the enemy had three entire platoons, (about 80 boys) against us. We lay down behind a ridge and fired as hard as we could, the old Lewis gun popping away as fast as it could. But soon, although we had 50 round of blank each, we soon ran out of ammunition, at least all except the Lewis gun which still went on. In about a quarter of an hour J Mendl arrived with his lot, and together with them, we charged the enemy and drove them back into the wood, and soon we had them surrounded on all sides. And the umpire, Colonel somebody-or-other, stopped the fighting, saying that the Leys had been utterly defeated!

A mess, showing our Route.

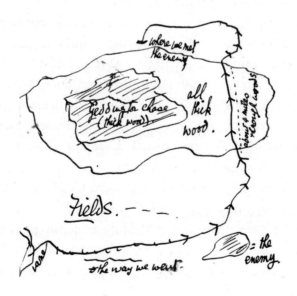

On that diagram, if you can make any thing of it, is only the actual spot of the action. You see we had to march 5 miles back to the station.

Going home, we went by a different line, going through Uppingham & Oakham, where Highton is; I saw both the schools . . .

I have ordered rather a fine photograph of one of the school buildings, it is a very large one. I will send it as soon as it is ready.

Love from
Roald

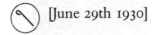 [June 29th 1930]   Priory House
                                                                            Repton
                                                                            Derbyshire

Dear Mama

Thanks for your letter. Yesterday was quite hot and very fine, and I spent most of my time either in watching the match, which we lost, or in going up and down the church steeple. The latter amusement is unknown to the majority of boys, but if you get on the right side of the old woman who looks after the church, she will let you go up. You go through a tiny door in a corner, and up a very steep narrow stone winding staircase. After going up for about a solid five minutes you arrive at the belfry, and you are able to see all the bells (colossal things) and if you are unlucky, they strike while you are there. To begin with it gives you such a shock that you nearly fall all the way down again, also it nearly deafens you. The first time, I went up with Palairet, (that boy who sat next to us) and when we got to the belfry he managed to step on a rod which he shouldn't have, and we saw the hammer slowly rising, then crash down upon one of the bells, it having struck 'one' at ten minutes to eleven! From the top, you get a wonderful view of the surrounding country . . .

Love from
Roald

Speech Day at Repton, June 1930. Roald (highlighted) looks out at the camera as if in a different world from the people around him

 [postmarked July 11th, 1930]

Priory House
Repton
Derbyshire

Dear Mama

Thanks awfully for the parcel which I got this morning, the eggs were alright too. I also got the shoes from Daniel Neil. They are fine. Very comfortable, and just the right size, so I am wearing them. That Dainite sole is jolly good stuff, it wears much better than leather, and is much lighter than crepe-rubber. Here is a photo of some of the spectators at Speech Day, watching the match. The arrow points <u>to your</u> black hat, and my hat can be seen just on your right, or nearer to the foreground of the photo.

Love from
Roald

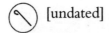 [undated]

The Priory House
Repton
Derby

Dear Mama

By the monthly order, I am 15th in my form out of 21 boys, however my form master, Mr. Wall is the most bad tempered man on the staff, but otherwise he is very nice.

When he looses his temper he goes completely mad, he rushes round the room, tips his desk clean over, with everything on it, kicks all the furniture in the room as hard as he can and especially his grandfather clock, which is gradually ceasing to exist. He shouts and yells, rushes round the room, and on Wednesday he nearly threw himself out of the window! I've never seen anything so funny in my life.

Love from
Roald

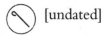 [undated]
The Priory House
Repton
Derby

Dear Mama

Thanks awfully for the cake you sent me at the beginning of the week, it was awfully good. And the parcel I got yesterday. Everything was all right. No eggs broken, or anything; that Tobler choclate is simply marvellous; I like the coffee one best, I think.

Last Tuesday was the sale of work, we got off prep, and went into Pears School, (the big hall, where the school assembles for films, etc.) It was full of all sorts of stalls and amusements. One thing which was rather subtle was as follows: a kind of horse, with a long body: as the long body revolved, and you got on at the back, and had to get to the other end and get the coconut suspended above the horse's head. It was jolly hard though, because whenever you tried to get along the horse its tummy started revolving and you tumbled off. I only got one coconut.

There were heaps of other things. One rather subtle one; you had to drop pennies into a glass tank of water; the tank was full of sixpences, and if you covered one you had it. Only when you dropped your pennies into the water they went all squiggly, instead of falling down straight.

. . . I am now in training for House Matches, and I have got to observe the following things:

'No eating between meals, except fruit which you may eat as much as you like.'
'No fizzy drinks.'
'A certain amount of "charged" exercise every day' (when there is no football I play fives.)
'Skipping after prayers in the evening.'

'No soaking in hot baths.'

'A cold shower after baths.'

'No playing on the yard.'

'A good walk on Sunday afternoon.'

I don't really mind any of it a bit. It means that I eat more fruit & less sweets which I suppose is really good . . .

Love from
Roald

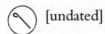 [undated]

The Priory House
Repton
Derby

Dear Mama

Thanks awfully for your letter and the parcel. My cold has gone, but it took about six days, and I used nearly a whole bottle of Mistol on it. At any rate its gone now.

The cream was marvellous. We had it last night with Force. We also had fried potatoes and two fried eggs each. Jolly good supper . . .

The new matron arrived last Tuesday, she comes from London, has got hair like a fuzzie-wuzzie, and two warts on her face, otherwise not bad! I think I shall offer her of my corn paint . . ..

Love from
Roald

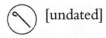 [undated]
The Priory House
Repton
Derby

Dear Mama

Fire! No one here's talking about anything else. I'll tell you the whole story: Last night at 6.15 we all went to Pears School (you know, the huge hall into which we went for the speeches) to see a film called 'When Knights Were Bold,' a very funny film. When the whole thing had finished, and we were all waiting to go, Major Strickland (the head of the O.T.C.) came rushing in and yelled for the gramophone to be stopped, so that he could make himself heard. He was very red in the face and sweating. Then he bawled 'All fire brigade outside!' (The school fire-brigade consists of 4 boys from each house, who have been trained and each knows his job.)

The rest of the school, in fact all the school – minus 36 boys stayed in Pears School. There we were kept waiting for fully 20 minutes. Then – 'All houses except Priory go back at once'. So we were left in there, wondering what had happened. Then we were told that the Priory had caught on fire, and that the whole of MacBrayne's study (the one I am in!!!!) had been burnt to ashes!

Mr. Carter (house-master of the Orchard) took us all there and gave us some supper. Then we went back to the Priory. The flames were really enormous, and the heat was colossal. All the Minimaxes in Repton were fetched, and we banged them on the floor and fairly poured it on.* After 45 huge Minimaxes had been emptied on to it, it began to show signs of going out. There was also a long double string of fellows passing water cans back and forward from the nearest tap. It was then that the Burton fire brigade arrived and finished the thing off.

---

* A fire protection company, founded in Berlin in 1902. They quickly became world-wide brand-leader in fire extinguishers, developing the foam extinguisher in 1926.

I thought that the whole place was going to burn down, but I think that 45 Minimaxes was too much for it. The whole place stank of burning and Minimax, and it got in your throat. I coughed all night. However, we got to our bedrooms which the firemen assured us were safe, but to us it looked as though they were being held up by about 2 thin planks. We picked our way gingerly up the stairs, (which was all black and charcoaly) of course all the electric light had fused long ago. We got into our beds which were brown and nasty, and I don't know how, but I managed to get to sleep.

The place looked grimmer than ever by daylight. All the passage was black, and in our study absolutely nothing was left. I luckily was wearing my new coat, but my new mack has completely gone. Mr. Jenkins has made us all write out a list and prices of what we've lost. Mine comes to £25 at the very least. The sort of thing it consists of is:

Mack £5 Hockey Stick, Squash Racquet, Fives gloves, Corps boots, house shoes. Writing case, hair brushes, books etc.

I wonder how much we will get back. Please don't write to him or anything because it will only make him more worried.

Now I have got some 'getting money news' for a change. We had a house sweepstake on the Grand National, and the tickets were 1s/ each. I only had 6d left, so I shared with Montgomery who also only had 6d. We drew a horse – Annandale, which came 3rd!! So we got 3rd prize 10s/-. Jolly good.

Right, I'll be coming by the usual train (leaves Derby at about 8) on Tuesday, and will look out for Louis. I suppose you'll be letting me know for certain if he is meeting me.

Sorry, no time for any more, I've got the whole of Grey's Elegy to learn by tomorrow, 124 lines!

Love from

Roald

[postmarked May 13th 1931]   Addressed to:
Cardinal and
Mrs Wolsey 'Oakwood'
Bexley
Kent

Dear Cardinals

Graggers on your eggs. For goodness sake don't go eating them or pushing them into the goldfish pond.
Love from
Roald

 [undated]   The Priory House
Repton
Derby

Dear Mama

Thanks awfully for your letter and the collar. Gosh, my new bat is marvellous. The first time I used it was on Thursday, in league house matches. I made 70. The side made 150. Then they went in and made 60. So we won easily. I have been doing quite a lot of photographing lately. Here are some photographs. I have taken a lot out and given to the house photograph book. That one of the cow just after it has done piss has come out rather well. Those sheep are rather nice too. I had a devil of a job to get close to them because they are so timid, and had to keep going ba-a-a the whole time!

. . .

Love from
Roald

P.S. Please return the photos.

A photo of Roald's study at Repton which he took in 1930.
Photography became a serious interest while he was at school
and he spent hours on his own in the school darkroom. 'I was
the only boy who practised it seriously,' he would later write, and
after the summer of 1931 the subject dominates his letters home

 [undated]   The Priory House
                                          Repton
                                          Derby

Dear Mama

Thanks awfully for the cake and the Radiostoleum. Did those
dates only cost 1/3, there were an awful lot in the box, 4
layers . . .

See if you can make sense of the following. There are no stops
or capital letters put in.

If you go to the zoo you will see elephants playing the
saxophone you first take a breath and swallow the mouthpiece is

then taken between the lips and firmly to boot polish people are proud to be or not to be is what hamlet said when bathing the baby care must be taken to clean up his sparking plugs should be the regular practice of every driver who wants easy running does are female wives may forgive husbands never tell took a bow and shot the apple through the inside left raced down the field and shot a gaol civilization being what it is is still necessary for locking up the undesirable flies fly and pigs don't brown is a dentist and can be seen any day drawing stumps is a sign that the match is over.

DON'T OPEN

Until you have tried to make sense of the other
    Correct version, punctuated.

If you go to the zoo you will see elephants. Playing the saxaphone, you first take a breath and swallow. The mouthpiece is then taken between the lips and firmly to boot. Polish people (people from Poland) are proud. To be or not to be is what Hamlet said. When bathing the baby care must be taken. To clean up his sparking-plugs should be the regular practice of every driver who wants easy running. Does (animals) are female. Wives may forgive husbands never. (William) Tell took a bow and shot the apple through. The inside left (in football) raced down the field and shot. A gaol, civilization being what it is, is still necessary for locking up the undesirable. Flies fly and pigs don't. Brown is a dentist and can be seen any day. Drawing stumps (in cricket) is a sign that the match is over.

[postmarked April 25th 1932]   Priory House
                                                                    Repton

Dear Mama

I arrived here alright at 3. and went on by bus.

Had rather an amazing lunch on the train. First while I was
having my soup I leaned my Daily Mail I leaned it up against my
bottle of cider, and the bottle promptly decided to fall over:
much good cider on opposite seat. The next course was an egg
(poached) covered in Spaghetti!! Jolly good. Next a chicken with
breast meat on its legs! Probably a crow. It was during this course
that the waiter spilt a lot of bread sauce over my Daily Mail. Very
funny, but I couldn't read any more about Hitler for he was
covered with bread sauce.

Binks was very perturbed because at least six boys are not
coming back yet for various reasons. I had tea with him.

Love from
Roald

 [postmarked May 30th 1932]   The Priory House
                                                                    Repton
                                                                    Derby

Dear Mama

. . . There is the very hell of a thrill here today. Last night we
had nearly 4 inches of rain! A record, with the result that the
Stinker (i.e. the small stream which runs through Repton) has
burst its banks and poured forth its vengeance and its water all
over the country side. Every field is about 3 feet under water.

Some of the streets here are or were this morning about 3 1/2
feet under water and hundreds of people have been flooded out
of their houses. Several masters were completely cut off from the

School this morning, and had to come to school by boats! People can be seen going about fetching bread, milk and other things on floating sofas or wooden bedsteads, You'd think that I was exaggerating but I'm not. Several houses had no milk this morning because the farmers couldn't get to their cows. We did.

The Priory is in no danger for it's standing on the top of a sort of gradual hill. It is the street below it on the right & left that gets it. But it's going down rapidly now because it's not raining any more. The Stinker which is usually a little stream is now a raging torrent! Generally about 6 feet wide, it's now about 50, going through gardens & farms. But worse is to come for the fields at the moment have only been flooded by the Stinker. But the Trent is rising at the most colossal pace, because it's receiving the

Roald with his camera watching a school cricket match, 1932

waters of the Dove & the Derwent. Tomorrow the complete
Trent valley will probably be about 4 or five feet under water. It's
a very dull day indeed so I won't be able to do much
photography. I hope it'll be better tomorrow. A Brick wall on the
side of the stinker and a Bridge have been completely swept away.

. . . Yesterday, as cricket was out of the question, I played fives
with Binks. He's very humorous, rushing about the court
shrieking out what a little fool he is and calling himself all sorts
of names when he misses the ball.

I have a plunge in the plunge bath every morning it is
frightfully cold, but it freshens you up like any thing.

I must go and develop some plates in the dark room with
Michael.

Love from
Roald

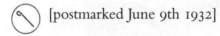 [postmarked June 9th 1932]   The Priory House
                                                                  Repton
                                                                  Derby

Dear Mama

. . . We haven't got a study-holder in our study yet because
Kelsey hasn't come back, so we are going to decorate the study
ourselves. Everyone's getting some flowers, so do you think that
you could bring some down in the car. Sweet peas etc. There's
one more thing I'd like you to bring. My three Fives cups. They
have to go on the mantlepiece. By the way please don't bring any
yellow flowers, because they wont go with our curtains &
hangings, which are a sort of bright orange.

I don't think that they are altering the date of the inspection
after all. I'm afraid that it's still being held on the Tuesday before
Speech Week. Yes, it would be a good idea to go to Dovedale or

to Ma Sharp. Turton, Reuss, Michael (you mustn't call him Arnold) and myself are going crayfish fishing this afternoon! We're going to some ponds called 'Orange Ponds' where there are lots of crayfish. We are making a big net out of wire netting. We tie lots of bits of string to this and with a nice rabbit's head or something tasty tied in the middle of it, we lower it in to the pond. Then we shall pull it up and with luck pull up some crayfish at the same time. We want them for two reasons:

(a) To try to eat them.
(b) To put in a boy's bed.

Rather funny, don't you think so.

By the way; last Sunday we went for a fine walk. About 12 miles. Binks signed us off school call (roll call), (which he is always willing to do if you want to go for a long walk). We walked to a place called Woodville, quite a big town. We went passed this, and lay down in a wood to eat our cake, which constituted our sole rations. We started out at about 2 o'clock and got back at six. Our return was not without excitement, for in one field a bull saw Turton's red hair, and proceeded to chase us for rather a long way. The worst of it was that we couldn't run very fast because we were laughing so much. But we got behind a hedge in time . . .

The weather has been fine this week and we've started bathing. I've bathed twice in the school baths.

In the midst off all this good weather, it suddenly clouded over yesterday, and I'm sure a cloud burst. The worst of it was that we were watching the match but luckily I had my umbrella with me as a sun-shade. The rain fairly poured down for about a quarter of an hour. The cricket square which had been surrounded by a mass of boys lounging in deck chairs was suddenly surrounded by tents. Very curious tents made of rugs, macs, umbrellas and deckchairs. We just lay there and waited for it to stop.

My six shilling umbrella kept it out very well, and Turton proclaimed in a loud voice how good his 4/- Irish self-opening umbrella was, for this time it had only let 'quite a lot' of the rain through and not all of it!

As the sun is shining I must now go and put our rabbit head outside, to make it a bit more appetising for the crayfish.

Love from

Roald

P.S. We've been doing quite a lot of enlarging etc. and are getting on fine.

 [probably October 2nd 1932]   The Priory House
                                                    Repton
                                                    Derby

Dear Mama

Thanks for the telegram and the parcel. We have eaten multer* once more last week, and have felt no ill effects. But it is quite probable that Michael's illness was caused by them . . .

At any rate they weren't frightfully good to eat, so we took a 2lb jam jar full of them, put them in a handkerchief (clean), and squeezed all the juice out of them into another jar. We got quite a lot of juice, and into that we put an ounce of yeast, bought at the grocer's, and 18 spoonfuls (tea) of sugar. You see the Repton sugar is so inferior, that you will only get one teaspoonful worth of sweetness out of 4. We stirred it all up and put it in the drying room for about

---

* Norwegian cloudberries..

36 hours. It's pretty warm in there. All this time it bubbled like hell and gave off heaps of Carbon Dioxide. When we took it out, a glorious smell was coming from it, a sort of very strong sweet potent multer stench. But it was very thick & full of yeast, so we filtered it through some blotting paper, through which it is still dripping. It comes out as a clear light yellow liquid, tastes lovely & is jolly alcoholic. I think multer wine is a very original drink. But you needn't be frightened for we will neither imbibe it in vast quantities, nor will we get drunk; our distilleries are too small.

Those plums are marvellous, thanks a lot for them. But there is still something else I would like you to send me – a Tek toothbrush (hard) and a <u>Jew's Harp</u>! A good one with a <u>nice high note.</u> I walked all over Derby trying to get one when I was coming here. I went into a grand-piano shop & tried to look as if I looked like I was the sort of fellow who would be likely to buy a grand piano! Then I asked for a Jew's Harp. The man told me politely that he'd never heard of them, but he had Bechsteins!, 'was it a baby grand? You would, sir'!!!

At last I managed to get a rotten little one for 3d. I play it a lot, but it's rotten. There are several in the house (Oakwood) but I don't think any of them are much good. Louis will get one for me. By the way, how is Louis, how many German girls has he got engaged to. I hope you've told him about my motorbike.

Tragic news: all my hard collars are much too small for me, they are the same size as my shirts' necks were before they were enlarged. So I bought 6 bigger ones at 9d each & had it put on the bill.

Also one or two of my winter shirt necks are much too tight, so I'm going to get the Grubber to send them away to be enlarged. The others are O.K. Funny that they should be like that, because I've <u>hardly</u> got a neck like a bulldog!

I'm going for a walk now.

Love from

Roald

October 23rd 1932

The Priory House
Repton
Derby

Dear Mama

Thanks awfully for your letter . . .

. . . Michael & I saw some stuff advertised in a Paper the other day – 'No more razors, no more frequent shaves. Use Snow'. You just put it on your face and take it off again & it takes the toughest of whiskers off with it. Se we sent 3/ !!! up & got a tin of this stuff. It proved to be a white powder, which you have to mix into a paste with water. Well, we did it in the bedder a few nights ago, and on mixing with water the most disgusting smell (i.e. Hydrogen Sulphide) was given off. It stank the whole bedder out & it stank the whole upstairs passage out with a smell likened unto the greenest & stalest of turnips. But we put it on our faces, and very little happened. It hardened on Michael's face, & he had to chip it off with a nail-file. It did absolutely nothing to me at all. So it was a bit of a failure. We had all the prefects coming in in turn cursing & asking what the smell was.

The next night we thought we'd do something else with it. So when a boy was out of the room we put some in his Pi-jerry (Po). He pumped without seeing it, & the foulest of all foul smells came out. I don't know what action uric acid had on it but it was much worse than water. The whole place was stunk out. Windows were opened & doors used as fans with a vengeance. The offending Pi-jerry was rushed outside & poured down a sink. It was most frightfully funny, & and we fairly rocked with laughter . . .

Love from
Roald

[probably November 7th 1932]   The Priory House
                                                      Repton
                                                      Derby

Dear Mama

Thanks very much for the box of apples, bananas & pears. They are all fine, the pears were a bit squashy, but very good. But far better was the news of the motor-bike, it acted on me like a squitter pill acts on a constipated man, i.e. a complete revival; your letter might even have been a dose of Kruschen Salts!* An 'Ariel' too; one of the four kinds I was hoping he would buy for me. What have the insurance people let me off with; they oughtn't to charge £4.

Last Monday we had a field-day, a jolly good field-day. It was a marvellous day & after an hour's train journey we arrived at a place called Rugely in Staffordshire. From there we marched to Cannock Chase, stopping on the way to eat our lunch . . .

Cannock Chase is a marvellous place: thousands of acres of heather & bracken on a deeply undulating plain: Deep valleys etc. Then we had tea here at some barrack huts, – quite a good tea, except for the tea itself, which they chucked about the place in dirty buckets. It had a distinct and glorious flavour of cow dung . . .

Been playing quite a lot of football & fives this week.

What pity about Else's fingers but she was a fool not to have seen doctor at the beginning. I hope it will soon be better.

Love from
Roald

---

* An old-fashioned remedy for constipation.

[probably November 14th 1932]   The Priory House
Repton
Derby

Dear Mama

Thanks very much for your letter. Glad Else's finger is a bit better.

Also glad that a bit more progress has been made towards the insurance of the motor bike. I'll undertake not to take anyone on the pillion alright as long as they will insure it at a decent price. They all seem to be absolutely absurd about it. Dash me, what the hell's an insurance company for. They can't make all their own rules & fix all their prices to suit themselves. They seem to think that a motor cyclist aged 16 is merely going to take his bike & run it into a brick wall as a matter of course. Call for the manager of the next insurance co. you go to & tell him that I'm quite willing to bet him sixpence that I wont have a smash. He'll say 'are you trying to be funny'. Then you ask him what his premium is for me & my bike & he tells you some exorbitant price. Then it's your turn to say 'Are you trying to be funny – You're merely a damn fool frightened of losing a penny even if you gain double the amount in losing it' is what you should say to him. Please let me know about further progress.

Love from
Roald

P.S. I've got an expensive shopping list for you: a Tube of Nostroline & a tin of Kalzana.* Could you please send them.

---

* These were remedies for colds and calcium deficiency. Even as a boy, Roald was obsessed with proprietary medicines.

[probably November 27th 1932]   The Priory House
                                                        Repton
                                                        Derby

Dear Mama

 . . . I'm glad you told [the insurance company] that I would only
ride [the motor bike] in the country, etc. etc. If they aren't decent
about it now they ought to be shot. You can also tell them I'm
terribly nervous, and show them as proof the hole in the floor of
the car which I have made by pressing with my feet as Alf takes a
corner. If they then say, 'Well, why has your foolish son chosen such
a powerful bike for himself?' You can say 'Why not, he's frightened
of cats'. At any rate please let me know as soon as they tell you.
 . . . Does Else honestly want to go to school in Switzerland. I
suppose it's damn nice there. Only it's a hell of a way away. I
expect she's getting quite a connoisseur on Schools!
 Just been confirmed by the Bishop of Derby. There are quite a
lot of parents here, but I didn't ask you, because it's a long way and
damned expensive. I hope you don't think I'm going to become a
religious fanatic. Talking about religious fanatics – this new Boss is
one. He's most frightfully nice, but he's a religious fanatic.* Far too
religious for this place . . .
 Love from
 Roald

* The new headmaster was John Christie, who would you go on to beat
Michael Arnold savegely before Arnold was expelled.

[? January 30th 1933]   Priory House
                                                         Repton

Dear Mama

Thanks awfully for all the parcels. I fitted the skates on to my corps boots all right, but of course they were on all wrong. Last Wednesday, the first day of skating Michael & I, wishing to skate apart, as he was learning, wandered off about 5 miles, and found a marvellous pond near some old caves – Anchor Caves . . . Everywhere we skated, we were preceeded by a long crack along the ice. But it didn't quite give way. When we got home I changed the skates, (pointed them inwards more). The next day we went in a Charabanc to Melbourne where there is a huge lake, about the size of Danstone Park, hardly huge, but large for round about here. By then Michael had also got some skates, from the Grubber. Gosh it was funny to see him learning. He spent most of his time on all fours. Instead of complaining of aching ankles, his wrists ached!

    . . . On the edge of the lake, Crummers, a fat master, was patiently instructing his small daughter to skate. Suddenly the ice gave & they both went in. Of course they were pulled out, but the only thing that Crummers said to his daughter while they were in the freezing water was 'keep cool' . . .

    Love from
    Roald

 [probably February 21st 1933]   The Priory House
                                                         Repton
                                                         Derby

Dear Mama

    . . . we had a grand time yesterday, The Maynell hunt met at the Cross here yesterday at 12 o'clock, We got off last hour to see them. Michael took his lunch with him and ran after them in football clothes. I was going to, too, but I asked too late. So I changed immediately after lunch and set off alone to find them. When I'd got to Crewe's Pond, Ma Binks came along in her Austin Seven, & told me to hop in. I got in & the mudguards almost rubbed against the wheels on my side, & the springs made the most alarming noises. But she didn't seem to notice this. She drove me along about 2 miles, when I got out and went across country, because it was no good following them on the road any more. It was a lovely day, except that the wind was a bit cold so one had to keep running. There wasn't a soul in the country except a few ploughmen. By asking them I was able to follow the hunt up, and take a few shortcuts. One ploughman was very excited – it appeared that the 'bloody forx' had run right between his plough and his horses, 'an I could 'ave slain the devil dead with t'stain, but I thought me better of t'it'.

Eventually I got up just after the 2nd kill. (Michael saw the first but not the second.) After that the hunt dispersed and set off home along the roads. I was then about 8 miles away from Repton, and could just see the spire in the distance. So I set off – heading straight for it. When I got to Orange Ponds, where I saw 23 skinned moles hanging neatly upon the barbed wire fence, – it started to snow like hell. When I say 'like hell' I mean exactly the opposite. At any rate it came down so hard that the ground was white in no time. It was pretty grim running home against this. Halfway I sheltered behind a steam roller for 5 minutes, but I saw that it wasn't going to stop so I ran home. Had a hot bath. In the changing room, I found Michael who said he had had the deuce of a good time, & had seen the first kill, which I had missed, but had missed the second kill which I had seen. By the way, Sir William Bass, the man who makes a little beer, was the master. I've just measured on a map & I make it that I went 23 miles!

. . . It was damned funny the other day in the study. You see we aren't allowed to cook supper on the fire on weekdays. But Michael & I had put a small tin of Pea soup in front of the fire to heat – one hour before supper – which was quite within the law. When I came to take it off, the tin was bulging at both ends. Hellish pressure inside owing to the steam of the boiling soup. I covered it with an umbrella & pierced it from behind – then took away the umbrella & stood at a safe distance; an enormous jet of steam & pea soup shot out, and continued to shoot for about 2 minutes. – All over the study, the place was covered with condensing pea-soup.

. . . Please can you send me a Tek Toothbrush.

Love from

Roald

 March 26th 1933   The Priory House

Dear Mama

Thanks for your letter. I'm going down to the house today, this afternoon. All this week I have been perfectly well, but still infectious, so I have wandered about the place with another fellow called Beaumont, who is up here because his nose is always bleeding. We've played Golf every day on the fields with some old clubs we found here, and Hodder gave us some old balls. Darn good fun. We each put our hat in the opposite corners of the field & played into them as holes. There's also a billiard table here. Last night Beaumont & I played Hodder & Sister for a shilling each. Hodder is marvellous & frequently makes breaks of 50. So they beat us, & we had to fork out a bob.

I lost another bob to Hoddy last Friday, on the Grand

National. I betted him a shilling to £1 that Annandale would win. If it had won he would jolly well have paid me £1, But it fell over another horse early on. I went down to his house to listen in to it on his wireless.

By the way, I asked him about riding my motor-bike to Tenby; & he said that it would be quite alright, because the only glands that I had swollen were a few just under my ears, and those only slightly, and that when 2 weeks have elapsed since the swelling disappeared they will be just the same as they were before. It is over a week already, so two weeks will be just as I get home.

. . . It's marvellous weather here now, & I was going to play golf with Hoddy in a field nearby, but Sister, – who is grossly religious, stopped us because it was Sunday.

Is Kari coming to Tenby? You never said anything about it before. But it will be fine if Ellen & Ashley come for a week. Jolly funny to see Ashley on Louis' motor-bike too.

I'll probably write or postcard again before Friday.

Love from

Roald

Roald with his friend Beaumont, smoking 'bowls' in the Derbyshire
countryside, in summer 1933. Earlier that year he told his mother:
'All this week I have been perfectly well, but still infectious,
so I have wandered about the place with another fellow called
Beaumont, who is up here because his nose is always bleeding'

May 14th 1933

The Priory House
Repton
Derby

Dear Mama

Do you know what has happened; Michael has had a severe mental breakdown and has had to go away for the rest of the term before he goes to Oxford. He is staying in a lonely inn, up in Westmoreland all alone + perfect quiet, which is essential for him to have. I don't think he'll mind it, because he rather enjoys tramping about on moors & things alone all day. I have had quite a lot to do arranging all his things, returning all his books to the masters from whom he had borrowed them, packing a crate full of his books, & putting everything else in his trunk. I'm very sorry he's gone, but now I go about with Smith, that fellow from Bromley. To show how darned popular he was – half the house has written to him already.

... By the way, has Else gone back to school yet. If not when is she going. I expect I shouldn't speak too much on them dropping my summons* if I were you. They obviously won't. I should have thought that they had got it all filed up, & were just waiting for its turn on the list. Of course, there is just the tiniest chance that they forgot to put it down or something.

... Last night after lights I was shaving in the dark, when Palairet whose bed was within reach of my basin, said, I'll strike a match for you, so you can see. I had my back to him, & when he struck the match, as it was still fizzing he pushed the end against my bottom, burnt a hole in both me & my pyjamas. – He had to be sat on.

Love from
Roald

---

* Roald had got a court summons for speeding or dangerous driving on his motorcycle.

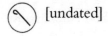 [undated]

The Priory House
Repton
Derby

Dear Mama

Thanks awfully for your letter & the parcel. Has someone been sending some Norwegian chocs? The fishing hooks will be fine; I've never seen so many in all my life.

. . . By the way, about speech day, I gather you are all coming down. I expect Alfhild will drive the car. I've just had a letter from Kari to say that she has received her permissions to come down as well. If Louis wants to come he could go & fetch Kari on his motorbike & sidecar.

May I take Kari to the Speech Day dance on Friday evening? I promised to do it jokingly last holidays, but there are lots of people in this house going & I think it would be good fun . . .

My gosh, it's hot, I simply can't write any more. I'm lying out in the Deer Park in my shirt sleeves, thinking of nothing but a bathe.

We're going fishing too this afternoon.

Lots of love from

Roald

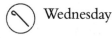 Wednesday

The Priory House
Repton
Derby

Dear Mama

Thanks for your letter. Yes, I knew Michael had been expelled, and had asked Binks what I should say to you about it, and he said that it would be by far the best for all concerned to conceal the fact under a pretext of mental breakdown. But please don't think that I had anything to do with him in that way at all. I was his friend and I knew that he had a kink about immorality. I had tried to stop him, as Binks knew, but it was no good. I have asked Binks, who knows my character here a good deal better than most, to assure you that I had nothing to do with it at all. By your letter I concluded that you thought I had been behaving badly and might be expelled if I was not careful. Well, please believe me when I tell you that I had absolutely nothing to do with it. But it was for the sake of everyone's feelings that Binks and I thought it best to conceal the fact of his expulsion. The boss told me that it was <u>not</u> homosexuality but merely the natural outlet for a rather over sensuous mind often met hand in hand with great brain. He has asked him to come down to the school again in a year's time.

If the scarlet fever stays in the Hall only, there will probably be a speech day, but I think that the dance will very likely be cancelled.

Lots of love from
Roald

PRIVATE AND CONFIDENTIAL

Repton

June 14th 1933

Dear Mrs. Dahl,

Roald came to me last night in considerable distress, because you thought that he must have been concerned in the unfortunate events which led to Michael Arnold leaving Repton.

He had not told you about that, because he did not want to distress you; but owing to the turn that events have taken, I think I had better tell you about it. Early this term it came out that Arnold had been guilty of immorality with some small boys last term. As he was a prefect and in a position of trust in the house, and as his acts had been quite deliberate, we decided that he must go. It was a very unpleasant business for everybody and especially for Roald; not only because he lost his chief friend, but also because people were likely to think that he was implicated. But as a matter of fact there was no sort of suspicion attaching to him, in fact I am convinced that he had done his best to make Arnold give up his bad ways; but the latter is very obstinate and would not listen to him.

When boys are sent away for this sort of thing, there is naturally some difficulty in accounting to their acquaintances for their leaving school. As a matter of fact Roald consulted me at the time about what he should say. I did not think it necessary to tell you about it – as he was not himself implicated – at least not at present, when he could only communicate by letter. So when Arnold's father ascribed it to a mental breakdown, I thought he had better use that explanation.

I may have been wrong in this – if so, I am sorry. But in any

78

case you may set your mind at ease about Roald. I am convinced that he is perfectly straight about it all and has not been concerned in Arnold's misdeeds.

As to the latter: Some of these very clever boys have an abnormality in their minds, which makes them resentful of authority, and difficult to deal with, and may lead to disaster as in his case. Arnold was apparently convinced (quite wrongly) that he was not appreciated at his true worth here, and took up a defiant and revolutionary attitude to assert his independence. It was of course a very wicked and selfish method of doing so, as he deliberately tried to start small boys off wrong. It is a sad business, as he has many good qualities: I only hope he will be able to control his 'complex' in future –

But my chief object in writing is to set your mind at rest about Roald – I'm sure he is straight and I hope you will tell him that you trust him to go right. It is of great importance that he should feel you believe in him.

Yours sincerely
SS Jenkyns

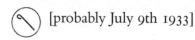 [probably July 9th 1933]   The Priory House
                                                                 Repton
                                                                 Derby

Dear Mama

. . . Last Tuesday we had a field-day. It was terribly hot. Just about the hottest day we've had. We didn't leave until after breakfast, because we hadn't so far to go as usual. Then at about 9 o'clock we all got into buses and started off for a place called the Weever Hills in Staffordshire. It took about one and a half hours in the bus – the coolest part of the whole day, because all the windows were open. It was rather a pleasant kind of country that we finished up in – all hills and stone walls. We messed about the whole day, firing our blank cartridges (of which we each had 110 rounds) eating our lunch and getting extremely hot. Then there occurred a thrill, which alone added spice to an otherwise dull and hot day. Some fellows in Trent College fired five live rounds (actual bullets) at us. We heard them whizzing overhead and hitting a wood behind and we went down behind the wall like shot rabbits. An umpire standing near on a horse heard the shots, and knowing them to be live rounds, rushed along and caught this boy in the act. He must have been mad – at any rate there's been the deuce of a row about it. I'm not sure that the War Office isn't going to do something about it!!! We all had tea in a field at about 5 o'clock and got back in time to have a much appreciated bathe.

On Wednesday we got off all the morning's work to go and welcome George and his wife.* We had uniform on of course and had to line the streets 15 paces apart in front of the pavement to keep the crowd on it. It was jolly hot, but few of the people were obstinate. Quite fun seeing George + Spouse, but even the old boy himself didn't arouse in me those instincts which prompted a woman on my right to fling her arms around Hooper as the King came past, exclaiming 'the King, the King', (much to the embarrassment of the unfortunate Hooper, whose face took on the delicate hues of some of the finer beetroots, which by the way can be bought quite cheaply at any grocer (green, of course) Hooper, by the way, was the boy standing 15 paces to my right . . .

Working for the ruddy Certificate now, which begins in about 2 weeks . . .

Love from
Roald

* King George V and his wife Queen Mary of Teck.

A montage of Roald and three friends at Repton with
a background of school landmarks. It was made by
Roald in his darkroom at Priory House in 1933

[undated]

Addressed to:
Mrs. S Dahl
10 Sloforks Hotel,
Larkollen
Norway

The Priory House
Repton
Derby

Dear Mama

I suppose that you are in the North Sea now, and judging by the weather here you aren't having a very rough time. Both yesterday & today it has been as hot as a ruddy furnace, and Smith & I have gone to Parson's Hills behind Latham House to Sunbathe every day. Yesterday we took off our shirts & immediately became the centre of attention in the ant world. The little devils crawled all over us, taking a particular fancy to my ears, where, no doubt they found a delicious food hitherto unknown to the ant. Then a large cow nearly mistook Smith's head for a thistle, so as a punishment we tried to milk it. But it wasn't having any nonsense and it was far too hot to chase it. We've done half the exams now; they weren't so bad, I may enclose some of the Papers as they might interest you or Alf . . .
    Love from
    Roald

P.S. Beastly nuisance having to pay 2½d for this letter, the family coffers can scarce stand such a drain upon their resources.

February 4th 1934 The Priory House
Repton
Derby

Dear Mama

. . . We are having a great fives match this afternoon in the
courts on our yard . . .

We are also planning a gigantic fire balloon, to be 18ft high,
with a diameter of 12 feet, outer surface area of 3,501 square feet!
It should lift at least one boy, but we are going to have it on a
rope (that is if it ever comes off).

Do you think you could find a pipe of mine & give it to me on
Thursday. It is one I often smoked, one you gave me in Norway
(not the light coloured one) It is well smoked in & has a fairly long
stem, fairly dark, with a little chip out underneath. If you can't find
it will you please bring the other one you gave me in Norway (still
not the light one) It is in the rack in my bedroom, a fairly fat one
with a longish stem & a short mouth piece!

Love from
Roald

P.S. Let me know fairly soon what you think about meeting on
Thursday, so I can answer.

[probably February 21st 1934]   The Priory House
                                                         Repton
                                                         Derby

Dear Mama

Thanks for your letter & the cheque thing to sign; I enclose it
here. The wireless came as you expected on Friday afternoon. It is
marvellous. It will get all the continent at any time of the day, and
Oslo easily. You know exactly what you are getting because all the
names are on the dial. The dial is accurate too and the tone is
excellent; now I think it is a good deal better than the Ferranti tone.
. . . I do Boxing twice a week now from 7–8 in the evenings. The
boxing competition will be starting in about two weeks. There are
only two of us in for the Senior Heavyweights, Downs & I. He
weighs 15 stone, but I hope the burden of his fat will slow him down
    Just been out for a walk with Reuss. Had a good smoke a long
way away; also rescued a cow that had fallen into the stinker, (the
method used was to grasp the tail of the beast and pull very hard.
It was awfully grateful to us afterwards . . .
    Love from
    Roald

 March 4th 1934   The Priory House
                                                         Repton
                                                         Derby

Dear Mama

Thank you for your letters. What a pity we can't go to Tenby.
Did Alf know that we wouldn't be able to go if she acted – tell
her she's a fool.
    At any rate I've got something else I want to ask you: next
summer hols there's a Public Schoolboys Exploring Expedition

going to explore the centre of Newfoundland. I'm wondering if it wouldn't be really worth going. It's led by the same man who led one to Finland last Summer, Surgeon-Commander Murray-Levick, one of the men on Scott's Expedition. It lasts six weeks, four of which are spent in the wilds of Newfoundland! which hasn't been mapped before so a bit of surveying would be done for the Government too. Total costs + journey & everything is £35. Is that a lot? There's a friend of mine in Brook House called Horrocks also thinking of going; the summer climate out there is good, very sunny & not over hot. What do you think of it & is it too expensive? I wouldn't be paying next Xmas term school fee, & suppose the Norway holiday usually comes to about £25 each, doesn't it.

Six of us have started work on our giant balloon; made out of bits of tissue paper 2½ft x 1¾. We've bought 80 sheets (1/-) & lots of grip-fix & have started, in fact we've done ½ of it. We've got it all worked out, its volume inside is 3000 cubic ft, & it stands 15ft high.

Lots of masters + Ma Boss have told us to tell them when it goes up, & are coming to watch! But it will not be ready for at least a week. We're having 4 lots of cotton wool fires in the structure underneath:-

Wonder if it will go up!!

Love from

Roald

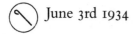 June 3rd 1934

The Priory House
Repton
Derby

Dear Mama

Thanks awfully for the figs & biscuits etc. Those figs will <u>keep me going</u> in more sense than one for quite a long time. They're jolly good; but one fellow in the study, who claims to have licked an Arab's foot said he recognized the taste on the surface of his fig. I said: 'not really', and he answered 'No, on second thoughts perhaps they were Italian's feet.'

At the moment all the fags are busy behind me devising cunning traps to catch mice alive. The study is being invaded by mice, they are eating our cakes & apples and everything except the good old figs. One fellow has put sawdust on top of treacle, and he swears that the mouse will think that it's terra firma, will walk thereon & will stick. But our latest device is a basin (my wash basin) greased all around with Priory butter (guaranteed to kill any animal after the second dose); and in the middle of the basin stands a piece of choice plum cake, a chunk of the very cake on which the mice have been feasting for the last week – so they are bound to like it! We maintain that the mice won't be able to get out, but it only remains to be seen whether they are fools enough to go into it.

Love
Roald

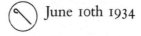 June 10th 1934   The Priory House
                                                    Repton
                                                    Derby

Dear Mama

Thanks awfully for the cakes – the remnants of the Norwegian party I suppose. But they are jolly good.

I had another letter from Parrain, after I had thanked him for lending me his trout rod. He said he wasn't lending it, he was giving it; and I was to take it in to Farleys in St. James; to have proper line & flies at his expense! Jolly decent of him. – I expect Ellen will be able to get it into her trunk.

Our baths have been filled, I had my first bathe yesterday – it wasn't at all bad. We've got a new device. A colossal filter has been fixed up behind the baths, and it is certainly drawing water out, cleaning it and sending it in again at the other end. It is a jolly good thing by the looks of it and it may save us bathing in a sort of green swamp towards the end of the term.

We've made an awfully cunning trap for catching mice alive; it's like this

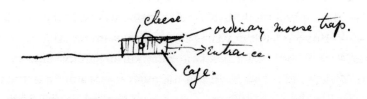

The mouse goes in and nibbles the cheese which is hanging by a bit of cotton. Have you ever tried nibbling an apple hanging by a bit of string, well the mouse puts his paws on the cheese to steady it & pull it down. The cotton is attached to the thing which lets off the trap. The trap springs down like a door & is stopped halfway, (it has been made into a door with wire.) The second night we caught a big one, but as we were emptying it into a box the darn thing jumped out before we could clap the lid on!

I'd like the remaining figs if no one else wants them

Lots of love

Roald

Furness Line
R.M.S. Nova Scotia

Thursday. At sea.
Dear Mama

This is Thursday and we are due in at St. John this afternoon at about 5 o'clock. We've had a marvellous voyage. Woke up on Saturday morning to find ourselves off the coast of Ireland. It looked a marvellous place. Later Scotland appeared on the other side & I took some photos of the Giant's Causeway.

After lunch, when we left the coast of Ireland it started to blow & we didn't feel so good. However we remained on deck, and caught the wireless operator being sick over the side! We are sharing a cabin with 2 fellows from Uppingham – very nice chaps – in fact everyone with the exception of an odd tough here & there, are very nice. We all lay down in our bunks that evening & at 12.15 midnight I awoke & found us all fast asleep & fully dressed!

Sunday was a lovely day. We discovered Sam amongst the crew. Sam is a Negro who hails from British Guiana in South America, and he's a marvellous fellow, black curly hair & a blue beret. After supper that night we went up to the bar & found Jimmy Horrocks, gloating over a Manhattan cocktail. After that he had a glass of sherry & then lo & behold he was tight as a drum. He called for more & got tighter & tighter. He was wearing an Old Reptonian tie & we asked him if that was the old school tie – 'Yes,' he said – 'What school' 'the old Pentonvillians' he answered terribly seriously.

We eventually got him down to the cabin & shoved him on his bunk; he slept so we left him & went to the service. When we went down again afterwards the bunk was empty. We thought he'd probably dropped himself quietly overboard, but when we went up to look, there he was sitting in the bar over a glass of port! After a long time we got him down again without Murray Levick or any of the leaders seeing him, undressed him & put him to bed. We sat in the cabin & when someone mentioned the pub 'The Pig & Whistle', Jimmie, lying in his bunk half asleep got up & sang 'Did you ever see a pig whistling' to the tune of 'did you ever see a dream walking'.

We were never sick at all after Saturday. On Monday we had fair weather. In the morning an old boy of about 80 came on to the deck in an amazing smock & started to show us how to play a game of his called Stoolball. Evidently he's absolutely crazy about it. He came on this ship especially to show us how to

play it. He travels on ships to India in order to introduce it on
the way. It's a damn silly game, & when he came down again in
the afternoon he found everyone playing cricket & so he went
away & we haven't seen him since – I think he's in the Atlantic
Ocean. The game has since been known as Toolball.

That evening the Captain attended dinner – speeches all
around. After dinner we dragged one fellow who had the most
atrocious black beard up to the bathroom and shaved it off. I
believe you saw him on the Station. Then as Murray Levick said
we were all to have our hair cut short I went along to Sam who
cuts hair in his spare time (there is also a ship's barber) & had all
my hair cut off! I've just got a tiny little bit of bristle on the
top – I look fine. I had to borrow Sam's blue beret to keep my
head warm & I've worn it ever since.

Tuesday was rough but we weren't sick. Took photos, & went
up to Captain's bridge. Entry in Log! 'Westerly Gale, much sea &
spray'. After dinner or supper in the evening we all went into the
men's quarters again (the two Uppinghamians Douglas & George
also Jim Horrocks) to watch Mike a fellow from Harrow have his
hair cut off by Sam. He lost courage at the last minute &
wouldn't have it all off! Sam's got a lovely wireless down there,
one of those tiny little 10 guinea sets bought cheap in America.

Yesterday, Wednesday fine weather, just played cricket & deck
tennis. In the evening we all went into the 1st Class room & saw
a film on Labrador by a silly little missionary there. He was
unbearably facetious but the film was good. After that they had a
mock trial. A man was accused of deserting his wife & flirting
with all the other girls on deck. Very amusing. The clerk of the
court told me to remove my beret, I refused, set 4 large police to
turn me out. I had a gang of 12 to defend me & the police
themselves got turned out instead!

Afterwards made acquaintance with one Miss Ruth Lodge an
actress from London, who's been acting in The Distaff Side.

Walked up & down deck with her etc, til one o'clock, & all 47 boys very jealous. Oh yes, at about 4 o'clock in the afternoon of that day we saw an iceberg in the distance; it looked marvellous, but too far away to photo.

It's now Thursday & we are due in at St. John at about 3 o'clock this afternoon, from where we will go straight to the station & get on a sleeper for a 14 hours train journey to Grand Falls. From there a 20 mile march to base Camp.& then the fun begins. You may only get short letters from me in future & you may get hardly any, so don't expect them. I'm on a party which is marching 100 miles inland where no one (so they say) has ever been before. The lakes on our map are all put down by hearsay.

What sort of a trip did you have. Thanks for your telegram, I got it an hour after you'd sent it!

Hope you have a good time in Tjöme, give my love to the Bestepeople & Finn & the Applesvolds.

Love from

Roald

Roald on the Long March in Newfoundland, 1934. He got so hungry there that he experimented with eating boiled lichen and reindeer moss

CHAPTER 3

'Another iced lager'

1935–1939

In 1934, after returning from his adventures in Newfoundland – a trip which concluded with Roald leading a 'mutiny' against its egotistical leader – he became a probationary member of staff with the Asiatic Petroleum Company, later to become a part of Royal

Roald on board HMS Nova Scotia *on his way to Newfoundland, summer 1934*

Dutch Shell, on a salary of £130 per annum. His hope, he explained later, was that he would eventually be sent somewhere exciting. He had few financial worries. His father's trust would provide him with a significant additional income when he turned twenty-five, and in the meantime he lived rent-free in Oakwood, the large, rambling family home in Bexley. His mother, 'desperate' at what she saw as his lack of ambition, sent off to have his horoscope professionally read. The psychic predicted Roald was going to be a writer. Sofie Magdalene kept that information to herself.[39]

For four years, however, there was not much adventure. Or indeed writing. Six days a week Roald took the 8.15 train into the City of London, where he passed his days in humdrum office administration. At home, he played golf, went greyhound racing,

The team of boys who went on the gruelling 'Long March'
in Newfoundland in the summer of 1934, charting the
landscape and collecting plant and insect samples. Roald is
third from right, with shaven head. He would later claim he
had done this because it reduced the chance of head lice

Roald resting on rocks in the Great Rattling Brook in
Newfoundland. It was cold, wet and eventually the expedition ran
out of food. As Roald recorded plaintively in his daily journal:
'honestly I don't think any one of us has ever been so miserable'

listened to Sibelius symphonies on his gramophone, read books
and developed photographs in the darkroom he had constructed
there. It was a safe, ordered and utterly conventional existence.

There were occasional breaks to this routine. In the summer of
1936 Roald was posted for a few days to a refinery on the lower
reaches of the River Thames. There, he told his mother that he
spent most of the day 'on top of an enormous petrol tank – very
hot and nearly suffocated by the fumes'.[40] A longer sales trip to the
West Country the following year gave him opportunities to take
some unusual photographs that revealed his eye for detail. Probably
the most enduring legacy of this strange hiatus in his life was the
weighty metal ball he constructed from the silver wrappers of the

chocolate bars he ate for lunch each day. He later kept it as a talis-
man in his writing hut.

Occasionally, during these four years, Roald did put pen to
paper – a comic article for the *Shell* magazine and a humorous
playlet called *Double Exposure* set in the future – but these literary
efforts were few and far between. Even letters are thin on the
ground. One written from Norway during this period however is
interesting in that it contains what appear to be notes for a story,
written quite self-consciously as a piece of prose. Roald sent it to
his mother, whose arthritic hips meant that she no longer took her
own holidays in Norway, preferring instead to vacation in Tenby
or Cornwall. This tale of Carl Christiansen, the mechanic, is probably Roald's first adult piece of prose storytelling.[41]

Roald's siblings were beginning to leave the family nest. His
half-sister Ellen had married an ambitious doctor, Ashley Miles, in
1930, and moved to Hampstead, while his half-brother Louis,
pursuing a career as a graphic artist, married Meriel Longland, a
clergyman's daughter, in 1936 and also relocated to London.
Alfhild, Else and Asta remained at Oakwood. Alf liked being near
London and, as her sister Asta recalled, enjoyed a 'fast' lifestyle. She
was often to be found, 'coming home on the milk train'.[42] Roald
spent a lot of his free time with her and her friends, who included
the composer William Walton, the historian Arthur Bryant, and
the flamboyant businessman and theatrical manager Alfred
Chenhalls. Alf would eventually marry a clever, but mentally
unstable Danish neighbour, Leslie Hansen, in 1940.

In the summer of 1938 Roald was finally posted to Africa. He
set sail on the SS *Mantola* in September, after a short holiday with
Michael Arnold in the south of France. A friend of Sofie
Magdalene's, who was also on the boat, wrote to her with news of
her son. Roald was 'very popular with everyone', she reported.
'Luckily for him he is fond of children & is good with them, for
they all swarm all over him.'[43]

BRITISH INDIA S. N. CO'S S. S. "MANTOLA" 9,065 TONS GROSS

A postcard of the SS Mantola *on which Roald*
sailed to Nairobi in September 1938

Roald thought his job was to be in Kenya, but when he arrived there, he was immediately sent further south, to Tanganyika, formerly German East Africa, but, since the end of the First World War, subject to British colonial administration. He was the most junior of the three-man team running a coastal oil terminal in the capital, Dar es Salaam. Most of the company's business there involved supplying fuel and lubricants for farm equipment, but Roald was particularly excited that he was put in charge of refuelling the flying boats that arrived in the harbour every two or three days.

For the next year Roald wrote to his mother and sisters almost every week and his letters are a wonderfully engaging chronicle of his time there and of life as a young expatriate in colonial Africa. 'I loved it all,' he reflected later. 'There were no furled umbrellas, no bowler hats, no sombre grey suits and I never once had to get on a train or a bus.'[44] Africa fired his imagination and these letters reveal his fascination with his new home as well as a delight in honing his skills as a storyteller and humorist. They also reveal his subversive madcap edge, whether poking fun at expatriate pomposity, or outraging German members in the Dar es Salaam Club by throwing darts at images of Hitler. In hindsight he would describe himself as 'a ridiculous young pukka-sahib',[45] admitting that he was 'mildly ashamed' of his tacit acceptance of certain British imperial attitudes that prevailed while he was there.

For much of his time in Tanganyika, he lived with two colleagues, Panny Williamson and George Rybot. They shared a large, spacious villa inhabited by various pets including the tick-infested Dog Samka and two cats, Oscar and Mrs. Taubsypuss, immortalised thirty-four years later as the US President's cat in his children's story, 'Charlie and the Great Glass Elevator'. The chronicles of their increasingly fantastical exploits show Roald's nascent storytelling imagination already beginning to take comic flight.

His raucous spirit was allowed free rein in the house – whether it was practising the healthy bowel exercises of Professor F.A. Hornibrook's *Culture of the Abdomen* or simply consuming large quantities of whisky with his friends. It was a life of endless 'sundowners', sport and visits to the club. There were occasional glimpses of leopards and snakes, but most of the exotic game he encountered was in the bar of the Dar es Salaam Club.

His spell in Tanganyika was formative for him in other ways. He learned to run a house, 'holding court' each morning with Piggy the cook and Mwino the head boy, paying wages, deciding menus, planning recipes and devising social events. He also indulged himself in the role of present-giver and treat-maker, regularly sending back jewellery, furs and curios to his family.

All the while, lurking in the background of these adventures, is the near certainty of the coming war with Germany and the later African letters give a fascinating colonial perspective on this. As Roald set sail on the SS *Mantola*, German troops were already occupying the disputed Sudetenland territory on the border with Czechoslovakia. By March 1939, when the German army marched into Prague, Roald had become convinced that war was inevitable. Repeatedly he urged his mother to get out of their house in Bexley, which he rightly believed would be directly under the flight path of any German bombers attacking London. He wanted her to move to their holiday haunt on the Welsh coast in Tenby. There he believed his family – who were all still officially foreigners – would be safe. But Sofie Magdalene was stubborn. Neither she nor her daughters were prepared to relocate. They stayed on, believing that Oakwood's large and well-stocked wine cellar would make an effective air-raid shelter against German bombs.

On September 3rd 1939, two days after Germany had invaded Poland, Britain declared war and soon Dar es Salaam began to fill up with soldiers. Roald at first enlisted as a Special Constable, but he instinctively disliked the army. So, inspired by his friend, the pilot Alec Noon, who flew small commercial aircraft out of Dar es Salaam, he decided instead to join the Royal Air Force and train as a pilot. At the end of November he drove 900 miles north to Nairobi. As he did so, he later recalled that he was transfixed by the gentle beauty of a family of elephants he encountered on the way. 'They are better off than me, and a good deal wiser,' he mused. 'I myself am at this moment on my way to kill Germans or be killed by them, but those elephants have no thought of murder in their mind.'[46]

[written on Shell Mex/BP notepaper]

August 11th 1936

. . . I have come across many examples of haphazardness on
the part of country yokels in the country, but I think that the one
I met with in Norway last month was the last word. We were
travelling down the Oslo fjord in a small motor boat with a one
cylinder engine. The day was windy but pleasant, with large
cumulus clouds in the sky. The boat was chug-chugging along
gaily when suddenly the engine spluttered, coughed a few times
& finally stopped. I was meant to be the mechanic on board, but
my knowledge of motors is essentially meagre; & after doing all
the usual things such as cleaning the plug, flooding the
carburettor & adjusting the mag we decided that we had better
row into the small village opposite which we had stopped. We
had no oars, only 2 canoe paddles, & Michael sweating in the
front kept asking when he was going to get his 'Blue'. We
awarded it to him after 10 minutes and his efforts were
accordingly increased. The village was called Filtvet, a small
village, just one of hundreds, dotted all along the fjord, apparently
doing nothing, and caring about nothing. We met an old man
with a red beard; I can talk Norwegian and enquired as to
whether there was anyone who 'understood engines' here.

'Well, yes,' he said slowly, 'Carl Christiansen is a mechanic.'
'Where does Carl Christiansen live then?'
'You see that hill?'
'Yes.'
'You see that white house at the bottom of the hill?'
'Yes.'
'Well, you see that yellow house at the top of the hill?'
'Yes, yes.'

'Well that's where Carl Christiansen lives.'
'Thank you – will he be at home?'
'Yes, he might be, and he might not be.'
'Alright,' I answered, 'we'll go and see.'

The door of the yellow house was open & a middle aged woman with a blue & red handkerchief over her head was cooking carrots & potatoes over a primus stove.

'Does Carl Christiansen live here?'
'Yes,' she said.
'Is he at home?'
'No – he's down in the village, by the sea.'

So back to the village & the sea we went; but there was no one in sight save the old man with the red beard to whom we had first spoken. Then some little white haired children with dusty bare feet pattered down the hill toward us.

'Have you seen Carl Christiansen?' I asked.
'No – he's probably in his house.'
'No, we've just been there.'
'Well,' they answered, 'we haven't seen him.'

For half an hour we sauntered round looking for the elusive Carl Christiansen. Then we tired of looking for Carl and wandered into the little general stores or 'landhandel' and ate 'vinebröd'. The girl behind the counter hadn't seen him since he came in to buy tobacco some 3 hours ago, but he was almost certain to be down in the village, by the sea. 'Ah, there's a party of men coming along – he'll be one of those.' We approached & after I asked – 'Excuse me, but is Carl Christiansen here?' 'Carl Christiansen the mechanic?' 'Yes,' (we were making headway) 'that's him over there' – and the spokesman turned and pointed to the old man with the red beard who was sitting half asleep on the wooden bench puffing gently at his enormous pipe. 'But it isn't,' I said, 'we've just spoken to him – he showed us where Christiansen lived.'

Without another word the spokesman walked quietly up to Carl, put a hand on his shoulder, and spoke to him for a minute or so, and having apparently succeeded in persuading him of his own identity, he called to us & introduced us.

'Are you Carl Christiansen?'
'Yes,' quite quietly & seriously.
'Will you please mend our boat?'
'I'll come & look at it.'

Well he mended it.

 [September 24th 1938]   SS Mantola

Saturday morning

Dear Mama

We've had a marvellous journey: fairly calm in the Bay of Biscay (at least I wasn't sick) then as soon as we came to the Spanish coast the sun came out, and it has stayed out ever since. We passed Gibraltar Wednesday morning at about 8 o'clock – magnificent sight with the sun just dispersing the mist over what looked like a very hot African coast. Since then there has been hardly a ripple on the water. We left the Spanish coast yesterday morning & we arrive at Marseilles tonight at about 9.00pm.

The boat isn't so bad – in fact I think it's very good. Some of the people are pretty dull, but I believe the best batch always gets on at Marseilles. There are four dogs on board which we exercise every morning – a great Dane – a mastiff puppy – a whippet (owned by Nina's friend) and a spaniel puppy. Also a horse!! The wretched animal is doomed to stand in his box (in which he can't even turn round) until we get to Mombasa.

The food is very good. Dinner jacket every evening & dancing afterwards & a bloody awful band (you heard it). I am considering offering my services as a pianist!

War news – as far as we can see – looks pretty bloody, so the quicker you get to Tenby the better. I'll address my next letter to the Cabin – it'll be from Malta, I expect.

There's not much more to say – the weather is marvellous & the sea is calm – you ought to do that trip to Marseilles & back one day.

Love to all

Roald

Thanks very much for the Elva plums – they're very good.

 Tuesday morning   Mantola

Dear Mama

We're now in the Red Sea, and it's bloody hot. The wind is behind us and going at exactly the same speed as the boat so there is not a breath of air on board. Three times they have turned the ship around against the wind to get some air into the cabins & into the engine room. Fans merely blow hot air into your face, the deck is strewn with a lot of limp wet things for all the world like a lot of wet towels steaming over the kitchen boiler. They just smoke cigarettes & shout 'Boy – another iced lager.'

I don't feel the heat much – probably because I'm thin. In fact as soon as I've finished this letter I'm going off to have a vigorous game of deck tennis with another thin man – a Government vet called Hammond. We play with our shirts off, throwing the coit as hard as we can – & when we have to stop for fear of drowning in our own sweat we just jump into the swimming bath.

We had an evening at Port Said, an amazing town. Wherever you go about 8 or 12 filthy Arabs run after you shouting & wanting to sell you something – but it's only shit.

. . . I bought a very nice Topee for 5/6. Then we took a Rickshaw thing and drove through the Arab quarter (just let me drink this lager . . . That's better).

Then we stopped by the sea shore & wandered down on to the beach. It was very dark, but before we knew where we were, there was a bloody great Egyptian policeman wanting to arrest us. Apparently the beach is used by lads who want to smoke opium and hashish on the sly – no one else goes there in the night. After half an hour's argument we managed to convince him that we only wanted to paddle! He only believed <u>that</u> after we had given him 5/–! You can do anything or get anything in these places if you keep surreptitiously slipping silver into the nearest oily palm that you can find.

Next day – Sunday – we went through the Suez canal. That was great fun. On the Arabian side just desert – hot yellow desert and nothing else. On the Egyptian side – more desert with, now & then a palm tree and a camel to break the monotony. Once we saw an Arab washing himself in the mud on the bank. We calculated by means of holding our little finger at arm's length & comparing it with a palm tree close by that his tool measured a good foot and a half in length – great excitement amongst the women passengers on board.

We stopped for a few hours at Suez to get some Shell Oil for the boat, whence we proceeded into this bloody frying pan in which we now find ourselves.

I'll post this at Port Sudan. Maybe you won't get another letter till we get to Nairobi or Mombasa. There's no airmail from Aden . . .

Love
Roald

P.T.O.

Asta

Many thanks for letters. I'm buggered if I'm going to write any more now.

There's a man sitting near me (a fat one) who is almost unconscious from the heat. He's flowing over his chair like a hot jellyfish – and he's steaming too. He may melt.

Hope you like your birthday present.

Love
Roald

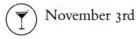 November 3rd   The Dar es Salaam Club
                                             Thursday evening

Dear Mama

. . . I get woken up by my boy at 6.30 – he brings tea and an orange (a marvellous orange tasting quite different to anything you've ever had – they're grown locally & cost about 2d a dozen, often much less I believe). I eat my orange & drink my tea – that is after the boy has removed the enormous bloody mosquito net that is suspended about 6 feet above you & tucked in under the mattress on all sides. Then I walk out onto my beautiful white verandah in my pyjamas & have a look at the harbour & the coast. Marvellous view. You look through a grove of coconut trees – all with bloody great coconuts on them – across the harbour where you get all the usual sort of stuff – mangrove swamps, mango trees, mangelwurzels and even mangles. Then my boy comes in & says 'bathee baridi' which probably means 'your cold bath is ready' – So I say 'homina gani' which means 'what the hell' & go in & have a bath. Come back & find suits & shirts & ties socks etc, all beautifully laid out for me, so I put them on. Go down & have breakfast, then drive to work in the Company's Buick with Joram Carey – who sleeps in the next room to mine – get to work at 8.00. Lunch 12/2p.m. & golf or tennis or squash or swimming or sailing at 4p.m. . . .

Drink bills come to about 2/300 shillings a month* – that is the average – & it looks as though mine may be a bit above the average this month – but as I said before – don't get excited, I'm not becoming a toper.

I was glad to hear that we get paid full salary since leaving London on the Boat, so at the end of October I got a chit from the bank saying that Nairobi had just paid 935 shillings to my account (about £47) which was the salary which had apparently accrued to me. Damn lucky too – it'll just see me out nicely, what with club entrance fees, new white suits, white shirt and goodness knows what else – expensive topees and mosquito boots – both of which one must have. The mosquito boots are long black leather boots going up to your knee (like riding boots), you have to wear them in the evenings to diddle the mosquitoes who, for some unknown reason, are particularly partial to ankle . . .

---

* There were about twenty Tanganyikan shillings to the British pound.

I'm going to buy a car soon, with my next allowance. I can't possibly buy one out of my salary, living is so bloody expensive. As a matter of fact it needn't be, but it's the way that you <u>have </u>to live. I believe you could live here very cheaply if you wanted to. Gold flake cigarettes are Shs 1/80 for 50 (100 cents in a shilling – no pounds) & you can get damn good cigarettes, full size, at Shs 1/20 for 50 or even 1/- for 50. Fruit costs next to nothing, but there's no fresh milk, it all has to be boiled – like us.

<u>8 a.m. Friday</u>
Knew I'd forgotten something – Xmas presents – you ask what I want – well – what the hell do I want. Don't know. I'll sign a few more of these damned invoices & things and then think again . . .

– Of course I know what I want. Large, good photos of all of you . . .

Love to all
Roald

A photo, taken by Roald in 1938, of one of the flying boats that regularly landed in the harbour of Dar es Salaam. One of his responsibilities was to refuel them

[postmarked November 25th 1938]   Dar es Salaam
                                    The Dar es Salaam Club
Dear Mama, Alf Else & Asta

How's Mama? I expect I shall hear by next mail. She'll
probably break all records for recovery like she did with her
tonsils – but it's bound to hurt like buggery afterwards.*
Tell her to rent Mrs R.B's house by the sea – just the thing.
And tell her the joke about the person who had all teeth
out & couldn't be fed through the mouth. So the doctor
said:

 – I'll have to feed you with a tube through your anus.
 – What would you like for your first meal?
 – A cup of tea please doctor.
 – Right, here goes.
 – Hi, stop doctor, stop!
 – What's the matter, what's the matter, is it too hot?
 – No, there's too much sugar in it.

Well if you (Alf) have heard that one, I had heard the one you
told; although I admit that it's a bloody good one. Let's have a
new one.

I'm just trying to select Else a 21st Birthday present. If she has
the jade necklace, I could get her a jade ring or jade earrings –
what about it? Or a thin gold carved bracelet or Rhino shit or
bullshit or elephant shit, Hippo shit – what?

The short rains are here & every now & then it fairly pisses
down, & then it stops & the sun shines. The whole place is full
of acacia trees with the most marvellous huge crimson acacias in
bloom all over them, flowers the size of your head. But they

---

* Sofie Magdalene had just had all her teeth extracted.

make you hot to look at them. Coconut milk & gin is a marvellous drink, you try it.

Love

Roald

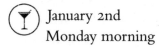 January 2nd   The Dar es Salaam Club
Monday morning   Tanganyika Territory

Dear Mama

Today is one of the <u>numerous</u> Indian holidays – thank goodness, so we've got a chance to recover from a week's solid, non-stop celebration. We'll start with Christmas Eve – Saturday before last. Being on the 25th of the month & thus the end of our financial year, all stock at the Depot had to be checked on that day. So Panny Williamson (one of our men here – very nice) Joram Carey & self spent from 11a.m. until 6p.m. down at the depot in those bloody corrugated iron godowns which are just like furnaces at midday.* We worked in shorts only – no shirts, unless we went outside to count drums – if you don't wear a shirt between 8a.m. & 4p.m. outside the sun will just burn your skin to a blister before you can say 'fuck'. Well we counted drums of Aviation spirit, drums of motor spirit, tins of Kerosene & cases of petrol & every bloody thing at the Depot. You see these have all got to be certified by a European once a year.

Then we went home & bathed & changed into our fancy dress – being Christmas Eve there was a big dance at the club. Our party consisting of Panny & I & half a dozen others (I can't write here, my sweaty hand has made the paper limp) had all

---

* Godown: in India and East Asia, a warehouse, especially one at a dockside.

ordered sailor suits at the local Tailors Messrs Haji Bros. of
Acacia Avenue. We looked very fine 5 sailor men & 3 sailor
women. Dinner at the Club with Champagne & then the
dancing & real drinking started. It was terrific. By 3a.m. about
three and a half per cent of those present were sober. The rest of
us (which would be 96½% so mathematicians inform me) didn't
go to bed. At 6a.m. we bathed & then went on to a Champagne
breakfast with a little man called Eric Fletcher. Then a party
before lunch at the Phillips's (British American Tobacco
manager) & then to bed until the evening. This was Christmas
Day. In the evening George Rybot & I thought we'd go to the
dance at the Africa Hotel. (George Rybot is now our manager
down here – Antrobus has gone on leave & George has come
down to take over for about six months – he's about 38 years
old – earns about £1500 & is known all over East Africa as the
biggest buffoon & yet a very clever man once he gets into the
office – which is occasionally.)

However we went to this dance at the New Africa, had a
bottle of Champagne each & then had a roaring time. I'm told
that all through the smart dinner, which was given at 2 long
tables with about 100 people – we kept getting up on the table &
singing 'Daisy Daisy give us your answer do'. However a good
time was had by all.

On Monday – bank holiday or was it Boxing Day – we
hired a couple of large motor boats & went out to the island to
bathe & have a picnic. Lovely bathing except that as 4 or 5 of
us were standing up to our waists in the water a shoal of flying
fish whizzed by – about ¾ the size of a ten bob note. One
went in Joram's mouth & another caught me across the cheek –
no damage but very amusing. They fly over the water like a
duck & drakes stone, leaping about 10/20 yards at the time.
Someone took some photos of this picnic. I'm getting some
prints & will send.

. . . Regarding Else's birthday present I'm much more excited about it than she'll ever be – afraid she won't get it for about a month – I'll tell you about it. Having selected 4 superb clear jade stones from old Haji, a big Indian dealer in the town, I got him to set them in 9 carat gold & make a chain bracelet – I didn't like the chain at all – so one evening I wandered into the Indian quarter of the town in my car & stopped the first intelligent looking Indian I saw & asked him if he knew a good goldsmith. 'Oh yes sir – just I know a very fine Indian gold worker who will just make you whatever will want' – so he got into the car & off we went down the most terrible side streets with natives & arabs & Indians all sitting about smoking hashish etc. & finished up outside an old shack where an old Indian wallah with an enormous beard was sitting with his legs crossed in front of a little urn with molten gold therein. I produced my

The Dar es Salaam Club, 1938, where Roald stayed for a while after his arrival in Dar es Salaam. 'I loved it all,' he reflected later in Going Solo. *'There were no furled umbrellas, no bowler hats, no sombre grey suits and I never once had to get on a train or a bus'*

jade stones, set together, & said could he make a nice bracelet for them – 'yes sir, just I will make you very beautiful bangle – just it will please the most beautiful wife who you surely want it for.' So I said O.K. – But this chap is very skilled & only works in pure gold. He melts down sovereigns to get his gold & will not adulterate it at all.

So Else's bracelet will be made of solid gold & I hope she jolly well likes it. It will be ready in 10 days' time & will be, so I am made to believe, very intricately worked. The snag is that I cannot send it home by airmail unless she pays 30% duty on it in England as it would be valued fairly high there I believe – I purpose to give it to someone who is going on a boat in the same way as Bob Bristow. So she'll get it in about a month or 40 days' time . . .

Lots of love

Roald

 [probably January 15th 1939]   Shell House
                                                             Oyster Bay
                                                             D.Sm.

Dear Mama

Thank you for your two letters; it seems ages since I wrote to you, but what with one thing and another – particularly with moving house, as you will see from my address. Panny Williamson has gone on safari upcountry for six weeks (in a box body Ford) and so I moved from the club last week to join George Rybot (our branch manager) in the Shell House. It is a lovely place, built about a year ago for £3000, it's outside Dar Es Salaam up the coast northwards, about 50 yards from the sea, with spacious verandahs all around it and an enormous boabab tree in the front. The view is marvellous – I get up in the

morning & stroll on to my verandah with my cup of tea and
survey the scene – bright sunlight – not yet hot, deep blue sea &
lots of surf & the coast line stretching away on both sides as far as
you can see – you'd go into ecstasies about it until about
8.30a.m., when you'd retire towards the refrigerator for a cold
drink, mopping your brow the while. Next week I'll take some
photos of it & send them along.

By the way, I'm the housekeeper. Every morning at breakfast I
hold my court. (Rybot hasn't got up by then.) First the head boy
troops in with his little book and I write the orders therein such
as soap, gin, whiskey, beer; and check up his previous day's
purchases. He is called Mwino and hails from the Kavirondo
province in Kenya; where Rybot goes he goes. Then Piggy the
cook enters with his little books. Piggy is a local native aged
perhaps 40/45 years – and a damn'd good cook at that. He's
called Piggy the cook because the Swahili for Cook is Mpishi &
it's just got turned into Piggy. We decide what we shall have for
lunch & dinner, & I write down orders for things like butter,
lard, salt, meat, rice etc. & then give him 2/- with which to buy
vegetables & fish for the day (and fruit). The food sounds pretty
cheap & it is but it's the whiskey that costs the money in this
house, because people are dropping in every evening for drinks
etc., and we consequently have to buy probably £10 to £15
worth a week. Don't get alarmed, we only drink a fraction of it.

Piggy has a smart electric stove on which to cook . . . Then
there is Mdisho my boy who I've brought along with me – he's
of the tribe of Mwanumweze (pronounce the 'e' at the end as in
Norsk) from Tabora way – towards Belgian Congo – you see
every native has his tribe – the Mwanumweze are the only tribe
that have ever beaten the Masai in battle – magnificent fighters.

– To go on with the staff, we have also a kitchen mtoto
(mtoto = young boy in Swahili) who helps in the kitchen &
washes and a shamba boy who does the garden etc . . . So we've

got 150/- a month to pay in wages. Other inmates of the house are Sam, known to his friends as Dog Samka, a guard dog with the biggest tool and the longest tail (always wagging) that I've ever seen. He's black & the size of a large sealyham, but he doesn't know who his parents were. Then there's Oscar, a large white Persian cat – very fine but very very Kali (Swahili for savage or truculent). If you offer him a bit of fish he'll bite your finger off just for fun. We attribute this attitude to repression & to the physical disabilities under which he labours – you see he had his pocket picked when he was young, if you see what I mean. Nevertheless Oscar is a very Kali cat, although no one can dispute his beauty. Then there is Mrs. Taubsypuss – or as she is referred to by the boys – Mem Sahib Taubsypuss (just as Oscar is Bwana Oscar to them). Mrs. Taubsypuss is a beautiful blue Persian like Mowgli, and she's not half so Kali as Oscar; but she too has her weaknesses. Hers (and here she's one up on Oscar) is sex. She has 2 kittens, 3 weeks old, which are no more like a blue Persian than my bottom – they, indeed, are Kali in the extreme and spit at you if you approach. You see she apparently took her pleasures with a wild cat (we were all agreed that to do this she must be very, very tough indeed, and we gave her full marks), and the result is more like a couple of baby tigers than anything else. However they are great fun and Mrs. Taubsypuss is very fond of them indeed.

That I think completes the household – except of course for the ticks on Dog Samka's back, we have to de-tick him every 2 or 3 days and he's so ticklish when we look between his toes that he just laughs himself silly.

. . . I got my allowance thank you, and I needed it. By the way don't think we live in this house free. We've got to pay the company rent at 15% of our salaries before we start to run it at all . . .

I started this letter at 6.30pm. Since that I've had my cold bath, & have now got my beautiful silk dressing gown on.

Mwino has just come up & announced 'Chakula Tayari' which being interpreted means 'Food ready' so we're off to dinner. Lovely being able to have dinner just in dressing gowns & bedroom slippers.

Love
Roald

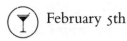 February 5th   Oyster Bay
                                                                          Sunday

Dear Mama

I've just finished bathing Dog Samka, who has got to look very smart as he's going to a Sundowner (cocktail party) with George & I in about an hour's time. He's getting a bit bald in the back & we're becoming worried about it as it's spoiling his looks; it makes him feel self-conscious too. I think that shortly we shall provide him with a toupee.

. . . Well, what's been happening here? Not an awful lot. The weather's just about getting to its hottest, and everyone sweats; Oscar is becoming more and more Kali every day; Mrs Taubsypuss's kittens are growing up; Dog Samka is sitting on the floor scratching himself in spite of the lovely bath I've just given him, and last but not least, I'm doing damn well as housekeeper of this mansion. I've been turning out some pretty slick meals just lately – things like hot curried crabs in their shells, sheep's brains in spinach, grilled koli-koli and barracuda, also prawns, lobster and crabs ad infinitum. They are all caught locally. The koli-koli & barracuda are huge fish usually, and provide local enthusiasts with very excellent deep sea fishing. I'm going out soon to do some with a fellow called Dicky Seal who is a fundi on fishing. Fundi is a much used word here – it's really the

Swahili for a plumber or carpenter, but is used to denote that you're an expert at anything . . .

Now please let me have some of your recipes for doing fish. Old Piggy the cook has no imagination at all, and I have to tell him exactly how I want it done every day (in my broken, but improving Swahili), and I'm running short of ways of doing it. We can match an English fish out here, so your recipes will do – Koli-Koli for example is just like Turbot; so send a few along or get Else & Asta to send a few plus other fairly easy recipes. I've ordered pigeon casserole this evening & before that cold crab in its shell –!

We had a damn funny evening last Wednesday. George & I'd been out to the cinema with some others & the two of us were driving home at 11.30 in the Company's car (large Chevrolet) which he always drives, when we whizzed passed an old car broken down on the side of the road. George said, 'I'm whistled as a coot, and I wish to get home to my bed, but many's the time when I've been broken down on the road miles from anywhere, and some Hindi has helped me out; and at any rate I thought I saw some lovely Indian women in the back of the car.' So we turned round & offered our services. The occupants turned out to be an educated native all done up in smart suit & trilby hat, his two wives & 2 children aged about 4 & 7. We drove them into Dar es Salaam & on the way passed a bloody great native fair which was going on. You see that day was the big Mahomeddan holiday of Id Ul Haj, and most of these natives call themselves Mahomeddans, although not many are practising. Well as I've said before, George was whistled as a coot, and I was not conspicuous for my sobriety, and it was therefore suggested that we should go in and partake of the fun of the fair with the rescued crew of the motor-car. They were all thrilled & thought it was a great joke, because only natives go to these fairs. So in we went; and damn'd interesting it was. There were lots of frightful old hand operated roundabouts (like the one at Havna)* made out of coconut trees etc, slipways down which you slid on coconut matting finishing up amidst a throng of yelling blacks; the most frightful sort of swing boats which were made, by some means or other, to revolve round an enormous coconut tree, and at full speed they stood out (that's the wrong word) parallel to the ground. Then there were native bands, with the players getting drunker & drunker on that frightful brew of theirs called Pombe, and beating the drums in the most weird fashion. But the best thing of all were the native dances. We saw the real thing – these blokes with nothing on except a bit of coconut matting & masses of white & red paint, yelling & swaying their hips in a manner which would make Mae West look like a fourth-rate novice. As each dance progressed, the dancers got more and more worked up, & yelled & shouted & leapt about until they just couldn't go on any longer and another tribe came on and took their place. The way they wobbled their tummies would have earned for them the fullest approval of our friend Professor Horniblow. As George drunkly remarked as we were watching the proceedings – 'Old boy, the buggers have been reading old Horniblow.'

I forgot to tell you that the native whom we picked out of his broken car leant over as we were driving in earlier & said to me, 'Thanks very much Mr Dahl.' I'd never set eyes on the fellow before, but apparently most of these natives all around here know you & all about you before long.

A bad bloomer I created in the office the other day: sometimes Piggy the cook calls into the office to consult with me regarding culinary matters, and on this occasion he brought in the duck he had bought for dinner that evening to

----

* Norwegian fishing village which the Dahl family often visited on holiday.

ask me if I thought it was big enough. It was dead & plucked; so I held it up by the hind legs or rather by the legs, and shouted to the nearest clerk – one H.V. Pandya – 'Is this duck enough for 5 people Pandya?' Whereupon he covered up his face and shrank rapidly into the far distance with a murmur of 'just sir excuse.' I went & asked George about this & he said, 'Good God, you mustn't do that. Pandya is a Brahmin, and they never touch or look at meat, fish or even hen's eggs.' So one lives & learns.

 . . . It's now 11p.m., have been to the sundowner & Samka enjoyed himself very much thank you, he said . . . Alec Noon

Roald's guard dog, Samka, whose exploits he would chronicle in his letters. Dog Samka is 'such an important person in this house,' he told his mother, 'that when he is ill or off colour the whole household is disorganised'

crashed his airplane up at Luinga last week but didn't hurt himself much.

Love to all

Roald

Kali Oscar says 'I'm not Wilde!' –

Dog Samka wishes to be remembered to you – Mrs. Taubsypuss sends her regards. –

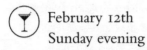

February 12th   Oyster Bay
Sunday evening   Dar es Salaam

Dear Mama

I've just been climbing the enormous Baobab tree in front of the house in a pair of shorts & gymshoes. We're going to build a little house up there in which to give sundowner parties and I was prospecting. You've never seen such an enormous tree; the branches very smooth, grey and hard, and lots of them – even the ones high up – have about the same circumference as your dining-room table. There are quite a lot of lizards up there, which don't hurt you at all, but I don't think there are any snakes – at least I didn't see them. But it's a marvellous tree, right on the edge of the sea, and you get all the breezes which are there to get – if any, but the bark is so smooth, and the boughs are so enormous that it's very difficult to climb – Louis would spend most of the day up there.

It was a very good dinner party. We had the Colonel – an old boy of 76 who has been hunting orchids in the forests of South America, mine-prospecting in the forests of Malay, buggering about in Hong Kong & fucking about all over the world. We like him – and he's called 'Iron Discipline', always to be pronounced together with a hearty thump on the table with your fist. That's because he keeps thumping his old wizened fist on the table – rattling the glasses and upsetting the whiskey – exclaiming the while, 'Iron discipline, that's what we want, Iron discipline.' He tells some incredible stories about his escapades – they make Lord Dunsany pale into insignificance.

. . . There are so many lovely moths out here that I'm going to start collecting them quite seriously. Has Louis got any books on the elementary things like setting them etc. If not could you please buy me one & send it out airmail, deducting from my next allowance. Also any books you can find regarding East African Moths (don't suppose there are any). And if I have got to get any implements – tweezers or anything, please send those too. Sorry about asking you to send all this, but you can't get a thing here.

There's no other news except that the sun's still shining & the natives are still black.

Lots of love
Roald

 April 9th 1939   Dar es Salaam
Sunday 3.30p.m.

Dear Mama

I've just been down to fetch two letters from you & one from Asta. The most sensible idea I've heard yet is that Bexley will be evacuated in time of war; it'll have to be done quickly though. I'm very glad to see that you are all ready to shoot off to Tenby – that should be as safe as anywhere. And if Alf, Else or Asta want to go nursing they can do it anywhere in England in one of the numerous country houses which will be converted into hospitals, without going buggering off to the front wherever that may be. We hear the news perfectly every evening at 8.45 pm our time, 6pm your time, on my superb wireless. I think I'm going to buy it. It's a Phillips 10 valve 1938 with a cracking good tone; and it's extremely powerful. Even in the afternoon I can get the English Empire broadcasts (short wave) perfectly – just like you get London at home. On the short wave I can get the news from England (fairly authentic), from Italy in English (very garbled), from Germany in English (more garbled still) and from America in American (very detailed, but not too reliable). So you can see that we know all that's going on as soon as you do. Funny I should be talking about this; at this very moment the bells of St. Martin in the Fields have just stopped and the velvet voice is saying, 'Here is the news, copyright reserved etc'. This is 1.15pm your time.

I learn that 2 hours ago Lord Halifax called on Chamberlain; there are crowds of holiday makers in Whitehall (it's Easter Sunday); Count Ciano has flown to Tirana etc.* It's a bugger. Why doesn't Mussolini take up some useful hobby; he could collect bird's eggs instead of countries; he'd probably say that it was cruel. As for Hitler, if he must keep his mind on guns, why doesn't he concentrate on a little vigorous fornication. Wasn't it Hitler who said to Göring after a piss up one Saturday night, 'I am ready for a whore.' Goering answered, 'Do you want a Great Whore, Adolf like the one you had in 1914?' Hitler hiccoughed and answered, 'I want a whore in the air, but don't give me a Civil Whore, they bore me, whereas it should be the other way round.'

---

* Gian Galeazzo Ciano was Italian Minister of Foreign Affairs and Benito Mussolini's son-in-law. Lord Halifax was British Foreign Secretary from 1938–1940. In 1940, he would become British Ambassador to the USA in Waashington. Roald would work for him there between 1942 and 1944.

. . . Everything goes mildew here during the rains, including most of our delectable inhabitants. I found my camera case and the bellows of the camera covered in green stuff this morning, and had to spring-clean the whole shoot. Golf balls go yellow, but that's nothing – mine do too, like everything else that's not used.

Many happy returns of Tuesday.

Lots of love to all

Roald

 Sunday 16th or 15th I'm not sure   Dar es Salaam

Dear Mama

Many thanks for your letter and all the newspaper cuttings . . . We all read them with much interest etc. I'm a bit drunk so you won't get much of a letter. I had meant to write to you this afternoon because I knew I should be drunk by the evening because we had a darts match on. But someone asked me to go bathing in the Indian Ocean, so I did that instead & said well I'll write my letter after dinner. We had a lovely bathe – David Powell, a girl called Moira who looks like Kari, and self – the water is rather like tepid bath water but apart from that we'd all seen a bloody great shark on the beach this morning which some fisher boys had caught. David kept shouting that there was a shark just behind, and what with lobsters nipping our toes & sharks biting the old balls – However, I am not yet talking falsetto.

Then we had a darts match against the Gymkhana 'A' Team in this house – it only finished ½ an hour ago, & a great deal of liquor was consumed by all concerned. You see the result in my handwriting for which many apologies, but the alternative is that I wait until I'm sober & miss the bloody mail & you'll probably think I've been eaten by a rhinoceros or a white ant or something equally dangerous.

. . . Last night we had a good party in Penny Burgess's house & went to a little dance afterwards. From 2pm Saturday afternoon until 2am Sunday (today) morning I consumed the following variety of liquors:–

Beer
Gin
Whiskey
Rum
Champagne
Sherry
Crème de Menthe
Brandy

And I felt a better man this morning, Gunga Din.*

I expect you think this is awful, but it's O.K.; it's only our weekend blow out from a lot of hard work, & tomorrow things will be running as usual – oiled wheels, etc etc.

Herewith a bloody great moth I wonder what the hell it'll look like when it gets to England – I hope you don't have to pay customs duty on its balls. Tell its parents it died fighting for its country & giving the Nazi salute.

. . . Apologies for the frivolous note, but better next time, and now there is nothing I'd like better than to fall straight into my bed and Hitler can go & fuck himself.

Love to all
Roald

---

* Gunga Din was the long-suffering Indian water-bearer, 'a better man than I am', immortalised in a poem by Rudyard Kipling. Roald, like many of his had to memorise it at school.

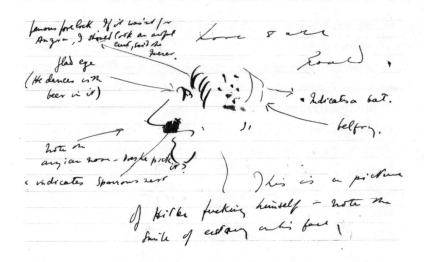

This is a picture of Hitler fucking himself – note the smile of ecstasy on his face.

[Notes on this illustration are as follows]

Famous forelock. If it wasn't for Angora, I should look an awful cunt, said the Führer.
Glad eye (He dances with beer in it)
Note the Aryan nose – Does he pick it?
X indicates sparrows nest
• indicates a bat Belfry

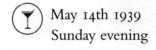 May 14th 1939   Dar es Salaam
Sunday evening

Dear Mama

I got your post-card from Tenby this morning, and you certainly seem to have got a fizzing house. I expect you're having a cracking time picking primroses, & going to Manobier & Caldy & all those places, & don't I envy you.

Here there's not much news. The rains are still going on – it rained solidly & heavily without a simple pause day or night from Monday to Friday evening and everything was just bloody wet. Our lawn's under water and so is my car almost. Dog Samka goes about in a bathing costume all day and thinks he's the Empress of Australia.

Frightful show here last week. George, David & I got a bit whistled at the Gymkhana Club after a Darts match. We'd won it and were celebrating our victory in the usual manner; there's an enormous blackboard in the club for chalking up darts scores, &

Roald and his friend George Rybot pose in front of a dartboard, on which has been pinned a picture of Joseph Goebbels, Hitler's Minister of Propaganda. A similar prank throwing darts at a photograph of Hitler got Roald banned from the largely German Dar es Salaam Club

one of us – I think it was yours truly – drew a picture of Adolf Hitler thereon, and we three invented a new darts game. Hitting his balls with a dart counted 10, hitting his tool counted 15, his navel counted 5, his moustache 20 etc. etc. This game progressed merrily for an hour or so and it was not until the next day that we heard that there had been a German bloke present at the time. He had watched us throwing darts at Hitler's balls for about an hour without saying a word, but the little bugger whipped straight off to the German Consulate afterwards; these people got in touch with the Government, & the Club Committee were called to an extraordinary General Meeting and all that sort of bullshit and now it only remains for us to ring the bell and ask for paper.

There's the hell of a showdown – you see there are so many Germans in this place & everything is rather on the boil – we seem to have squeezed the bugger. However we're just watching the fun at a safe distance.

Moral: Don't throw darts at Hitler's Balls in public they're private parts.

Love to all
Roald

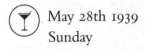 May 28th 1939   Dar es Salaam
Sunday

Dear Mama

. . . It's now 4.30pm. I'm just having tea of toast and marmite, and Dog Samka likes it very much. He had a big adventure yesterday. You know <u>he</u> comes to the office every day; well, yesterday David went across the road at about 12.00 to buy some special ointment for my leg and Sam followed him.

That was the last they saw of him, so a search was immediately instituted. At 2pm he was located sitting in the window of the chemist's shop wagging his tail (being a Saturday, the shop had shut at 12.00). But they couldn't find the proprietor, because he didn't live on the premises. At 3.00pm David & George came back for lunch with the news that Sam was in the window of the Chemist's shop & it seemed likely that he would have to stay there over the weekend. We consoled ourselves with the thought that by now he would probably have had a very good meal of vanishing cream with a dessert of orange skin food and perhaps a bottle of 'Nuits de Paris' or 'Blue Grass' to wash it down. After lunch they went out again and at 5pm they located the owner of the shop and Sam was released. They say that when he trotted out his lips were rouged and he'd powdered his balls, but I don't believe that. What I do believe though, is that the angry chemist has promised to send us a bill for damage to his furniture – Apparently there are a lot of little stains on the chairs and counters. George said that they'd match the ones on his character, so that didn't help matters.

When interviewed later by reporters Dog Samka was heard to remark: 'I found french letters fried in liquid paraffin very nourishing, I shall always carry a packet with me in future in case of emergencies' – this was immediately cabled to Hitler under the heading 'Strength through Joy', and his reply is eagerly awaited in official circles.

Hope you had a marvellous time in Tenby. I expect you'll be home again by the time this arrives.

Love to all

Roald

Here's another moth for Asta – Is she setting them?

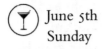 June 5th
Sunday

Dar es Salaam

Dear Mama

Many thanks for your letter and the 2 post-cards of Caldy Islands. You seem to have had a very decent time but I suppose that you're back by now; probably glad to be back.

I've had a bloody week. The poison seemed to have cleared up out of my leg and foot last Monday, so Doctor Ehrlich said I could hobble to work on Tuesday so long as I sat still with my foot up on a chair. Anyway it was more or less essential that I should go because David went upcountry on safari on that day for 2 months. I hobbled about with the help of a hockey stick and it looked as though it was getting better, but then 4 days ago it got worse again & gave me hell. Old Ehrlich scratched his head and gave me some very potent injections, and put something else on it, and today it seems to be better. But I'm having a very quiet-weekend and haven't got out of my dressing gown today.

. . . I'm afraid there's not much news, as I haven't been doing much this week. My wireless and gramophone are the greatest relief you can imagine. I borrowed Beethoven's 3rd (Eroica) and 5th Symphonies from a little man called Finnis and I'm not talking bullshit when I say that I now get the hell of a kick out of them. I studied the analysis of them at the beginning of the album very carefully and I now know them pretty well. I shall buy them and some more as soon as the next allowance rolls along. It's pleasant lying back and listening and at the same time watching the antics of Hitler and Mussolini who are invariably on the ceiling catching flies and mosquitoes. Perhaps I should explain that Hitler & Mussolini are 2 lizards which live in our sitting room. They're always here, and apart from being very useful about the house they are very exciting to watch. You see Hitler (who is smaller than Muss and not so fat) fixing his unfortunate victim – often a small moth – with a very hypnotic eye. The moth, terrified, stays stock still, then suddenly, so quickly that you can hardly see the movement at all, he darts his neck forward, shoots out a long tongue; and that's the end of the moth. They're quite small, only about 10 inches long, and they've taken on the colour of the walls & ceiling which are yellow & become quite transparent. You can see their appendixes, at least we think we can . . .

Love to all

Roald

 Sunday   Dar es Salaam

Dear Mama

Last week I finally succumbed to malaria and went to bed on Wednesday night with the most terrific head and a temp of 103°. Next day it was 104° and on Friday 105. They've got some marvellous new stuff called Atebrin which they straightway inject into your bottom in vast quantities which suddenly brings the temperature down; then they give you an injection of 15 or 20 grains of quinine and by that time you haven't got any bottom left at all – one side's just Atebrin and the other's quinine. On Saturday, yesterday I was O.K., and today I'm up, feeling none the worse except for a slight loss of weight through sweating. If any of you want to do a bit of slimming hire an anopheles mosquito and ask him to bite you. You sweat so much your sheets have to be changed several times during the night. I discovered that it was an excellent scheme to sleep between two enormous bath towels.

. . . The funny thing about my getting fever was that, George being upcountry, and Pakenham-Walsh having broken his right wrist, I still had to sign all letters and cheques. Without knowing it I'm told I signed cheques for 20,000 shillings – I only hope the Bank recognized the signature. Anyway we know the Bank managers etc. here so well personally that there's never any trouble.

. . . You'll be extremely surprised to hear that I'm expected to win the Tanganyika Golf Championship, which takes place down here in a few weeks. If it was Peggity I might stand a chance. People have been foolish enough to back me – but as you know I never bet myself, I never did hold with gambling – or didn't I? What's going to win the St. Leger?

. . . I hope there's not going to be a bloody war – but if there is all you people have got to pack into the car and drive for Wales as fast as possible, whether you've got a house or not. Those aeroplanes will be over just as quick as it takes them to get there. Will you please write and confirm that you'll be doing that.

Love

Roald

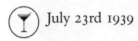 July 23rd 1939   Dar es Salaam

Dear Mama

. . . We've had the hell of a week. Two darts matches, a snooker match at the Railway Club, and a piss up last night . . . A small dinner party, a cinema, then the club till 2am. Then we all came back here and I distinguished myself by inventing a new game called strip-darts, run on the same principles as strip-poker. You each throw 3 darts at the board, and at the end of one round the person with the lowest score has to discard one garment. If you throw a double or a bull you can put one garment on again. Well, the first crisis came when Scottie only had his trousers left and threw the magnificent total of 3 (quite pie-eyed). We were all waiting for him to take off his pants, when he solemnly extracted his false-teeth, placed them on the table and said, 'That's foxed you, you buggers.' Scottie (being more whistled than the rest) continued to throw the lowest score with amazing consistency, and each time carefully removed one of his fly buttons with a pair of nail scissors. At last came the 'moment critique' when he had no more buttons left, and the manager of the East African Central Line Sisal Estates was compelled to remove his

The staff of Roald's house in Dar es Salaam. Roald was
housekeeper and greatly admired his nineteen-year-old 'boy'
Mdisho, on the left, who came from a tribe of 'magnificent
fighters'. Mdisho travelled everywhere with Roald,
showing 'absolute loyalty' to his 'young white master'

ravaged trousers. There were no pants underneath – only the usual things.

. . . When I said I wanted to photo the boys, there was terrific excitement. The Shamba boy (gardener) who never wears anything except a pair of trousers dashed round the place trying to borrow a Kansa (the white robe the houseboys wear) but he couldn't get one. Then Mwino approached and asked if I would take a photo of him and Mary, his wife, who as you will see is quite an elegant creature. I had to wait 10 minutes while she did her toilet.

I must fly and get some clothes on; someone's coming up for a drink.

Love to all

Roald

I may send you some leopard skins!

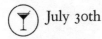 July 30th   Dar es Salaam

Sunday

Dear Mama

. . . This hasn't been a very eventful week, except for one terrible incident which happened yesterday. George & I were asked to go and have a drink at Mrs. Wilkin's house. Mrs. Wilkin is a frightful old hag who weighs 19½ stone (and is proud of it) and looks like a suet dumpling covered in lipstick & powder. Well George went into the drawing room & I went down to the basement to have a widdle. Down there I came across the most marvellous <u>crimson</u> tin pi-jerry, so with a whoop of joy I seized it to dash upstairs to show it to George, entering the drawing room waving the thing above my head. Well, I wasn't to know that there were 20 other people in the room, sitting primly around sipping their pink gins. There was a horrified silence then George started giggling – then we both got a fit of giggling while I pushed the frightful apparition under the nearest sofa and muttered something about 'what a pretty colour it was and didn't they all think so'. No-one answered & Dr. Wilkin said 'what will you have to drink'. We didn't have one; I said we had to go to the office at once to send a telegram which was very urgent, and George said, 'By God yes. I'd forgotten that,' and we dashed out. I don't think we'll be invited to the Wilkins' again. Got to go to golf . . .

Sorry this is such a bloody awful letter, but I'll write again soon.
Love to all
Roald

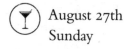 August 27th   The Dar es Salaam Club
Sunday   Tanganyika Territory

Dear Mama

This will only be a very short letter, because there's rather a lot to do here in these times of crises. I suppose that by the time you get this letter war will either be declared or it'll be off, but at the moment things, even here, are humming a bit. We're all Special Constables, with batons, belts & all sorts of secret instructions. If we leave the house we've got to leave word where we've gone to so that we can be called at a moment's notice. We know exactly where to go if anything happens, but everything's very secret, and as I'm not sure whether our letters are being censored or not I'm not going to tell you any more. But if war breaks out it'll be our job to round up all the Germans here, and after that things ought to be pretty quiet. Perhaps the Germans will allow themselves to be rounded up quietly too.

Many thanks for your letter which I got yesterday. You must try to sell the house for anything you can get now. If war breaks out it will be worth absolutely nothing, being where it is; so if that borrowing scheme (from Alf) has materialised go right ahead, pay off the mortgage & sell the house for £200. It seems a frightful shame, but I don't see what else you can do.

Grand fancy dress party last night for the British Legion. George & I were actually in our baths (me after cricket & he after golf) before we decided what to go as. Eventually we were a couple of sportin' parsons; white trousers tucked into our mosquito boots – Black waistcoat back to front and the usual stiff collar turned the wrong way round. Then he wore my old Reptonian blazer & I wore one of his tweed jackets (He's about 5 foot 6 inches). He carried a butterfly net & I an umbrella & that was fizzing – we won a prize of a bottle of whiskey, which, I regret, was empty by the time it came to leave. I woke up in the sitting room at 8am this morning in my sportin' parson's clothes feeling a little the worse for wear, but everything's O.K. now – Bar Hitler.

Lots of love to all

Roald

P.S. My records haven't arrived yet!!

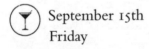 September 15th
Friday

Dar es Salaam

Dear Mama

. . . I'm very sorry I haven't written to you for such ages – (that's why I put on Alf's letter 'To be opened by Mrs Dahl . . .') but you can guess that things have been humming a bit here. Now all the Germans in the Territory, and it's a pretty big place in which to try to catch them, have been safely put inside an internment camp. And we Special Constables were the people who had to collect them. The moment that war broke out at about 1.15pm on Sunday the alarm was given on a series of telephones and certain key men dashed round and collected their squads, & proceeded to the police lines to be armed and to receive orders. At the time, I was actually out guarding the road going down the South Coast to Kilwa and Lindi with 6 armed native troops (Askaris) and an enormous barbed wire blockage across the road. All I heard was a grim voice down the field telephone which said – 'War has been declared – Stand by – arrest all Germans attempting to leave or enter the town.' Then the fun started, and after a bit when I was relieved, I went into the town to help with the work there, rounding them up in their houses. I better not say any more or the ruddy censor might hold up the letter.

Well most people here have been called up by the K.A.R. (Kenya army), but as we're an essential service we've got to go on working for the moment – and working like buggery. When I was guarding the road, I used to sit under a palm tree all night with a gun across my knee & being bitten absolutely to death by anopheles mosquitoes, get home at 6am & go to the office for the whole of the day – then on again at night. It was no joke. Now all we do is work like buggery from 7 or 8 until 6 or 7 or often longer.

. . . I may have to move about all over the place, in which case my allowance will be very essential if you are able to remit it to me – I hope so. If you can't let me know and I can make arrangements with the Company to pay me here if you'll pay them there – will write again v. soon.

Lots of love to all
Roald
Please move house!

September 30th 1939   The Dar es Salaam Club
Saturday   Tanganyika Territory

Dear Mama

Many thanks for your letter and the second batch of
newspaper cuttings which caused much amusement in the club
bar on Thursday evening. Your letter was opened by the Censor
here, who probably thought it was one from Alf full of dirty
jokes; no doubt he was disappointed. Glad to learn that you're
all still O.K., but I say once more that you've no right to be
sitting in one of the most dangerous places in the world at the
moment, quite happy in the mere thought that you've got a
cellar – That cellar's no good once the real raids start, which
presumably they must before very much longer. And if they start
with a vengeance, Oxford won't be any good either. You'll have
to go to Wales; but enough of that – by now you must know
what I think.

. . . There's absolutely nothing one can do out here at the
moment. There's no point in joining the local army, who do
very little, having very little to do; and one's not allowed to leave
East Africa – anyway for the time being. If I get the chance I
think it might be a good idea if I trained for flying up in
Nairobi; I believe they're taking a few blokes soon. But for the
moment, as far as I can see we shan't be doing anything for at
least a month or two.

As for Dar es Salaam it is exactly the same as usual except for
one or two things. Firstly, as I believe I've told you before, there's
been an invasion of women from Nairobi to work for the
military down here as stenographers, typists, telephone operators,
secretaries and making the colonels' tea. They belong to an
organisation in Kenya and are quite seriously called the somewhat
unfortunate name of 'Fannies'. Each letter in the word stands for

something but I don't know what – you know, same idea as ARP or D.O.M. These girls go about in the most gruesome khaki uniforms you ever saw, and all have to be in by 8.30pm in the evenings; but the one I know is not so dumb – you should see her shinning up a drainpipe to her room at midnight – her name is Lance-Corporal Higgins and she's got one stripe on her uniform. She deserves promotion, but I daren't suggest it to the Colonel because he may start wondering why, and then she wouldn't only be making his tea. We had a game of mixed hockey with them yesterday and they certainly are tough, but they were very out of position because there's only one they know. Actually that's not true – they're very prim really.

Then the second thing about Dar is an invasion of the military. Fellows in uniform and cockade hats all over the place and a frightful lot of snobbishness. All bullshit. Talking about Bullshit we've invented an instrument called the <u>Ox-ometer</u> which is designed to measure the amount of bullshit talked and written by the military and by the Government out here (this letter'll probably be stopped by the censor – if it is you'll know why you haven't got it!).

. . . What is everyone at home doing? Let me know, and let me know what things are like – here there's rationing only of petrol – I get 2 gallons a week. We could of course take as much as we want but we're being strictly honourable about it. The only chance of any fighting out here is if the Italians come in against us – then it'll be pretty hot what with Abyssinia.

Lots of love to all
Roald

October 14th 1939   Dar es Salaam

Dear Mama

. . . Nowadays one flying boat a week comes in from the
North on Thursdays, and one a week leaves for England on
Sundays but the bugger of it is that even if we post on Saturday
mornings we may not catch the mail because the censor has
perhaps not thought fit to go to the Post Office and do his
censoring, so one's letter has to wait for the next mail – that's
why you're getting my letters at such odd times. The last but one
I received from you had been opened by the Censor! And – oh
bugger!! I've just spilt a bottle of ink on the floor – just hold on
while I call a boy to try to wipe it up –

That's better. You see, it's now 3.30 on Saturday afternoon.
We've got through most of our work, have been to the club
for the usual Saturday morning beer and gin and have just had
lunch. And I'm lying on top of my bed with nothing on (it's
getting really hot again) writing this letter. For some weeks
past I've always written in pencil, but I thought that it was
time that I used ink. I hate ink in bed anyway because it
always gets on the sheets, however careful one is; but
nevertheless I balanced the bottle on the end of the bed and
proceeded to write. Then I sneezed and over it went and now
there's a horrible black mark on the floor, but there's luckily
some ink left in the bottle. I'm getting fed up with talking
about ink.

. . . WE had a terrific snake hunt the day before yesterday.
David & I had just rolled up to the house in my car and David
got out and went up the steps. I was just going to follow when a
huge black mamba shot past. Now these black mambas are real
bastards. Not only are they one of the few snakes that will attack
without provocation, but if they bite you, you stand a jolly good

chance of kicking the bucket in a few hours unless you receive treatment at once. Any way the old Mamba shot into a corner just where the steps join the house, and having jumped onto the roof of my car I shouted to David to have a look over the verandah. You should have seen the look on his face. All he saw was a horrible head waving in the breeze and looking up at him, and he knew bloody well that it was a black mamba. He rushed into the house & got a couple of hockey sticks and threw one to me on the car. Then the bugger darted into the garden in some grass and we followed, because you can't possibly leave a thing like that lurking around. Shouted to all the boys, 'Nioka, nioka kubwa njo upesi' which means 'snake, snake big, come here quick', and out they came, Mdisho with a thing like a bargepole, Hosmani with an axe, Abdulla with a bread knife. Only Omari, David's boy stayed inside ironing because if there's one thing he hates like hell its 'nioka'.

We surrounded it but it shot out and away like a flash; surrounded it again, and this time the sod came at us, and I just managed to catch him with my hockey stick and break his back before it was too late. Then there was much rejoicing and the boys danced around and got very excited because he was a big bugger (for a Mamba) about 8 feet long and as thick as my arm and black as soot. I'm getting fed up with talking about snakes.

Last Saturday we had the best party we've had for a long time. A week of hard work and only a strict ration of 3 or 4 whiskeys in the evenings had left us just right for a real heat up – And we had it. At the Dar Club in the evening I'm told that I tossed each glass over my shoulder à la Henry VIII as soon as I'd finished the whiskey therein, and worst of all a dame I know told me that every time I danced with anyone I just said, 'you dance like a goat, so stuff me full of sage and onions'. Well, that was awful, but one gets excused for doing things like that because there's a war on. The worst thing about that night was waking up next morning on the floor underneath my bed. For 3 awful minutes I wondered where the hell I was, and wondered whether I'd been buried alive. It was indeed a bugger. I'm getting tired of talking about drink.

This income tax sure has played hell with all of us. I knew exactly what it meant as soon as I heard it on the wireless. What about the car; wouldn't it be better for you to sell it for what you can get – No, on second thoughts, you must keep it; it will perhaps be your only means of getting away from London if those air-raids start. You can all get into it and just beetle off with the dogs and a suitcase as soon as things begin to look dangerous. Nevertheless I think you could live cheaper and very much <u>safer</u> on a farm in Devon or Cornwall, or would that be too bloody. Mind you do that if things start to happen.

. . . I must get up and get ready to play in a big football final against the Sudanese which will be watched by a crowd of about 800 natives who, I'm afraid never cease to rock with laughter at me when I trip up over my own legs, which I do frequently. Then up to Penn's house for some Shove Halfpenny and some beer and bugger the war.

Lots of love to all
Roald

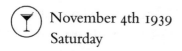

November 4th 1939
Saturday

The Shell Company
of East Africa Limited
P.O. Box 343
Dar es Salaam

Dear Mama

. . . Things are moving: on Tuesday or Wednesday next – 7th
or 8th Nov., I'm packing a suitcase and flying to Nairobi for a
'medical' for the R.A.F. If I pass, which I think I certainly should,
I shall be drafted into a flying course somewhere in Kenya and no
doubt will have learnt to fly after about 6 months. Then as far as
I can see there's a good chance of going to Egypt . . .

You needn't get alarmed about this flying business out here –
it's just very good fun, and anyway the chances of getting sent to
any scene of action for at any rate 9 months or a year are pretty
remote. I hope the war will be over by then. When I fly over to
Nairobi on Tuesday I shall first go due west to Dodoma (it'll be
on the map), and after my 'medical', and assuming I pass it, I
hope to fly down here again for a few days to clear things up i.e.
sell my car & wireless and pay my bills (which are pretty well
up-to-date) resign from clubs and 101 other things. Unless you
have already sent my lovely cake and the ham, perhaps you'd
better wait a week or 2 until I can give you a proper address; but
until further notice please continue to send my letters to Dar es
Salaam. If I get a semi-permanent address in Kenya soon I may
cable you just saying 'Address . . . so & so . . .'.

I'm certainly looking forward to getting into a decent climate
(4000ft) after being down here on the coast for a year without a
holiday.

Everything here is still very normal; I've been playing a lot
of soccer and hockey, and doing quite a bit of Golf organising,
and life is altogether quite pleasant. Tonight I'm going to a
Dance at the Dar Club with the Chief Secretary of Tanganyika,

who is at the moment acting Governor, as the Governor has gone to Kenya for a conference. I suppose I'll get drunk, – Saturday night.

We've got 2 hens in our garden now, and they make the hell of a noise at 5.30am. I bought them in the native bazaar for one shilling each. But they won't lay because there is no cockerel. David and I refuse to buy because we do not countenance immorality on our property. I came home from soccer yesterday evening and found the bloody hens perched on the edge of the sofa in the sitting room. If they'd shat on my wireless they wouldn't be alive now. I think we'll have to kill them soon as they encourage snakes. I don't think there's any more news, I'll write and let you know what I'm doing next week – from Nairobi, I expect.

Why don't you sell the car, now that you get so little petrol – or do you think you'll get a better price for it later on.

Poor Louis seems to be having a tough time – there's little use for artists in wartime. I'm going to send him some native wood carvings for Xmas if I can get them shipped.

Lots of love to all

Roald

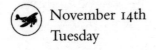 November 14th   P.O. Box 1221
Tuesday   Nairobi

Dear Mama

I believe I missed the mail, but that was because I was on my way to Nairobi, where you will see I now am. I didn't come up by plane because there wasn't one going, so I got on our little coastal tanker last Thursday morning and had a lovely trip to Mombasa, arriving there on Friday morning. We didn't call anywhere on the way, but just went through Zanzibar harbour to let them know who we were. I slept on the deck and also distinguished myself by catching a large barracuda (fish) from the back of the boat for the evening meal. Got on the train at Mombasa on Friday evening at 4pm, had dinner, went to bed and woke up to find we were chugging along through the plains of Kenya about 4000 feet up. Looking out of the window while having my breakfast I saw literally hundreds of buck and antelope of all sorts, a herd of zebra, ostriches, buffalo and best of all four enormous giraffes and a baby giraffe so close you could almost lean out of the carriage window and touch them. The country was nothing to look at just a bare brown grassy plain with a few leafless trees, but once I caught a glimpse of Mt. Kilimanjaro in the background, and very fine it looked, with its pointed snow covered peak.

Anyway, arrived at Nairobi station at about 9.30am and George Rybot was there to meet me. We drove to the office which is a magnificent building. All the rooms are parquet floored and panelled, and everyone is connected to everyone else with these Dictograph things by which you can talk to anyone you like. At 11 o'clock I was up at the aerodrome having the stiffest medical test I've ever had in my life. I held my breath for 2 minutes; blew a column of mercury up a tube till I thought I was going to burst; lifted trays up to eye level without letting the long wobbly things balancing on them topple over – (you stand a fountain pen or an unsharpened pencil on a piece of wood and try to lift it up high and put it down again with one hand). The most incredible instruments were produced for testing eyesight and all sorts of nervous reactions, and I weighed 14.00 stone and measured 6ft 5¼ inches.

Ultimately I passed with flying colours and was classed as 100% fit to fly. The result is that I must report at the aerodrome (R.A.F. headquarters) at Nairobi on the 24th November – 10 days' time, when together with a few other blokes I will be made an aircraftman on the princely salary of Shs 5/- per day, and be put through an 8 weeks flying course. After that, if one has shown an ability to fly, we are sent to some God-forsaken place in Egypt called --------, where still more flying experience is gained, and finally in about 4 to 6 months from now to join the R.A.F. Middle East Command in Cairo. Now I don't know what you think about all that, but personally I think it all sounds fairly exciting and interesting and a bloody sight better than joining the army out here and marching about in the heat from one place to another and doing nothing special. Further more one learns to fly free,

Roald, shortly after he began his RAF flying training in Nairobi, 1938. Of the sixteen people with whom he did his initial training, only three survived the war

Roald with two other trainee pilots in Nairobi, 1938. He was taller than most pilots and his head stuck over the wind shield of his Tiger Moth so he had to duck down every few seconds to take a breath. His love affair, however, with this new element was immediate. 'I've never enjoyed myself so much,' he told his mother

which is a very great commercial asset in these days. It would certainly cost one about £1000 to obtain a 'B' licence. So much for what I'm going to do, but I'll let you know more about it later; but I'm certainly looking forward to 8 weeks in Nairobi . . .

Lots of love to all

Roald

CHAPTER 4

—

'Thoroughly good for the soul'

1939–1940

ROALD DAHL'S WAR
1939–1941

KEY

 ROALD'S HURRICANE

 ROALD'S GLOSTER GLADIATOR

 ROALD'S PLANE CRASH

 CONFIRMED ENEMY
KILL BY ROALD

 UNCONFIRMED ENEMY
KILL BY ROALD

 FIELD HOSPITAL: ALEXANDRIA, EGYPT

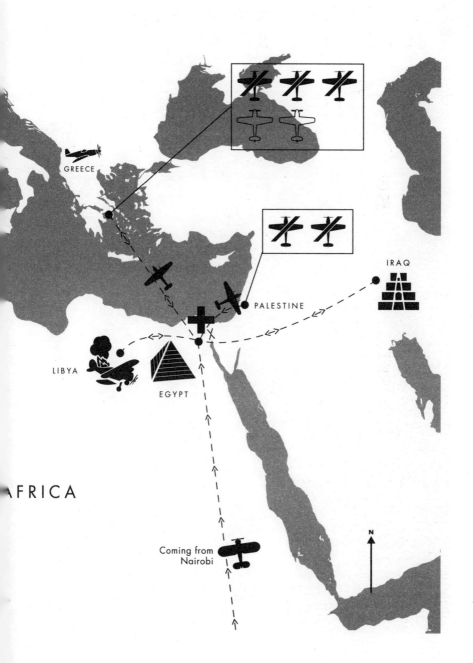

GREECE

IRAQ

PALESTINE

LIBYA

EGYPT

AFRICA

Coming from
Nairobi

N

It was undoubtedly Roald's experiences as a wartime flyer that finally made him into a writer. Right from the beginning, swooping over the Kenyan bush, the sense of being alone and free in an unfamiliar element stimulated his sense of the mystical. The sky became an alternative world: a place of tranquillity and gentle beauty that could be magical, transformative, even redemptive. Most of his early adult stories are profoundly connected to this spiritual dimension of flying, and it is a feature of much of his children's fiction. In his final book, *The Minpins*, a small boy rides on the back of a swan, flying 'in a magical world of silence, swooping and gliding over the dark world below, where all the earthly people were fast asleep in their beds'.[47] Similarly, in *James and the Giant Peach*, the child protagonist stands at night on the surface of the giant fruit as it flies across the Atlantic. Contemplating the heavens, James is filled with a similar sense of wonder: 'The peach was a soft, stealthy traveller, making no noise at all as it floated along. And several times during that long silent night ride high up over the middle of the ocean in moonlight, James and his friends saw things that no-one had seen before.'[48]

His training began in the idyllic surroundings of Nairobi in Kenya. Soon he was flying over the bush and exploring the Rift Valley. He delighted in the RAF lifestyle and was thrilled to have left the humid world of sundowners and expatriate life on the coast behind him. The final stages of his training however took place in the remote desert air base of Habbaniya in Iraq, some sixty miles from Baghdad.

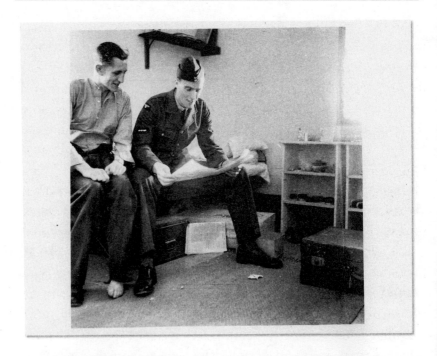

*Roald with his friend Alec 'Filthy' Leuchars while completing his
flying training at RAF Habbaniya in Iraq, 1940. Roald would later
describe Habbaniya as possessing 'the worst climate in the world',
where the trainees lived 'only for the day we will be leaving'*

Its many buildings included churches, a cinema, a dental hospital, a
swimming pool and a mineral water factory. Writing to his mother,
Dahl praised the good food, including fresh fish from the River
Tigris, and the central heating in the billets, but later he would recall
it as 'an abominable, unhealthy, desolate place . . . a vast assemblage
of hangars and Nissen huts and brick bungalows set slap in the middle
of a boiling desert on the banks of the muddy Euphrates river miles
from anywhere'.[49] Roald was one of the top trainees on his training
course and also one of the few who occasionally ventured out, visiting Baghdad to play poker and haggle in the marketplace for gifts,
and driving to see the ruins of Babylon.

All the while, he continued to worry about the welfare of his mother and sisters. The 'phoney war' that followed the declaration of war in September 1939 had continued through the winter, and despite Roald's attempts to persuade his mother to move to Tenby, Sofie Magdalene had stubbornly refused to budge. Bexley lay close to two potential bombing targets: Woolwich Arsenal and the Vickers Armament works in nearby Crayford. Roald knew that Oakwood, the family house, would almost certainly be hit by any German air raid. He was also concerned that his mother's status as an alien might make life difficult for her – particularly when Norway was invaded by the Germans in April 1940. But from 4,500 miles away he was powerless to do anything but cajole, hector and browbeat.

His chronicles of the dusty tedium of life at Habbaniya make vivid reading, as does his description of what happened when the Euphrates flooded and the entire station had to be rebuilt three miles away as a tented encampment atop a sand mound. The scorpions, sand vipers and incessant sandstorms brought out the stoic in his personality and made him reflect on the good things of life. He had little inkling that far greater travails lay ahead for him.

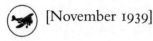 [November 1939]   P.O. Box 1071
                                                 Nairobi

Dear Mama

. . . Well, I drove up from Dar es Salaam on Tuesday Wed and
Thursday. And it really was marvellous fun . . .

. . . Left Korogwe at 8am Wednesday (by the way Dar to
Korogwe was 300 miles) and had the most lovely journey right
up into the mountains. The road climbed to about 7000 feet,
marvellous scenery; but after I'd gone about 100 miles it started
to rain like hell, and miles away from anywhere the car decided it
couldn't get through the muddy road. It slithered from side to
side and ultimately finished up in the undergrowth. After what
seemed hours some wandering natives came along & helped to
get it out, none the worse for wear.

At 3pm I sighted Kilimanjaro looking simply marvellous with
its huge snowcapped peak, and 2 hours later I arrived at Moshi,
which is a town literally at the foot of Kilimanjaro – marvellous
place, with air just like that of the mountains in Norway. I stayed
at the Lion Cub Hotel and left again next morning for Arusha.
This bit was one of the most interesting parts of the trip because
I came into the Masai country. You probably know all about
these natives which are quite untamable and still walk about with
paint and mud on their faces and hair and bows & arrows and
spears. They are great fellows for hunting lion, and very few of
the men stand under 6 foot 2". I stopped and talked – as best I
could because they don't speak Swahili – to some of them on the
road. One had the most lovely bow and arrows I've ever seen. It
was so tight I couldn't stretch it more than 2 or 3 inches, but at
my request, and for a cigarette, he shot an arrow into a small tree
literally 60 or 70 yards away. He said he killed a lion last month.
Arrived at Arusha at about mid-day, and went straight on to
Nairobi where I arrived at about 6.30pm. Saw lots of game on or

just beside the road all along the way. Giraffe, rhino, zebra, antelope and thousands of lovely little buck. I took some photos, including one of Giraffe & will send them by next letter.

The next day – Friday, I reported at the R.A.F., and immediately became an aircraftman, we've been issued with uniforms – blue & 2 khaki, socks, boots, shirts, towels – everything. I live in a barrack with 18 other fellows, who seem very pleasant indeed, and we start flying on Monday, and attend a lot of classes about flying, Morse code and all that sort of thing.

I can't tell you much more yet because these letters are carefully censored and it would probably only be crossed out any way, but it looks as though it's going to be very good fun. No more nonsense with boys doing everything for you; you wash your own knives & forks & mugs which you own, call everyone sir, and in short lead a life which I think will make me extremely fit and be thoroughly good for the soul . . .

Now it's Monday – I couldn't get this off yesterday. Great fun today – did my first flying with extremely pleasant instructor . . .

Must go and polish my kit now.

Lots of love to all

Roald

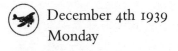 December 4th 1939   P.O. Box 1071
Monday   Nairobi
                           Kenya

Dear Mama

. . . I'm having a lovely time; have never enjoyed myself so much. I've been sworn in to the R.A.F. proper and am definitely in it now until the end of the war. My rank – a Leading Aircraftman, with every opportunity of becoming a pilot officer in a few months if I don't make a B.F. [Bloody Fool] of myself . . . The flying is grand

and our instructors are extremely pleasant and proficient. With any luck I'll be flying solo by the end of this week.

These details are rather meagre, but I can't say any more. We never wear ordinary clothes, except for games. My dinner jacket and tails and nearly all my clothes are stowed away in a camphorwood chest (moth proof) which I had made before I left Dar. If we go out before 4.30pm (Wednesday is a half day) we wear a Khaki RAF uniform. After 4.30pm wherever we are, be it walking, talking in a club or dancing in a hotel we must wear the RAF blue uniform with a little blue cap on the side of the head – you know it.

. . . I don't think there's any more news. Hope everyone's O.K. – for all we know I might be in England before 1940 finishes, but that's a bit optimistic. Thank goodness the bombing hasn't started yet, but when it does, you've all got to shoot away to Wales without wasting any time.

By the way, will you please send my next income instalment (if any!) to my account Barclays Bank Nairobi. I must go to bed – it's only 9 o'clock, but late nights just don't work with this life.

Lots of love to all

Roald

Herewith some photos of my trip from Dar to Nairobi, see backsides for comments.

 December 11th 1939   P.O. Box 1071
                                                         Nairobi

Dear Mama

. . . You needn't address my letters Aircraftman . . . and anyway that's the wrong title because I'm a Leading Aircraftman now! The flying's going fine, it really is great fun. I can just about manage a plane for elementary things such as taking off, cruising around, climbing turning and landing. The landing part of it was jolly difficult, largely I think because there's always such a hell of a wind blowing across the aerodrome. It's in a great flat plain, and you've only got to look over the fence a bit and you see all sorts of things wandering around – wildebeest, zebra, buck etc. Also the fact that one is 5½ thousand feet up before one starts doesn't help matters. We're starting to fly at 6.15am now in order to avoid the wind.

. . . I'm trying to write this letter in the Naafi* when there are about 100 aircraftmen drinking and making merry, playing the piano and singing some very beautiful songs, and it's not very easy, so I think I'd better stop.

Anyway, I want to drink and sing too.

Lots of love to all

Roald

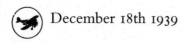 December 18th 1939   P.O. Box 1071
                                                        Nairobi

Dear Mama

. . . Well, everything here is also going very smoothly. I did my first solo flight some days ago and now go up alone for longish periods every day. I've just learnt to loop the loop and spin and the next thing we've got to do is flying upside down, which isn't quite so funny. But it's all marvellous fun. Nairobi looks very small and funny from the air; it's in the middle of a huge plain on which you can see all sorts of weird animals roaming, and if it's not too cloudy you can see Mt. Kilimanjaro on one side and Mt. Kenya on the other – a marvellous sight.

---

* The Navy, Army and Air Force Institute was an organisation created to run recreational establishments for servicemen. It was essentially a glorified bar.

The peaks of both are covered in snow the whole time – even out here.

I'm afraid there's absolutely no news – this is just to say that I'm still here and everything's fine and it's bloody cold at 5.30am in the mornings and dammed hot at midday and I'm tired and I'm going to bed although it's only 8.30. Never in my life have I continually gone to bed so early and got up so early as we do these days; I'm sure it's very good for one . . .

Sorry this is such a short letter.

Lots of love to all

Roald

I'm writing to Bestemama tomorrow.

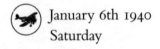 January 6th 1940   P.O. Box 1071
Saturday   Nairobi

Dear Mama

I'm afraid that I haven't written to you for years – not since my Xmas telegram – if you call that writing.

Anyway, what with Christmas and New Year there's been quite a lot to do. At Christmas I had a great 4 day holiday: stayed in luxury at a marvellous farm house just outside Nairobi with two old ladies and a fellow in our flight called Alec Leuchars (who's a friend of theirs). Alec used to be in Dar es Salaam with me as Imperial Airways man. George, who went to Mombasa lent us his car, and we went to Brackenhurst (7500 ft) every day to play golf and dance. Nothing very much happened but it was very enjoyable and extremely restful . . .

On New Year's Eve we had the best party that I've had in East Africa – and that's saying something. I went with a fairly large party to the Muthaiga Club whose annual New Year's party is famous. I got special permission to wear a dinner jacket, which was in itself a bit of a relief, and after polishing off about a bottle of Pol Roger 1926, I didn't remember very much else about the party – not in detail anyway. I remember dancing around the most enormous bonfire on Muthaiga Golf Course at midnight, and kissing all the unfortunates who came within reach. The next thing I remember was ordering breakfast at 7 a.m., and then going home to bed – only to get up again at 9 a.m. to play in a golf competition, which, believe it or not, I won. In fact I won this very smart 40/- fountain pen with which I'm writing this letter, and which, in my opinion makes my writing look a little less spidery than usual.

And now we're flying again, and as far as I can see everything is going O.K. I was the first in our batch to do the more advanced solo aerobatics such as slow rolls and inverted gliding – and it's bloody good fun. (We always wear parachutes for that.)

I'm not allowed to tell you where we're going or when we're going, but in a very few weeks' time we'll be on the move.

I seem to remember that either Alf, Else or Asta knew some people in Cairo. I may be wrong, but if they or anyone else you know does, you might let me and them know, because it would be useful. This doesn't mean that we are actually destined for Cairo, because we are <u>NOT</u> . . .

There's no more news. The weather here is a very pleasant change from the coast, and I was told the other day that I was looking <u>really</u> fit for the first time since I'd been in Africa. (They only sell beer at the canteen – no whiskey!)

Lots of love to all

Roald

 January 29th

P.O. Box 1071
Nairobi

Dear Mama

The time is now drawing very near and we're all feeling fairly excited about leaving this country. All our exams are finished and so now all we do is to fly the whole time. Yesterday I had a great time. I flew someone up to Nakuru about 90 miles, dropped them there and went on to a place called Eldoret, another 100 miles or so. It's a grand country to fly over, because the scenery is so interesting. Escarpment going into the Rift Valley is amazing. You fly along merrily over woods, fields and native villages and things when suddenly you see below you what is little less than a bloody great cliff about 2000 feet high, and the whole country in front of you suddenly assumes a level of 2000 feet less than it was before. This Rift Valley, which you've no doubt heard of in your geography lessons, is full of extinct volcanoes with huge craters, and lakes and flocks of pink flamingos and giraffes and ostriches and many other things which force you to take your eye off the compass too long and lose your bearings. I've seen quite a lot of Africa already; it really is marvellous fun.

Else keeps asking what sort of machines we are flying but I haven't mentioned any names because I don't think I'd be allowed to. Anyway up to now we've only been flying fairly small trainers, but as soon as we arrive at our next destination we get straight on to bigger and more serious stuff. Whether it be bombers or fighters. If we get any choice, which I believe we do, I shall choose fighters straight away . . .

We've had rather a tough week. Friday we 'held an airman's ball' in our hangar, at which about 200 airmen and their molls participated. We got a bit drunk and I went to bed in my shoes and socks and a shirt – at least that's what I woke up in. The others in here seemed to think it was very funny but I didn't feel in any mood to laugh . . .

I haven't got the cake or the pullover yet! But I'm leaving instructions for it to be forwarded – so by the time I get it that cake will have done a bit of travelling.

Lots of love to all
Roald

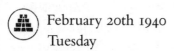 February 20th 1940   Address: L.A.C. Dahl
Tuesday   774022 (!)
                             Pupils Squadron
                             4 F.T.S.
                             Habbaniya
                             Iraq

Dear Mama,

Well here we are in Iraq. We flew from where you got my last letter and arrived 2 days ago. On the journey we called in at the most remote places in Palestine that you could ever imagine – a small aerodrome in a vast desert with perhaps a pumping station for the Iraq petrol pipeline – an icy cold wind blowing, and a group of incredible Bedouin folks all in about 6 huge sheepskin coats and furry hats. Altogether we saw a lot of country but it was mostly sand. The river Jordan looked picturesque and so did one or two of the oases, but otherwise, as I have said before, it was just sand; and for that matter it still is!

This place is miles and miles from anywhere – it is literally IN THE DESERT. Sixty miles away is Baghdad, but, except for an exceptional weekend, no one ever gets there – I expect we'll go sometime. On the other hand it is a rather marvellous place – an enormous R.A.F. camp – so enormous that you could not possibly visualise it. Churches, cinema, hospitals, mineral water factory, a street of shops, and hangar upon hangar and billet upon billet; all these things there are, but women do not come this way, so amongst numerous other things, they, during the next 4 or 5 months will have to be completely forgotten. But that will not be difficult because we are working and flying so hard.

Lake Habbaniya is very close, and the River Euphrates wends its very windy way past us only a few hundred yards distant. Otherwise there is sand all around us; in one direction it is flat sand, and in the other it's a curious mountainy sort, and when the wind blows as it invariably seems to at this time of the year you breathe this sand in a rough proportion of 50/50 with the air. Then, so they say, you get Gyppy Tummy and spend the next 3 days on the lavatory seat hoping that you haven't got dysentery – you usually haven't! There's hardly any malaria, but there's sand fly fever which has almost exactly the same effect – high temp. for 3 or 4 days and 8 days convalescence. They say one is bound to get sand fly fever because no mosquito nets are small enough to keep out the bloody little sand flies. Otherwise at the moment, the climate is lovely because it is meant to be springtime. Icy cold in the mornings, and warm in the daytime. In a month or so the summer comes along and it will be 120/130 degrees in the shade! Deserts, they say, get very very hot.

Because of these inconveniences, they have built here one of the finest R.A.F. Stations in the world; up to date and beautifully equipped. Excellent sleeping quarters and good food; marvellous canteens and Naafis, tennis, squash, cricket, rugger, soccer, hockey, and golf of a sort! A good swimming bath . . . It appears that we'll be stuck here for 4/5 months, after which time, with luck we should be drafted to a squadron with a commission. We should get our wings fairly soon. By that time I should imagine that we shall be pining for a bit of civilisation and a little less sand.

So much for Habbaniya. We had 4 days in Cairo and had the hell of a time from which we are only just recovering. We had unfortunately to stay in a large R.A.F. camp outside the town, but we went in each day. Wine, women and song were the order of the day or rather of the night, and by day we scrambled up the pyramids, gaped at the Sphinx, rode camels from place to place, and galloped about the desert on frisky Arab steeds (I did not fall off). We saw King Tutankhamen's treasures in the museum and King Farouk driving through the streets. They were all cleared at his approach, and he passed at 55 mph surrounded by men and motorbikes.

Then we called on your old friend Dr. Omar Khairat, who gave us a very cordial welcome. Four of us Leading Aircraftmen were invited to dinner at his brother's house where the most incredible orgy took place. Course upon course of rich Egyptian delicacies were piled upon us, and we were forced to eat until we could literally hardly stand upright. Dr. Omar, as we called him, was extremely kind to us . . . Jock Dick, who had toothache was whisked off by him in a taxi to a good dentist, where his rotten tooth was removed, and he was informed that it would be taken as an insult if he attempted to pay for anything – even the taxi. He gave me 2 photographs – one of Else and Asta tabulating blood transfusions and one of Ellen working in the labs, both very good. His other photos were absolutely marvellous and if Ashley had known the number of University College nurses that he had photographs in the nude he would have had a shock – very beautiful women and very beautiful photographs. We sent him an enormous box of chocolate-covered marron glacés because he likes sweet things . . .

Here is an unposed and not very good photo taken of me in the streets of Cairo by one of those men who pop up from behind a public lavatory and snap you and hand you a bit of paper telling you to call tomorrow for the print. What do you think of the uniform! Jock Dick is in the background, and Geoff Pelling's arm is in the left foreground. Also some snaps taken in Nairobi on our last day at the aerodrome.

Lots of love to all

Roald

 [postmarked March 8th 1940]

Pupils Squadron
4 F.T.S.
Habbaniya
Iraq

Dear Mama

. . . The post is doing funny things these days – witness the fate of your beautiful Christmas pudding and the Air Force blue pullover, which are now probably being eaten and worn respectively by some Gyppy postmaster in some outlandish Egyptian village.

On the other hand the watch turned up last week. Thank you very much indeed. It seems to be really quite a good one, and keeps excellent time. It comes in particularly useful here and is in great demand because we can time at how many words a minute we are sending our Morse code. I hope it won't get worn out. Talking about watches – I couldn't resist spending what was virtually my last penny in Cairo on another wrist watch, merely because it was such a bargain (there's no duty here on Swiss watches). My gold waterproof is going perfectly but I thought I'd like a standby, as I lost my silver Stauffer in Dar es Salaam some time ago. Anyway the one I bought is a very small waterproof stainless steel Longines – who are I think the finest watch makers in the world. I paid £8, but you couldn't have got it in England under £12 or £14. I know because I looked at some Longines when I was going to buy the gold one you gave me, or rather before I bought it. You may think it rather extravagant, but I've got rather a weakness for watches with good movements. My gold one and the Longines both keep time to the second.

. . . I went on a cross-country flyer today and saw a bit of Iraq from the air. Saw the Tigris meeting the Euphrates; saw Baghdad; saw, down in the desert, one of the seven wonders of the world – the largest unsupported arch in existence at Ctesiphon; saw one of the holy cities with an enormous gold domed mosque. You could see the same glittering in the sun many miles away. Also saw lots of desert.

You ought to be able to find a photograph of it in your photographic encyclopaedia.

Naturally the people who live in the desert round here are most curious types. It is literally dangerous to wander far out of the camp either into the desert or along the bank of the river. By far I mean only 3 or 4 miles, because they are quite liable either to fall upon you and hand you over to their womenfolk, who take good care that you do not get away with your balls; or to have a shot at you with a rifle from the top of a date palm! Not long ago they murdered a Pilot Officer who was riding to the lake on his bike because they wanted his bike and he wouldn't give it to them. I've taken some photographs of these people and will send you them when they are developed . . .

(Pause while I eat my orange, which are very good here.)

. . . I hope the cold weather has disappeared. How awful not being able to get any coal. I expect you'll get a warm spring to make up for it. My Christmas presents seem to have been very well chosen.

When we go to Baghdad I'll see if there's anything interesting there for your birthday, also for Alf and Leslie's wedding present. Am writing to Parrain.

Lots of love to all

Roald

Photographs of Iraqi desert-dwellers taken by Roald on a trip from Habbaniya to Baghdad, 1940. Roald was fascinated by the Bedouin, but sometimes alarmed by them. These 'blokes with guns and knives', he told his mother, 'don't think twice about cutting your balls out for the sake of getting your brass fly buttons.' They were, he reported, 'a treacherous crowd'

A photograph of the Arch of Ctesiphon, the largest unsupported arch on earth, taken while Roald was flying over Iraq. 'I was flying over the desert solo in an old Hawker Hart biplane,' he wrote in Going Solo, *'and I had my camera round my neck . . . I dropped one wing and hung in my straps and let go of the stick while I took aim and clicked the shutter. It came out fine'*

 March 27th 1940

Pupils Squadron
4 F.T.S.
Habbaniya
Iraq

Dear Mama

Many thanks for your letter – I'm glad you've given Harrods the raspberry about the Christmas Cake – although I don't suppose that it's their fault. John's a lucky bugger having Else and Asta keeping a pub for him at Havant – tell him he can thank his stars he's not here. He'd only get his balls cut off if he wandered out of this camp!*

Anyway we've just had a marvellous Easter weekend – probably the most expensive I've ever had in my life – I've got no more money left! But what's the use of saving it. There were three of us altogether – Alec Leuchars – whose home is in West Byfleet Surrey: Peter Blignant, who hails from the gold mines of South Africa, and myself.

We hired a taxi and beetled into Baghdad on Thursday evening and stayed at the Semiramis Hotel again. That evening we beat up the Cabaret and most of the rest of Baghdad, finished up at 4 a.m. in a filthy top storey attic playing poker with 5 of the crookedest Iraqi gents I've ever seen. They were all wearing hats and smoking yellow cigarettes and eating raw onions. Anyway they were shouting and grabbing and kept fingering their knives (all these blokes carry them) so we buggered off after we'd lost about £5 each.

The next day we decided that we must see the ancient city of Babylon, an opportunity which would probably not occur again, and which after all is not granted to many. It's so difficult to get to that very few of the average travellers or sightseers go there. We hired a taxi and drove out across the most desolate looking country for 2 1/2 hours and finally arrived at what looked like a few large slag heaps on the banks of the Euphrates. But lo and behold; on approaching closer, there beneath the ground which had been excavated to some 150 feet lay part of the old place itself.

It really was most interesting and absolutely amazing. The most marvellous brick walls still in perfect condition, the bricks cemented together with ordinary bitumen or tar. There was no-one there to look after the place, except an old Arab who had

---

* John Logsdail, also in the RAF. He would marry Roald's sister Else later that year.

been with the German expedition which had been doing the excavating, but had packed up when the war broke out. We wandered round, picking up pieces of beautifully glazed pottery, blue and green, and I found a bit of brick with cuneiform writing on it – you know the stuff like this.

I translated mine to read 'Dear Nebuchadnezzar, I'm in pod, what are you going to do about it?'* But the others said that that was wrong. However they are a good 6000 years old.

Meanwhile I got the old camera going, and got some good shots, which I rather treasure, because apparently no-one has taken many good ones of the place. They are enclosed herewith plus explanations on the back. The ones of the three of us are very successful considering they were taken by the old Arab. I fixed everything and told him what to press, and he did it very well, particularly the one of us in the Lion's Den where Daniel was thrown.

By the waters of Babylon we sat down and ate – our lunch of sandwiches and beer, and drove home again, to have another beat up in Baghdad . . .

I think I must buy a Persian carpet before I go – they cost very little – and they <u>are</u> Persian, hand made . . .

Many happy returns, and the same to Louis.

Lots of love to all

Roald

---

* In pod: contemporary slang for being pregnant.

Roald, Alec Leuchars and Peter Blignant exploring the ruins of
Babylon, and the den where the biblical Daniel was purported
to have been thrown to the lions. 'I got the old camera going,' he
told his mother, 'and got some good shots, which I rather treasure,
because apparently no-one has taken many good ones of the place'

April 26th 1940   Same address as before
                                         'The Desert'

Dear Mama

I don't think that I'm very good at writing letters on the
floor of a tent with eight other blokes in it, pitched on top of a
bleak sand mountain in the Iraqi desert. I think it's nearly over
now; more I cannot tell you, but I've probably witnessed one of
the most extraordinary episodes in the history of the
R.A.F. . . . Anyway it's an excellent thing to experience
discomforts which are so intense that you can be tolerably
certain that you will never have to experience ones which are
worse. Putting up tents at midday of an Iraqi summer in a
desert which consists not of ordinary sand, but of a form of dust
which is so thin and light (I expect some will get into the
envelope of this letter anyhow) that the slightest puff of wind
whips it up in your face.

Anyway the wind doesn't seem to have dropped since we have
been here, and many times it has blown at 40 mph for hours on
end. That means a proper sand (dust) storm. You can see about
20 yards if you dare to open your eyes. You certainly cannot go
about without special dark glasses with side bits on them. I was
on guard duty on the river for 7 hours last night in the middle of
it, and staggering back to my tent to find my blankets under 2
inches of sand. Five scorpions and 2 sand vipers were found in
the tents on either side of ours this morning, and a fellow or 2
here have been bitten – I believe a native died – but we are
keeping a careful watch in our tent.

I had a grand shit in a petrol tin this morning with 3 other
blokes doing the same within a space of 4 yards. One of them
suddenly leapt up, shrieking, 'Gor – a fuckin' scorpion's got me
balls.' A lengthy examination followed, and after a muttered,

'Thank shit, it's only a bloody sand fly,' he sat down again and resumed his duties.

I can't write any more because it's absolutely dark – for the last 5 minutes I haven't been able to see what I'm writing, and there's only a tiny little lamp in the tent.

Please thank Else for her letter. Hell of a pity about the bracelet – but let's hope it'll turn up sometime. If I ever go to Dar es Salaam again we'll have another made. I think and hope we'll be back and flying soon – Advanced Training this time – I'm told I collected an Above Average for I.T.S.

Love to all

Roald

Am on guard duty from 11.00 p.m. to 6 a.m. Bugger it.

 May 8th 1940

4 S.F.T.S.
Habbaniya
Iraq

Dear Mama

At last I'm able to write to you under fairly normal conditions. I'm sitting in a chair, at a table; and there is no sand in my eyes, ears or mouth. To us, this camp, which a month ago was a pretty bloody uncivilised sort of place, now appears to be the very height of luxury. The beds seem uncommonly soft and sheets dazzlingly white. You no longer find a little heap of sand in the bottom of your mug after you've drunk your tea – and last night I wore a set of clean clothes.

That we should have come to regard Habbaniya in the light of a luxury city is a very excellent and I am told, quite unprecedented thing – but I'm afraid that it will not be so for long. Soon, no doubt we shall once more be so spoilt that we shall be crying out for a drink of whisky, a taxi or a theatre; or a dance and the company of women. But at present we are very thankful for small mercies – and comforts.

I don't know how much I may tell you of what happened, but I don't think that the Censor can object to a bare outline. It is after all common knowledge by now in Baghdad.

The ancient River Euphrates chose this singularly inopportune moment to flood its banks to an extent previously unheard of, due to the melting of the snows up in Turkey where she has her source. (You can no longer argue that we too have not felt the effects of your cold winter.) As this camp is on the river it was, said the authorities, assuredly in a very dangerous position in spite of the fact that enormous bunds* some 20 feet high have been built all around. It was generally assumed that the whole camp would be 20 feet under water. It was very difficult to imagine so vast a place being completely inundated – but was it not the Euphrates that submerged the proud city of Babylon.

What to do? Get out quick. So the whole camp, plus every item of equipment, stores, food, planes, chairs, tables, hospitals, dental chairs started a grand trek up on to a huge sand plateau situated on some mountains some 3 miles from the camp. To visualise the magnitude of the operation you've got to realise the size of the camp. I don't know how many people there are here; probably some 4000 British men and about 6000 Iraqis from the civil cantonment, who act as our servants, shopkeepers, labourers, etc.

Anyway this vast camp was set up. Tents appeared, and we all bundled in. I drove an Albion lorry for 3 days transporting crates of dried fruit, marmalade and ammunition up there. The temp. was well over 100 degrees in the shade and the dust was everywhere.

---

* Bunding or bund walls were flood defences.

The camp itself was many miles in circumference, and you could well walk about in it for an hour without finding the squadron for which you were looking. Beside it were lines of aircraft pegged down in the open on a flat piece of desert, whither they had been hurriedly flown.

Once installed, we spent our time working in gangs on the bund, reinforcing it with sandbags. I worked every night from 10 p.m. to 6.30 a.m.! Every day there was a dust storm up on the plateau. The sand all around the camp had been churned to powder by the lorries, so that even the lightest wind would raise it in a cloud. This dust and sand is guaranteed to get anyone down, and in a tent and eating in the open – doubly so. There were times when the cookhouses just couldn't function.

Then came the old scorpions and tarantulas to add to the excitement. They loved the tents, and many were killed (scorpions, not people). The secret was never to walk about barefoot, and always to look into your blankets before going to bed. Nevertheless several people were bitten. One fellow went to bed with a sand viper – I asked him if it was for want of a more suitable companion, but he swears he didn't do it on purpose! I killed a 4 ft sand viper on the bund the other evening just as it was approaching Peter Moulding who was sitting down having a rest and a cigarette.

The net result of our labours was that we beat the river. The night on the bund we saw the water creep up to within 2 feet of the top – lorries were waiting to rush us away if it broke; but it was not to be. Breaches were made in the banks at other points to relieve the pressure and no doubt many wandering Iraqis and Bedouins were drowned, but Habbaniya was saved. And now we're all moving back and trying to wash ourselves clean. I am told that the river has burst its banks lower down and is flowing across the plain to the Tigris and Baghdad is going to be flooded to buggery.

I've just received a letter from you and one from Asta enclosed. I'll bet you the Bestes are still in Josefine* quite safe and sound. I'm sure things aren't so frightfully bad in Oslo. They are only bombing the aerodrome. But I don't think you've much hope of hearing from them for a long time. As for old Finn and all the others – goodness knows. It's pretty bloody.

As far as I can see you're doing too much work, Ellen says so too. You simply must get a maid – and <u>keep</u> her. Why don't you take that holiday?

Tell Asta I've just told her story about the Mississippi at supper and it lifted the roof off. People spluttered custard all over the place through laughing with their mouths full.

I must stop to catch the post. They tell me there's a parcel for me at the P.O. May be my shoes – or even the Christmas Cake and pullover! I'll let you know next post.

Lots of love to all
Roald

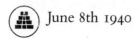 June 8th 1940

A.T.S.
4 S.F.T.S.
Habbaniya
Iraq

Dear Mama

I expect your last letter has been held up somewhere again, as I haven't heard from you for about 9 days. I'm afraid you'll have to get used to short non-newsy letters from me now, firstly because there is so little news, and secondly because when there is some it seems hardly worth mentioning at the

* Roald's grandparents, Bestemama and Bestepapa, Karl Laurits and Ellen Hesselberg's Oslo apartment was in Josefinegate.

175

present time. The only news we listen to at the moment is the home news on the wireless. It's pretty frightful – at the moment anyway – but there's no point in discussing it. Here as usual the news is just flying (which is going quite O.K.) and the heat, which is not so O.K . . .

However, I expect it's better than having to be running in and out of the cellar the whole time, as you're probably doing. You really must move – and move soon. It's absolute madness to stay in Bexley. The Germans will probably do their bombing from about 30,000 feet because they are frightened of our defences, and from that height the bombs will be dropped absolutely indiscriminately – they can't possibly aim accurately at their targets. Tell Alf, Else and Asta to think about it a bit. They won't be helping Leslie or John by staying. On the contrary, they'll only be worrying them. And what's more – I don't think Sussex is any good really, do you? Somewhere like Wales or Cornwall are the only really safe places. You might all just as well go there as not. Once again, please let me know what you're doing.

We had a large snake in the swimming bath last week. About 100 people swam quicker than they had ever done before, and the whole bath was empty of airmen in about 5 secs. The wretched animal was ultimately killed, and bathing continued, but it was very funny while it lasted.

No more news I'm afraid.

Lots of love to all

Roald

Dated August 19th 1940

DAHL

OAKWOOD

BEXLEY

KENT

> ADDRESS R.A.F. ISMAILIA,
> EGYPT STOP
> PILOT OFFICER NOW PASSED
> OUT SPECIAL DISTINCTION
> HOPE ALL WELL
> LOVE
> RONALD DAHL [*SIC*]

 August 28th

P/O R. Dahl
Officers Mess
R.A.F. Station
Ismailia
Egypt

Dear Mama

Today I sent you a telegram telling you where I am and I hope you got it. Really this is the loveliest (that's lovely, not lousy!) place I've yet seen anywhere in Africa. My views are probably a bit biased after being in Habbaniya for 6 months, but I think that anyone, wherever they come from, couldn't fail to be impressed. You've probably seen on the map that we're about half way down the Suez Canal – in fact Ismailia (pronounced ISMA-LIA or Ismer-lier) is the home of the Suez Canal Company. It was practically all built by them and is consequently overflowing with French Suez Canal Co. families. There's a French Club and a larger French bathing place, to both of which all R.A.F. officers are admitted as Honorary Members. The beach is frequented by hordes of the most lovely women I've ever seen – and coming after 6 months of terrific abstinence in the desert at Habbaniya it has come as a bit of a shock.

As I told you in the telegram, I got a 'Special Distinction' which is one better than a 'Distinguished Pass' and exempts one from taking any exams for promotion. In our reports they have to classify you for 'Ability to become an officer' and I, by some extraordinary chance, got the only 'Exceptional' on the course.

I should say at a guess that we're only spending a very short time here, learning to fly modern type fighters, and shall no doubt be having a crack at the Italians before this reaches you. Hope so anyway. I'll try to keep you informed telegraphically of my movements.

You must be having the hell of a time with bombing raids. I do hope you're all all right – where is Asta? Is she in a London hospital?

I'm afraid I can't make this letter half as interesting as it should be, because the censor will only cross everything out, so you'll have to use your imagination. At the moment anyway, and I'm afraid it will only be very short lived – though well earned – we are having a marvellous time – flying in the mornings, bathing and perhaps dancing in the evenings. The climate is perfect. How we got here I can't tell you, but it was a marvellous trip. I saw Lake Galilee, Nazareth, and all the lands of the Bible.

Do look out for yourselves in the raids.

Love to all

Roald

September 10th 1940

P/O R. Dahl,
Officers Mess
R.A.F. Station
Ismailia
Egypt

Dear Mama

This place Ismailia is indeed a marvellous place.

. . . Every morning we have been getting up at 5.30 a.m. and started flying at 6 o'clock. At eight we go back to the mess for breakfast. But breakfast in the Officers Mess is a little different to breakfast in the Airmen's cookhouse. No longer do we have to remember to give our forks and spoons an extra good lick on the last mouthful or to scrape our knives on the edge of the plate to make them easier for us to wash in the communal bucket of water and permanganate of potash. Nor do we have to queue up for the food while some Iraqi cook slops it on to your plate. No, we go back at 8 o'clock to an ordinary breakfast sensibly served and cooked. Stewed fruit, Force, eggs, bacon, kidneys, tomatoes – toast and Coopers Oxford marmalade – what a change.

Then some more flying until about midday; a drink in the Mess and lunch. After lunch some sleep until half past three in the afternoon. Then we drive down to bathe at Ferry Port. Ferry Port is a large expanse of sand actually on the edge of the Suez Canal, reserved almost exclusively for the employees of the Canal Company, who are of course legion here. British Officers are allowed there too – and I should bloody well think so considering that we're defending them. The bathing is marvellous. For about ten yards there's shallow water with a silver sand bottom then it goes sheer down into the Canal proper, where the dredgers have been at work. We bask on the beach for a while, then someone suggests a swim to Sinai . . .

The weekend before last – our first here – we <u>drove</u> to Alexandria in 2 taxis and had some marvellous champagne parties with all the friends of the 6 people on our course who originally lived there. Once again we bathed (this time in the Mediterranean) and basked in the sun. Last weekend we took taxis to Cairo to have another look at that. A very enjoyable but hectic weekend. I expect I'll soon be browner than I ever was in Norway with all this 'basking' and everyone has already, I should say, recovered nearly all they lost in health at Habbaniya. Yes – Ismailia is a good spot.

Lots of love to all and thank Asta again for her letter.

Roald

CHAPTER 5

———

'Don't worry'

1940–1942

In October 1940, on the way to his first day on active service, Roald got lost over the Libyan desert at night, crash-landing his Gloster Gladiator and suffering head injuries so severe that the RAF doctors thought he would never fly again. The crash itself would be the subject of his first piece of published writing, 'Shot Down over Libya' (1942), and was an event to which he returned several times, most notably in 'Missing: Believed Killed' (1944), 'A Piece of Cake' (1942–6), 'Lucky Break' (1977) and Going Solo (1986). 80 Squadron's accident report notes that, 'Pilot Officer Dahl was ferrying an aircraft from No. 102 Maintenance Unit to this unit, but unfortunately not being used to flying aircraft over the desert he made a forced landing two miles west of Mersah Matruh. He made an unsuccessful forced landing and the aircraft burst into flames. The pilot was badly burned and he was conveyed to an Army Field Ambulance station.'[50] Roald's own accounts of the incident, however, often differed markedly from this record. Sometimes the plane did not crash, but was instead 'shot down' by a German fighter. Initially these fictions were necessitated by the needs of Allied wartime propaganda. But the mythology persisted.

That crash was undoubtedly the key event in Roald's life. For the first time he tasted mortality. Blinded and trapped in his burning aircraft, he contemplated what seemed to be a certain death. 'All I wanted was to go gently off to sleep and to hell with the flames,'[51] he wrote. But some sort of life force, a 'tendency to remain conscious'[52] made him extricate his burning body from its parachute straps, push open the cockpit canopy, and drop out on to the sand beneath. Then the Gladiator's machine guns started to explode and bullets ricocheted around him. 'All I wanted was to get away from the tremendous heat and rest in peace,' he explained later. 'The world about me was divided sharply down the middle into two halves. Both these halves were pitch black, but one was scorching hot and the other was not.'[53]

Perhaps the most revealing piece of mythmaking associated with the crash involved another airman entirely. Douglas McDonald had flown with Roald from Fouka in a separate aeroplane and put his Gladiator down safely on the sand, close by the wreckage of Roald's plane. McDonald comforted his injured comrade through the long cold desert night, while they waited for rescue forces to locate them. It was, as Roald later told his daughter Ophelia, the worst moment of his life.[54] Roald, who liked to appear impregnable to the world, found himself supremely vulnerable, being nursed by another pilot and one, moreover, who had not crashed his plane. So, despite the fact that in the earliest versions of the crash McDonald is present in the narrative, he largely disappears from later accounts. Most tellingly, Roald fails to mention him in the first letter he wrote to his mother after the accident. Even for her, perhaps particularly for her, he needed to maintain that façade of strength. Yet, writing to Douglas McDonald's widow, Barbara, in 1953, eighteen months after her husband's death in a plane crash in the foothills of Mount Kilimanjaro, Roald shone a different light on the situation.

April 24th   9 East 62nd Street,
                                            New York City

Dear Mrs. McDonald

It was really very good of you to write to me like you did. I should have written to you first about Douglas, had I known where you were, because I heard the awful news from 'Mug' in Nairobi some weeks ago.* It shook me more than almost anything that has happened for a long time, because, although I hadn't seen him since the war, I always felt a strong personal bond – and also a very deep gratitude – to him.

I expect he's told you a little of what happened that evening in the desert when we both came down, and I crashed. But I doubt he explained how really marvellous he was to <u>me</u>, and looked after me and tried to comfort me, and stayed with me out there during a very cold night, and kept me warm. Well, he did. And I shall always remember it most vividly, even some of the things he said (because I was quite conscious) and most of all how, when he ran over and found me not dead, he did a sort of dance of joy in the sand and it was all very wonderful, because after all we were not very far away from the Italians and he had a great many other things to think about.

I'll never forget it. I tried to write a little of it in that story 'A Piece of Cake'. Of course you know that the 'Peter' there is Douglas. That appeared originally in the Saturday Evening Post and was read by 12 million people.

I hope you are not too sad about it all any longer, and I'm glad that you have a daughter to comfort you.

I'm staying out here for a while now, writing stories for

---

* 'Mug' was the gossip columnist of the Nairobi *Sunday Post*.

the 'New Yorker' magazine, and possibly a novel. If I come home soon, I'll call you up.

    Yours sincerely,

    Roald Dahl[55]

That letter to Mrs McDonald is a reminder that the 'fictionalised' version of events in Roald's life is sometimes closer to the truth than the front he maintained in his letters home to his family, which was generally one of the confident entertainer, the provider of gifts, the stoic, unflappable *pater familias*.

That image was certainly a long way from the reality of his situation in hospital in Alexandria. There, Roald lay concussed and sightless, uncertain of time or surroundings for many days. He told his mother that he was blind for a week, but later admitted that he was not able to see for 'much, much longer', altering the truth, 'so as not to alarm her'.[56] As he lay in his hospital bed, he also learned that Oakwood, the family house in Bexley, had been virtually destroyed by German bombers and that the tent in Ismailia where his air-force kit – including camera and photographs – was stored, had been destroyed in an air raid. It must have seemed to him as if one part of his life was over and an entirely new one had begun.

He left hospital after almost three months to convalesce in Alexandria at the spacious villa of a wealthy English couple, Major Bobby Peel and his wife Dorothy. For several weeks, he tired easily and suffered from severe and prolonged headaches, yet his letters make light of his lack of energy, describing instead how he slept on silk and linen sheets, listened to Beethoven, Brahms and Elgar on the gramophone, and was pampered by Dorothy Peel. As always, in his letters, he focused on the positive.

Roald often claimed that this 'monumental bash on the head' had changed his personality in some way and therefore turned him into a writer. Whether or not he actually underwent a psychological change as a result of the trauma is impossible to tell – he certainly believed he emerged from the accident a different person – but it undoubtedly gave him something powerful to write about. The comic chronicler of Dog Samka's adventures in downtown Dar es Salaam was now working on a much broader canvas.

Roald's first big decision when he was discharged from hospital was whether to be invalided home, or to stay in Egypt and try to recover sufficiently for him to fly again. He opted for the latter, returning to 80 Squadron to fight in Greece in April 1941. Roald arrived when the Allied forces were already in full retreat. The squadron had been stationed at Elevsis to defend Athens, but the odds against them were enormous: approximately 800 German and 300 Italian planes against a motley force of 192 British and Greek machines – or, as one of Roald's fellow pilots described it, 'all the wops in the world and half the Jerries, versus two men, a boy and a flying hearse'.[57] Defeat was inevitable and Roald witnessed the death of many of his comrades including his friend David Coke. He evoked that fatalism in his early short story 'Katina'. 'The mountains were invisible behind the rain, but I knew they were around us on every side,' he wrote. 'I had a feeling they were laughing at us, laughing at the smallness of our numbers and at the hopeless courage of our pilots.'[58]

Yet there was another side to these grim encounters. 'It was truly the most breathless and exhilarating time I have ever had in my life,' Roald would later write in *Going Solo*. These were also the sentiments he echoed in the brief description of the combat he gave to his family in letters or indeed in telegrams, where the telegraph operator almost always got his name wrong, signing him Ron or Ronald. He flew briefly again in combat over Palestine, before the headaches and blackouts returned and he was pronounced unfit to fly, returning home to England in late summer 1941. 'They never recede with time,' he wrote years later of his experiences in battle. 'They were so vivid and violent that they remain etched on the memory like something that happened last month.'[59]

YEAR 1941		AIRCRAFT		PILOT, OR 1ST PILOT	2ND PILOT, PUPIL OR PASSENGER	DUTY (INCLUDING RESULTS AND REMARKS)
MONTH	DATE	Type	No.			
—	—	—	—	—	—	TOTALS BROUGHT FOR...
APRIL	20	HURRICANE		SELF	—	TAKE OFF AFTER GROUND STRA...
"	21	HURRICANE		SELF	—	ELEVSIS TO ~~MENIDI~~ MEGARA SATELL...
"	22	HURRICANE		SELF	—	~~MENIDI~~ MEGARA SATELLITE TO ELEV...
"	22	HURRICANE		SELF	—	ELEVSIS TO ARGOS
"	23	HURRICANE		SELF	—	ARGOS TO SATELLITE
"	23	HURRICANE		SELF	—	DEFENSIVE PATROL ARGOS ...
"	24	LOCKHEED HUDSON		F/O GOODMAN	SELF	ARGOS TO MARTIN BAGUSH (E...
		SUMMARY FOR APRIL				
		IN GREECE.				
		80 SQUADRON.				
		Certified that the above is correct				
					E. Gordon Jones. S/Leader. D...	
					O/C 80 Squadron.	
		GRAND TOTAL [Cols. (1) to (10)] 208 Hrs. 45 Mins.				TOTALS CARRIED FOR... HURRICANE 33.

Roald's pilot log book covering his ten days of aerial combat over Greece in April 1941. It details his three confirmed 'kills' as well as the destruction of all the RAF planes there by ground strafing. 'No fighters left in Greece,' was his grim conclusion

139·25	0155	0135								1650	12·35	
0100												
0010		No petrol to operate. Much bombing all around.							40 JU's destroyed 2			
0010									Greek seaplanes			
0020									400 got away.			
0010		40 ME 110's attacked aerodrome. We remained over shipping as										
0200		unrequired, turned back Squadron of Ju 88's.										
										0330		

Evening of April 23ʳᵈ. All remaining Hurricanes
written off on ground by groundstrafing ME 110's.
The 5 Hurricanes which were up in the air
at the time (including mine) landed O.K. in the
dusk, and flew to Crete April 24ᵗʰ. No fighters
left in Greece.
    Total fighter defence of Crete
was thus augmented considerably and was thereafter
8 machines!

| 143·15 | 0155 | 01·35 | | | | | | | | 20·20 | 12·35 | |

Dated September 21st 1940

NLT DAHL
WOODLANDS FARM
AYLESBURY

PROCEEDING TO FIGHTER
SQUADRON IN WESTERN
DESERT IMMEDIATELY.
ADDRESS R.A.F. CAIRO.
YOU WON'T HEAR MUCH
FROM ME SO DON'T WORRY.
LOVE
RONALD DAHL

TELEGRAM TO ASTA

 Dated October 14th 1940

NLT ASTA DAHL
WOODLANDS FARM
QUAINTON

MANY HAPPY RETURNS AND
LOVE
CRASHED IN DESERT TWO
WEEKS AGO.
CAUGHT FIRE BUT ONLY
CONCUSSION BROKEN NOSE.
ABSOLUTELY OKAY SOON.
ADDRESS FOR

FEW WEEKS ANGLO SWISS
HOSPITAL ALEXANDRIA
DON'T EXPECT ANY LETTERS
LOVE TO ALL
ROALD DAHL

TELEGRAM

 Dated November ? 1940

NLT DAHL
WAYSIDE EDGE
LUDGERSHALL
BRILL

GOOD PROGRESS SITTING UP
READING WRITING.
ANY TIME NOW HOPE LEAVE
HOSPITAL FOR
CONVALESCENCE
IN TWO OR THREE WEEKS
TWO MONTHS BEFORE FLYING.
POOR OAKWOOD.
LOVE
ROALD DAHL

November 20th 1940

2nd/5th Gen. Hospital
Middle East Command
Egypt

The air raids here don't worry us. The Italians are very bad bomb aimers.

This address is the same as the one you have, but we're now not allowed to use the previous name or mention the town

Dear Mama

At last I'm allowed to write, but I'm told that it's got to be a short letter. Yesterday I received eight letters from you and one from Alf and one from Else and one from Asta, dating back from July right up to the last one you wrote in October from the cellar at Oakwood, when Mrs. Creasey arrived in the middle. They'd been all over Egypt and the desert before finally turning up, and are the first I've had for two months.

I hope you're well settled now at Wayside Cottage and that it's quite safe there. You seem to have had the hell of a time at Oakwood. I expect you've written to tell me what's happened to the house and the pictures and furniture. Did you take the best pictures out of their frame and cart them off. I hope so.

I sent you a telegram yesterday saying that I'd got up for 2 hours and had a bath – so you'll see I'm making good progress. I arrived here about eight and a half weeks ago, and was lying on my back for 7 weeks doing nothing, then got up gradually, and now I am walking about a bit. When I came in I was a bit of a mess. My eyes didn't open for a week (although I was always quite conscious). They thought I had a fractured base (skull), but I think the X-ray showed I didn't. My nose was bashed in, but they've got the most marvellous Harley Street specialists out here who've joined up for the war as Majors, and the ear, nose and throat man pulled my nose out of the back of my head, and shaped it and now it looks just as before except that it's a little bent about. That was of course under a general anaesthetic.

My eyes still ache if I read or write much, but they say that they think they'll go back to normal again, and that I'll be fit for flying in about 3 months. In between I still have about 6 or more weeks' sick leave here in Alex when I get out, doing nothing in a marvellous sunny climate, just like an English summer, except that the sun shines every day. We stay with rich people in Alex, who volunteer to take in convalescent officers. But for any letters or telegrams written about 3 weeks from now send to

c/o Barclays Bank Mess
97 Avenue Prince Ibrahim,
Sporting
Alexandria

That'll always get me at once.

I suppose you want to know how I crashed. Well I'm not allowed to give you any details of what I was doing or how it happened. But it occurred in the night, not very far from the Italian front lines. The plane was on fire and it hit the ground. I was just sufficiently conscious to crawl out in time, having undone my straps, and roll on the ground to put out the fire on my overalls which were alight. I wasn't burnt much but was bleeding rather badly from the head. Anyway I lay there and waited for the ammunition which was left in my guns to go off. One after the other, well over 1000 rounds exploded and the bullets whistled about seeming to hit everything but me.

I've never fainted yet, and I think it was this tendency to remain conscious which saved me from being roasted. Anyway luckily one of our forward patrols saw the blaze, and after some time arrived and picked me up and after much ado I arrived at

LOVE FROM BOY

Mersah Matruh (you'll see it on the map – on the coast, east of Libya). There I heard a doctor say, 'Oh he's an Italian is he.' (My white flying overalls weren't very recognisable.) I told him not to be a B.F. and he gave me some morphine.

In about 24 hours' time I arrived where I am now, living in great luxury with lots of very nice English nursing sisters to look after me. I was in a private room for some time, but now I'm in a big ward with some other blokes, which is more fun. The good ladies of Alex come and visit us and bring us flowers and one Danish one Mrs. Ludwickson has lent me a wireless. The Norwegian colony, consisting of 2 judges who sit on the Mixed Tribunal here, rallied round right from the outset and have been very kind. I believe you've heard from Mrs. Dahl, Judge Dahl's wife, who you used to know at school in Norway. I've been told I've got to stop now.

By the way, if there's ever any money due to me, please always cable it to my a/c with Barclays Bank (D.C. & O) Cairo. If there's any difficulty about getting it out of the country, telegraph me and I'll arrange it with the Shell Co. here. I've got an income tax reclaim form here to sign, but can't get a suitable witness till I get up.

Lots of love to everyone

Roald

Thank Alf for her offer of a birthday present, but tell her it's no good. I'll have it after the war. Don't bother about Xmas presents.

December 6th 1940

P/O R. Dahl
2nd/5th = Gen. Hospital
(The same hospital)

Dear Mama

I've just been told that all troops are allowed to send home a one page letter free which if posted by tomorrow evening will be guaranteed to arrive by Christmas. So here it is.

Merry Christmas to you all.

I've just received your telegram saying that you've sent me a parcel to R.A.F. Cairo. Many thanks – and I'll make sure of getting it this time.

I haven't written to you since my one and only letter some weeks ago, chiefly because the doctors said that it wasn't good for me. As a matter of fact I've been progressing very slowly. As I told you in my telegram I did start getting up, but they soon popped me back to bed again because I got some terrific headaches. A week ago I was moved back into this private room, and I have just completed a whole long 7 days lying flat on my back in semi darkness doing absolutely nothing – not even allowed to lift a finger to wash myself. Well, that's over, and I'm getting up today (it's 8 o'clock in the evening actually) and writing this and incidentally feeling fine. Tomorrow I think they are going to give me intravenous saline and pituitary injections and make me drink gallons of water – it's another stunt to get rid of the headaches. You needn't be alarmed – there's nothing very wrong with me; I've merely had an extremely serious concussion, they say I certainly can't fly for about 6 months, and last week were going to invalid me home on the next convoy. But somehow I didn't want to – once invalided home, I knew I'd never get to flying again, and who wants to be invalided home anyway. When I go I want to go normally.

Anyway instead I shall be going up to a big new hospital in Cairo as soon as I'm up and about (which won't now be more than about 2 weeks. I'm not pulling your leg) and from there I'll go straight to Kenya for a long sick leave of some months – 3 or 4 months I should say, my brain apparently must have a complete rest, so I'll probably find some friends with a farm in the Highlands and stay there, and perhaps travel about a bit. By the way, I forgot to tell you that all my belongings, plus my white suitcase were blown up in my tent in the desert some time ago.

A photo of Roald in 1941, taken on his way to fly in Palestine after he had been evacuated out of Greece. In reference to the plane crash the previous year when he had suffered severe head injuries, he told his mother: 'I'm enclosing another awful photograph of me – just to show you that I've still got a nose'

The only things we found were my cigarette case and gold watch (still going). So I've got to start all over again. The only other things I've got are my cameras, which luckily I'd left behind. I don't mind much because I am only too thankful that I wasn't in the tent at the time.

I don't think my eyes are affected but I'm not allowed to do any reading yet (11 weeks in bed so far) but I've got my little wireless beside my bed. At the moment they are playing Brahms Second Symphony from Jerusalem and it's very good too. Will notify you by telegram of all my movements.

Happy Christmas and best love to all

Roald (My nose is bent!!)

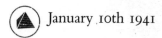 January 10th 1941

R. Dahl
Pilot officer
8 Rue des Ptolomées
Alexandria
Egypt

Dear Else

This is meant to be a sort of pre-wedding letter, saying good luck and all that sort of thing, although you may well be Mrs. John before it reaches you. You must have bought a lovely trousseau by the sound of it, although I hope you didn't waste any money on pyjamas; but I suppose they're necessary these days in case you have to go into an air raid shelter.

Lucky John's not a fighter pilot or you'd find he wanted to sleep in his parachute, and they're so cumbersome. Anyway I hope you have a decent honeymoon, and tell John he's a lucky bugger. I'm arranging for a wedding present but it'll take some time to reach you I'm afraid – something gold (oo-er!).

'What do you think it is, Asta?'
'Dunno, Vaseline I should think.'
'Silly you are to say that.'

By the way, Thank you, and Asta for your letters. Yes, living my life of luxury, I'm making goodish progress. I never get up till 10.30, and when I feel tired or have a bit of a head I go to bed before dinner. The old brain seems a bit sluggish still. Whereas before I used to play quite a moderate game of bridge, I find that at the moment I can't remember a single card or even formulate a simple plan for playing a hand. That however, is all only a matter of time so long as I'm careful.

I've started to play a tiny bit of golf. There are two lovely courses here with very good grass greens. (What a change from Dar es Salaam.) I drive down with Bobby Peel late in the afternoon and we play a leisurely 6 or 7 holes. Bobby and Teddy between them have 5 cars, 2 Cadillacs, 2 Fiats and a Rolls, so there's never much difficulty about transport.

Mrs. Peel weighs me regularly and contentedly watches me putting on the two odd stone which I've lost. I get masses of invitations from the good people of Alex, but I very seldom go anywhere except an occasional tea, although most of them have beautiful daughters. By the way, whilst I was up in hospital in Cairo I am told by Rhoda Hill, one of the sisters at the Anglo-Swiss that a young Naval fellow called to see me, saying that he knew the family at home; but he left no name or where I could find him. He must certainly have been Ian Patterson, so I shall try to get hold of him by making enquiries with the Navy.

My chief joy still is the gramophone. I play it all day. At this very moment I'm playing the last movement of Franck's D Minor Symphony. Before that I had on Dvorak's Fourth (not the New World) and as Cesar Franck is just coming to an end I must get up and put on something else. Excuse me –

That's fine, Beethoven's Trio in B flat – the Arch-Duke.
You'd be surprised – I could now tell immediately any of
Beethoven's nine symphonies if you played me a few bars of one
of them, or for that matter any of Brahms, Elgar, Franck,
Dvorak, Mendelssohn, etc. I know practically all of them
backwards. And although I still couldn't hum or whistle a single
bar of any of them in tune, I can 'think' through a symphony
with the greatest of ease. But you people who know about
music must I think get something extra out of it. For it means
nothing to me whether a thing's in B flat or C sharp; I fail to
appreciate a subtle change of key or skilful orchestration; and
although I can follow a score for a few seconds, I get left miles
behind as soon as it speeds up. In spite of all this, I think I enjoy
it more than many.

I remember, years ago hearing Ellen say that Ashley got a
funny feeling down his spine whenever he heard Wagner, and
what nonsense I thought it must be. But it's not – I get tickles in
the tummy – but not from Wagner, except bits. I get exactly the
same sensation from reading Matthew Arnold's Scholar Gypsy as
from listening to Beethoven's Pastoral.

Maybe it's nonsense, but anyway I've filled up another three
pages and if I stop in about a minute or so I shall just be in time
to turn over Beethoven's record.

Give my love to Mama, Alf, Asta, Ellen Ashley, Louis, Meriel,
John and Leslie.

My squadron is the famous fighter squadron in Albania; if I
can get fit quickly, I'll be there soon.

Lots of love

Roald

TELEGRAM

 FEBRUARY 10TH 1941

DAHL

WAYSIDE COTTAGE

LUDGERSHALL

BUCKS

> LISTEN IN TO WIRELESS ON
> THIRTEENTH FEBRUARY.
> CHECK UP IN PAPER
> MIDDLE EAST BROADCAST
> BECAUSE I MAY CALL YOU.
> LOTS OF LOVE
> RONALD DAHL

POST OFFICE TELEGRAM

FROM A.H.E. C3 SANSORAGINE

DATED MARCH 6TH 1941

TO

DAHL

WAYSIDE COTTAGE

LUDGERSHALL

BUCKS

> MESSAGE
> STARTING FLYING AGAIN NOW
> ADDRESS AS LAST SEPTEMBER
> VERY FIT
> LOTS OF LOVE
> ROALD DAHL

March 7th 1941

Officers' Mess
Royal Air Force
Ismailia

Dear Mama

It's simply ages since I had a letter from England – although I expect you are writing quite often. I suppose the trouble is that I keep jumping around from place to place. Whenever I leave one spot I always hopefully leave my next address with them for forwarding letters, but all in vain. I don't suppose you are getting many of mine either.

Well, as I telegraphed to you 3 days ago, here I am once more in Ismailia, getting the hang of flying once more after having been off it for over 5 months. I expect I'll be here altogether about another 4 weeks before rejoining my squadron which is incidentally the hell of a long way away – feeling the cold. Incidentally I'm now flying a more modern type of fighter thank goodness; I don't suppose I can mention its name, but it's the same kind as Douglas Bader uses.

It's very pleasant down here; warm and sunny each and every day, and once more our working dress is just khaki shirt and shorts.

Whilst I was at Heliopolis I tried in vain to find Leslie Pears, whom Alf had told me was coming out here to work for the Air Ministry. Then suddenly about 3 weeks ago she came up to me in the bar of the Metropolitan Hotel in Cairo one evening when I was tucking back a few quiet whiskeys with a fellow called Peter Fisher. She said aren't you Roald and I said Yes, who the hell are you, and promptly dropped a glass full of whisky and soda all over her feet and stockings. Well, after that we got on quite well; last Saturday she had a day off so I drove her down to Alexandria in my car to see Dorothy Peel and family and also incidentally to see Alex. We drove through the hell of a sandstorm the whole way but luckily on the way back the sand went although the wind persisted. Anyway we thought you might like a photo taken on the road, so we took the enclosed awful things when we stopped for me to have a pi. There was so much wind blowing that we could hardly stand up. I like Leslie because she's the first woman I've met since I left home to whom I can swear or say what I bloody well like without her turning a hair – trained by Alf I should imagine, and well trained at that.

Well I'm afraid I haven't got any news for you – I haven't heard that Else's been married yet; has she? I got quite a lot of news about you all from Leslie, but not enough. I wish they wouldn't lose your letters in the post.

Lots of love to all

Roald

P.S. Tell Asta she's not allowed to marry until I come home.

 [pencilled note – no date]

Handed in 12th

Many happy returns.
No letters for ages.
Rejoining Squad. imm;
northwards. A grandfather knew their language.
Love
Ron

April 12th

Officers' Mess
Royal Air Force
Ismailia

Dear Mama

A very short note to say that I'm going north across the sea almost at once to join my squadron. I telegraphed this to you today and told you where to send my letters. You may not hear much from me for quite a long while so don't worry.

Here are a few photos – we went on a trip in my car last weekend and took them.

Lots of love to all
Roald

TELEGRAM

POST OFFICE

R. PEEL TO MRS. DAHL

TELEGRAM ENVELOPE

DATED APRIL 29TH 1941

TO

NLT DAHL

WAYSIDE COTTAGE

LUDGERSHALL

AYLESBURY

POST OFFICE TELEGRAM

OFFICE OF ORIGIN &

SERVICE INSTRUCTIONS

ALEXANDRIA

MESSAGE
RONALD BACK SAFE LOOKING
VERY WELL
STAYING WITH US
RECEIVED YOUR LETTERS OF
MARCH 5TH
SEND LOVE
PEEL

*The wreck of a Hurricane destroyed by German ground strafing
at Argos. Roald had flown this very plane the day before*

May 6th 1941

80 Squadron
H.Q.M.E.
Cairo

Dear Mama

Thanks for your telegrams – we had great fun in Greece although I must admit I was pleased to get away safely. Once more I lost everything I had including my best camera, and arrived one evening at the Peels' house here looking like a tramp with nothing but my flying suit and a pair of khaki shorts. They reclothed me – I had a bath and borrowed a razor

Roald washing himself at the tented camp in Elevsis, Greece.
When he returned there after the Battle of Athens, he would
write: 'As I made my way slowly across the grass I suddenly
realized that the whole of my body and all my clothes were
dripping with sweat. Then I found that my hand was shaking
so much I couldn't put the flame to the end of the cigarette'

to shave off my beard after which I felt normal once more. Incidentally I got three German aircraft confirmed and 2 unconfirmed.

Lots of love to all
Roald

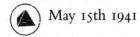 May 15th 1941

Alexandria
80 Squadron
R.A.F.
H.Q.M.E.
Cairo

Dear Mama

I've just finished my rest leave having had a lovely time staying with Dorothy and Bobby Peel and today I'm off to the place where the squadron is reassembling. It's not the Western Desert this time – it's very near the place we had our first big celebration after leaving Iraq about 9 months ago – you may remember. As I told you – once more I've lost all my kit, everything I had. I got no compensation the first time and this time I've so far got £12 which doesn't go very far – in fact I hope my income tax reclaims come along soon.

Well, I don't know what news I can give you. We really had the hell of a time in Greece. It wasn't much fun taking on half the German Air Force with literally a handful of fighters. My machine was shot up quite a bit but I always managed to get back. The difficulty was to choose a time to land when the German fighters weren't ground straffing our aerodrome. Later on we hopped from place to place trying to cover the evacuation hiding our planes in olive groves and covering them with olive branches in a fairly fruitless endeavour to stop them being spotted by one or other of the Germans or aircraft overhead.

Anyway I don't think anything as bad as that will happen again.
Lots of love to all
Roald

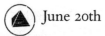 June 20th

80 Squadron
R.A.F.
H.Q.M.E.

Dear Mama

I had to have my photo taken the other day for an RAF pass. Here's a copy. Sorry about this note, but at present we're operating from a very obscure place, and such things as writing paper are difficult to come by. I shot down another JU88 and a French Potez last week over the Fleet, who as you will have heard over the wireless are operating up here.

It's pretty hot, but there's lots of every kind of fruit about – I expect you envy us there. But what a lot of flying. For the first 3 weeks we never stopped – you see there weren't many of us. Ground straffing, escorting, intercepting, etc. etc. Some days we did 7 hours a day which is a lot out here, where you sweat like a pig from the moment you get into the cockpit to the moment you get out. I'm writing this in a fig grove. Have a fig – there are lots here. Hope you are all O.K. Not getting any letters.

Lots of love
Roald

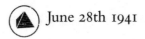 June 28th 1941

80 Squadron
R.A.F. H.Q.M.E.
Cairo
Egypt

Dear Mama,

I've suddenly received three of your letters dated 4th January, 15th January and 4th April! also one from Asta 4th January and one from Else 27th March for all of which many thanks. They give the first details I've had about the wedding which seems to have been marvellous. It'll obviously be a laud week in the history of Ludgershall and in time to come the locals will say 'It was in the year that Else and John were married . . . etc.'

Hope you never got your Lemoine 1927 Champagne – it's the worst year for champagne on record and is worth nothing, whereas the 1929 which Alf bought is one of the best. Still I don't suppose you can pick and choose.

. . . We've been doing some pretty intensive flying just lately – you may have heard about it a little on the wireless. Sometimes I've been doing as much as 7 hours a day, which is a lot in a fighter. Anyway my head didn't take it any too well, and for the last 3 days I've been off flying. I may have to have another medical board to see if I'm really fit to fly out here. They may even send me to England, which wouldn't be a bad thing, would it? It's a pity in a way though, because I've just got going. I've got five confirmed, four Germans and one French, and quite a few unconfirmed – and lots on the ground from groundstraffing landing grounds. We've lost 4 pilots killed in the Squadron in the last 2 weeks, shot down by the French. Otherwise this country is great fun and definitely flowing with milk and honey.

I sprained my ankle in the blackout yesterday!

The Germans are bombing us a bit, but they won't come over by daylight.

The sun shines all day and we are just by the sea – wish we got time to bathe.

Lots of love to all
Roald

P.S. Cheerful news: over 30% of our Habbaniya Training course have been killed or are missing here – it may be more now. Alec Leuchars was missing but walked out of a prison camp in Abyssinia when we captured it! He had baled out O.K.

Joke for the girls:

say quickly

Man walks into Pub.
'Give me a fucking beer fucking quick before the fucking
    trouble starts.'
Landlord pulls a beer and hands it over – Man drinks it.
'Give me another fucking beer fucking quick before the
    fucking trouble starts.'
Imperturbable landlord pulls another beer and hands it over.
Man drinks it.
'Give me another fucking beer fucking quick before the
    fucking trouble starts.'
Landlord starts to pull another beer, looks up and says, ''Ere,
    wot d'you mean, before the fucking trouble starts?'
'Well, it's sure to fucking well start soon because I haven't got
    any fucking money.'

[written on the back and underlined]

Private
Alf – Else or Asta

POST OFFICE TELEGRAM ENVELOPE
DATE JULY 21ST 1941
ADDRESSED
DAHL
WAYSIDE COTTAGE
LUDGERSHALL
BUCKS
TELEGRAM
OFFICE OF ORIGIN
ALEXANDRIA

MESSAGE
COMING HOME VERY SOON BY
SEA. VERY FIT. SYRIAN WAR
FUN. CABLE BY RETURN ANY
PARTICULAR MATERIALS OR
ANYTHING YOU WANT. ALSO
SIZES SILK STOCKINGS ALL
SIX OF YOU. EVERYTHING
HERE.
ADDRESS CABLE CARE PEEL
ALEXANDRIA.
LOVE
RONALD DAHL

POST OFFICE TELEGRAM ENVELOPE

DATE AUGUST 27TH 1941

TO:

MRS DAHL,

WAYSIDE COTTAGE

LUDGERSHALL

BUCKS

MESSAGE

RONALD IS VERY WELL AND

CHEERFUL AND

SENDS LOVE TO ALL.

The airstrip at Ramat David in Palestine, 1941. Roald was the first pilot to land there. It was a hastily prepared grass airstrip rolled out in a cornfield by residents of the nearby kibbutz

211

CHAPTER 6

——

'Teeth like piano keys'

1942–1943

Early 1942 found Roald living with his mother in a thatched cottage in the small Buckinghamshire village of Grendon Underwood, planting raspberry canes and wondering what to do with himself. He had returned from Egypt via Cape Town the previous summer and was still on extended sick leave. He was also dealing with a feeling of emasculation that he was no longer a fighter pilot. The RAF dangled the possibility of a job as a flying instructor in front of him, but that was almost like torture. As he was to write the following year, 'to a pilot, being alive but earthbound is worse than not being alive at all.'[60]

Then one evening in London, over dinner at Pratt's, one of London's smallest and most exclusive all-male dining clubs, his loud, raucous energy got him an unusual job offer. He was asked to work for the RAF at the British Embassy in Washington DC, where Lord Halifax was ambassador. His job title would be Assistant Air Attaché and he would be charged with using his charisma and flying experience to bring the American public behind the Allied war effort. He accepted it with alacrity.

His first weeks in the capital were among the most astonishing in his life. He met countless celebrities, had his moment of epiphany as a writer, and got his first story published. Before long he had befriended the US Vice-President, Henry Wallace, and was soon hobnobbing with the Roosevelts themselves at the White House. Within months of sitting under a tree in Grendon Underwood, telling stories about gremlins – strange little elves who RAF pilots held responsible for mechanical failures in the aeroplanes – to the children of a pilot friend who had recently been killed, he was working with Walt Disney as a writer on a major feature film about them.

His letters home chronicle the excitement of these dizzying new encounters. There is much name-dropping, as a host of film stars, directors and writers come into his office, all eager to support the war effort. It was the same with the many powerful and wealthy individuals he met, some of whom went on to become friends or lovers. Roald's shock at the contrast between the austerity of life in wartime Britain and the excesses he confronted in the USA is evident too and he sent home endless gifts of butter, sugar, chocolate, Norwegian cheeses, lipstick, stockings and other luxuries denied to his family by rationing in Britain.

There is an infectious delight in the pleasure he gets telling his mother about his literary successes, which began soon after a lunch with C.S. Forester. Forester had been commissioned to write a piece about the RAF for the *Saturday Evening Post* and took Roald out for a meal, so he could get some good circumstantial details for his story. Roald told him about his crash in the desert. The table was a small one and both men ordered rather messy roast duck. Forester found it difficult to eat and take notes at the same time, so Roald offered to write the story up for him when he got home that evening. He did. When Forester read the result, he was astonished. He told his newspaper editor that the story should be published pretty much exactly as Roald had written it. It was. A career had been launched.

Roald's letters reveal how seminal this moment was for him. From now on, in spite of all his other distractions, writing was what really mattered. The letters to his mother stress the role that luck and happenstance played in this transformation. And certainly the stars were on Roald's side. He was in the right place at the right time. But his official correspondence to agents and editors presents a contrasting picture. These letters reveal the intensity with which he was already practising his craft.

Roald did not find the embassy a convivial place to work. He thought it snobbish, humourless and hierarchical. The Air Mission itself was looked down on by embassy figures such as Isaiah Berlin, the information officer, who recalled that his colleagues regarded it 'rather as a grammar school was looked on by public schoolboys'.[61] Occasionally, in his letters home, one senses Roald's frustration with this working environment, but it is like light glimpsed through cracks in a wall. He would articulate that resentment more fully later on. 'I'd

Dignitaries inspecting Montgomery Blair High School Victory Corps, 1943. The programme focused high-school children on skills relevant to the war effort. Flight Lieutenant Roald Dahl however (fourth from the right) found it absurd. 'The things we do for England' he commented to his mother. On his left is the veteran playwright and farceur Squadron Leader Ben Travers. Roald described Travers as 'about the dirtiest little man I have ever met, but extremely nice and terribly funny'

just come from the war,' he told the writer William Stevenson in the mid-1970s. 'People were getting killed. I had been flying around, seeing horrible things. Now, almost instantly, I found myself in the middle of a pre-war cocktail mob in America. I had to dress up in ghastly gold braid and tassels. The result was, I became rather outspoken and brash.'[62]

It is sometimes hard to see this frustration in the letters, because all Roald's wartime correspondence home was censored. So there is little actual detail about his job in them. His unflattering opinion of the ambassador, Lord Halifax, is impossible to detect because Roald's comments about him are generally limited to their time on the tennis court. His intense dislike of his immediate boss, Air Commodore Thornton, is also scarcely apparent. Yet Roald's arrogance and intolerance was very discernible to those around him. Isaiah Berlin for example thought writing successes had turned his head. He became 'extremely conceited', Berlin recalled, believing himself 'a creative artist of the highest order, and therefore entitled to respect and very special treatment'.[63]

Roald was made a squadron leader in April 1943, but Air Commodore Thornton, who had always disapproved of his subordinate's maverick qualities, had by then decided he could tolerate them no longer.

◯ [probably April 1942]   On board

Dear Mama

We're due in this afternoon, although we can't see any land
yet. It's actually taken 2 or 3 days less than we thought it would –
we went pretty fast. All the same it has seemed almost as long as
the Capetown–England trip, I don't know why. We had some
fairly rough weather, and a lot of the types disappeared for a few
days, but it didn't affect me. One or two scares; a few depth
charges popping around but nothing, except when a ship going
the other way passed clear between us and our neighbours one
dark night. It hit a gap about 800 yards wide without knowing
we were there at all and that shook all concerned quite a bit.

As usual the food has been ordinary peacetime first class
passengers' food. Typical breakfast: stewed fruit – four kinds of
cereal – haddock or kipper – eggs, bacon, ham, tomatoes –
griddle cakes and maple syrup (a Canadian speciality) – rolls,
butter and marmalade ad lib.

At lunch and dinner always soup, fish, 2 kinds of meat and
pudding. Why the hell they do it, I don't know. All the types
have been eating themselves silly and are complaining of chronic
constipation, which serves them right. Plenty of whisky at 7/- a
bottle, I'm sorry I can't send any home. On the other hand, no
one's allowed to get drunk because they figure that it's easier to
get into a lifeboat when you're sober.

Old Bradbury, who was our Intelligence Officer in 80
Squadron at Haifa is on board bound for some training school in
Canada, and he's managed to keep us amused. He used to have
an Alsatian called Rex in the Squadron and he still likes to
pretend he's got him on board. For example yesterday he entered
the lounge when all and sundry were knocking back their
pre-supper glass of ale – carefully held the door open and said,

'Come on Rex old boy.' Then walked across the room saying, 'Rex, come here, good dog.'

The result was amazing. Strong men dropped their drinks and gaped wondering whether they were seeing things; complete silence until old Brad had walked out of the other door, again carefully holding it open and saying, 'Come on Rex, old boy.' We shook with laughter.

We've arrived. It's bloody cold, with a terrific wind blowing. It's even trying to snow. Otherwise looks rather like Norway.

Lots of love
Roald

 April 21st

British Embassy
Washington, D.C.

Dear Mama

I couldn't cable you many happy returns because we were only allowed to send three figure groups – one meant 'arrived safely' then 'all well' then 'love'. At least that's what they told me. So here's a belated many happy returns. I sent you a temporary present via a special messenger which should get to you pretty soon. The parcel contains a large tin of marmalade, 2 long slabs of cheese like the one John gave you, and some milk chocolate and lemons. Also 5lbs of sugar separately. I hope you got them.

We got off the boat and saw many extraordinary things at which we marvelled much. I bought a local small town newspaper – it had 40 pages. I had a hot dog and a milk shake. Everyone else was eating ice cream although it was bitter cold. At the railway station I bought handfuls of magazines for 50 cents (2/-). Everyone else was buying bottles of milk and drinking it out of a straw.

The train to Montreal which took 24 hours was luxurious. It was full of gadgets, air conditioning, floor heat, thermos, spittoons. Some Americans were arguing next door. One said, 'Aw let's talk about somethin' else.' Another said, 'Yea, let's eat foxes.' At meals the waiter gave you a pad and pencil and you wrote down what you wanted from a vast menu of pineapple juices and maple syrups. Everything iced. Then a very comfortable night in a huge bed to wake up and see lots of snow on the ground. Two more Americans came along; one said, 'Did yer sleep well?' Answer, 'Wal, there's no profit to be shown.' The first one then said, 'However, what's cookin'?' Sounded queer to me.

The train kept changing engines and drivers every 3 hours, and every now and then went backwards for 5 minutes, but we eventually arrived at Montreal in the evening. I was met and taken to the Ritz-Carlton, a swank joint where I did myself very well. Had a drink with Anna Neagle. All the Americans say your name after each sentence: Pleased to meet you Mr. Dahl, Thank you Mr. Dahl, Goodbye Mr. Dahl, and so forth. I now know their names anyway. The bathroom had floating soap in it, my suit was valeted in 5 minutes and the lift to the 10th floor took 5 seconds. You usually arrive at a place well before you get there, and you start to get ready to go after you've left. The food at the hotel was amazing. Lettuce hearts like giant cabbages, and steaks like doormats, only thicker. The females all have baby faces but when they walk you think they are strolling from the bathroom into the bedroom – and they usually are.

The men all wear fantastic gold and diamond rings, they look like Austin Reed posters and have teeth like piano-keys.

Came down to Washington by night train 12 hours. Stopped at New York, Philadelphia, Baltimore.

This is a lovely city. Spring is well advanced and the whole place is covered with the most magnificent double cherry blossom. It's very warm, almost too hot for these clothes already and for the moment I'm staying at the Willard – about the biggest hotel here. The cost is 21/- a day without food!

Meanwhile I'm finding a furnished flat and I've got to buy a goodish car. But this diplomatic business is very useful. I have a special diplomatic car licence so I can't be fined, pay no car tax, or for that matter, no tax on anything. My whisky, for example, is duty free which works out at 4/1 a bottle. Every time I buy something at a shop I get a special price, because the tax has to be deducted.

The people in the Embassy seem very pleasant. I've got plenty of secretaries, and there's going to be lots of travel. In three days I've got to fly up to Newark, New Jersey, and be guest of honour at the Masonic Lodge of West Orange, New Jersey, make a speech and give a lecture – probably on Greece.

People keep stopping you in the street and asking you what your uniform is – then they say, 'Thank you sir.' Tomorrow I'm attending the premiere of a new film 'Saboteurs' . . .

I've got to stop now because I've got a lot to do. I've got to write a lot of articles about Greece and Syria for papers like the Saturday Evening Post, Readers Digest, and Atlantic Monthly; hope they pay me well . . .

Let me know what you would especially like me to send; I can send parcels weighing up to 5lbs, one a month to each address. So I could send one to you and one to Alf, and possibly one to Asta. (Let me have Asta's address.) You cannot have more than 2lbs of each article, and the packing usually weighs about 1/2lb or more, so 4lb is probably more like it. But you can have literally anything, and you have to pay duty at your end. So let me know, and I shall just phone a standing order.

Lots of love
Roald

May 13th 1942

Air Attaché
British Embassy
Washington D.C.

Dear Mama

. . . As far as I can see I may be coming into large sums of money over here for those R.A.F. stories our British press people are getting me to write. My first one – a short thing of about 4000 words was sent up by C.S. Forester to the biggest agent in New York, and reply received yesterday. I was told that these agents are tough indeed and spend their lives sending stories back to aspiring authors with a polite or often an impolite chit of non-acceptance. However they said about mine 'It is remarkable – if he wrote it himself, he is a natural writer with a superior style; It will certainly sell'!! which shook C.S. Forester even more than it shook me. He said he'd never had a note like that from his agents in his life, and he gets $1000 for a short story. I'll let you know what happens.

They are trying to make me write a book re Middle-East R.A.F., also a play for Hollywood – but I've told them I won't run before I can walk. I'll send you a copy of the first one shortly; it's called 'A Piece of Cake' and is just about getting shot down. It's really purely in my line of duty, because they say it does a lot of good with the American public.

I move into my little house ($150 a month) on Friday next – the 15th May. I shall only be able to afford a half time negro servant I think – someone to come in and make the bed and wash clothes and dishes etc. Anyway I don't want a cook, because I've got to go out to most meals.

I've made about four speeches in the last 10 days. One in New York, two here in Washington and one in Newark, New Orange [Jersey].

I don't know what they were like – they sounded pretty awful to me, but everyone was very polite and stood up and clapped loads at the end – then started asking countless questions. I've had my photos of Greece and Syria made into lantern slides, so they can be shown on a screen if necessary.

The average size of the rather po-faced cod-eyed audience is three to four hundred – usually at a dinner. I get myself a little pissed before I start and that makes things a lot easier.

The only thing was, I told a party of rather staid Freemasons, in a happy moment that, 'someone had his balls sheared off because he had his finger in!' Whereas I meant to say 'he was reprimanded for inefficiency.' They pissed with laughter, as the President said afterwards, 'The Diplomatic Corps has a language all of its own.' Talking about Diplomatic Corps, I have a special number plate on my car which says D.P.L. in large yellow and black letters. It gets you a lot of places. Yesterday it got me into the White House in a hurry . . .

May 14th next morning
My story has been sold to the 'Saturday Evening Post' for 300 dollars which is about £76, which will help pay for some of my car – half in fact . . .

Apparently the Saturday Evening Post is the widest read magazine in America with a circulation of about 4 million. I am told that it's every author's ambition to get a story therein.

I've had an offer to write a film script but I simply haven't got time.

C.S. Forester has just sent me the letter he received from his New York agents – the first one – it says: *Dear Cyril, That's a remarkable piece. It is not much more than a fragment but I hope to be able to see it nevertheless. Did Lieutenant Dahl write it without any assistance whatever? If so he should write more. He is a natural writer of superior quality. I will let you know what happens. Yours, Harold Matson.*

Sounds funny to me because I didn't think it was anything special . . .

Must stop.

Lots of love

Roald

I hear Mrs. Harris has taken up bicycling.*

---

* Mrs. Harris was one of Sofie Magdalene's dogs.

Sort?; A gremlin walked
across the page
after bathing in my
ink bottle.

The first story, called 'A piece of
Cake' is appearing in about 3 weeks
time in the Saturday Evening Post. I'll
send you a copy when it comes out.
The thing is I have
to write all these things in the lunch
hour and in spare moments because I'm
pretty busy so I can't do many. That's
why my letters to you are such a
scrawl usually, but you'd rather have
3 pages scribbled than ½ a page
neatly written, wouldn't you.
The weather here is
now really damp and cold, and my little
house becomes an oven when I go back
to it in the evenings. But I don't mind
that. I've got a lovely radio gram with
already about 15 books of records
when I get time to play them, which
is usually when I'm dressing in the
morning or when I'm undressing at
night.
I've got a Squadron leader
Alexander staying with me at the moment;
he's a very nice type passing through
on his way back from Egypt where he
flew Wellingtons with great distinction.
As Hannah, my coloured maid, doesn't
put in an appearance until the afternoon,
Alex makes my breakfast, which is
all very nice.
I believe I told you
I have a tiny little garden at the back

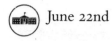 June 22nd

British Embassy
Washington

Dear Mama

I've just done another story, this time longer, about 7000 words, on 'Gremlins'. Maybe you don't know what they are, but everyone in the R.A.F. does. They are little types with horns and a long tail who walk about on the wings of your aircraft boring holes in the fuselage and urinating in your fuse-box. They have wives known as Fifinellas, and children which are Widgets or Flipperty-Gibbets, according to their sex. Widgets are masculine.

It's really a sort of fairy story, and I was very surprised to see it referred to by the British Information and Press Service over here and by Ronald Tree the Parliamentary Secretary to the Ministry of Information as 'one of the best literary efforts that has appeared on this side since the war began'.

It's going on the market shortly and I'm told that there should be no difficulty at all in selling its magazine rights for 500 dollars which is about £125, but I may get more. The other shock I got was that apparently Walt Disney is interested, but I'm not saying anything about that yet. If he really means business it will become worth many thousands of dollars. I propose to give a large proportion of anything I make to the R.A.F. Benevolent Fund. I haven't a spare copy of it at the moment, but I'll send you one as soon as I can.

Sorry; a Gremlin walked across the page after bathing in my ink bottle.

The first story, called 'A Piece of Cake' is appearing in about 3 weeks' time in the Saturday Evening Post. I'll send you a copy when it comes out.

The snag is I have to write all these things in the lunch hour and in spare moments because I'm pretty busy, so I can't do many. That's why my letters to you are such a scrawl usually, but you'd rather have 3 pages scribbled than 1/2 a page neatly written, wouldn't you?

. . . I believe I told you I have a tiny little garden at the back of the house, and a little flower bed which I water assiduously on my return from work every evening. My nice window-box is no longer a thing of beauty because the flowers have died and I haven't been able to deal with it. My front door and window shutters are pale blue, which is a very pleasant sight to be sure. But the dame who furnished the house was in the habit of using pink sheets and pillow cases, which look bloody awful.

Someone has lent me a large original Munnings horse picture to hang downstairs, which helps, but I want some more. I asked Mr. Guggenheim, whom I know quite well, if I could borrow one of his Titians (he has two in the drawing room) but he said he thought he'd like to keep them.

My head's not behaving badly at all. Occasionally I feel it, but not much. I think it's on the mend – although of course this climate is not exactly ideal . . .

Must rush.

Love to all

Roald

 August 7th 1942   Washington

Dear Mama

I'm getting a bit more used to this American business at last, although they are undoubtedly as different from us as the Chinese. Everything is done in terms of publicity and money. Aircraft manufacturers try to get film stars to autograph the wings of fighters; tank manufacturers get Clark Gable to ride one of their trucks out of the factory (with a battery of press photographers waiting outside). The wireless or radio as it's called here has no ordinary programmes at all. They are all advertisements, doesn't matter where you tune in, all you can get is some hot swing music for 30 seconds, then a smooth-voiced bastard comes on who says, 'Buy delicious creamy white vitamin filled double flavour bread,' or 'Put delightful smooth-tasting soft chewing Wrigley's chewing-gum in your mouth – the flavour lasts,' or 'Do you have stomach trouble: if you do take S.R.Tablets. Delightfully smooth working, pleasant tasting, quick acting S.R.Tablets. Take S.R. and there you are.'

So now you know why I've bought a lot of gramophone records.

The shops are still as full of everything as ever, so don't forget if you want any clothes of any sort let me know. I'd better send Asta some more films I think.

Petrol rationing has got quite serious. The average person gets a basic allowance of 3 gallons a week – which sounds a lot; but it isn't in these American cars which all do 10 miles to the gallon. So it's equal to one gall. a week for your car. I get a bit more because I've got to do a lot of special trips. But I don't use it at all for cruising out into the country or anything like that.

I started this letter the moment I got into my office this morning, before my secretary had started chucking stuff at me and before the telephone had begun to hum, but as you see I didn't get very far. It's now 7.45 in the evening and I'm still here and this is the first chance I've had of looking at it again. I kept a check today just to see, and I find that I've dictated thirty letters to a relay of three different typists – answered 55 phone calls, including one from Montreal, three from Miami, one from Seattle, five from New York and one from San Francisco (3500 miles away). So in a moment I'm going to trot home and have a quiet whisky and soda on my sofa and listen to some music.

I'll also send you the Saturday Evening Post with my story in it. In reading it you must remember that it was written especially to impress the American Public and to do some good over here – and also that my name's not on it.

The leading American newspaper man here in Washington told me last night, and much to my surprise that every newspaper man in the country would give his right arm to get an article in the 'Post'. He said once they've done that they're made. I'm not of course because no one knows who wrote it; and by the way the B.F.'s have gone and changed the title and half ruined it – it's now called 'Shot Down Over Libya' which is bloody, I think. Ask Asta to take a photo of Mrs. Harris for me.

Lots of love
Roald

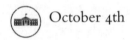 October 4th

Air Attaché
British Embassy
Washington, D.C.

Dear Mama

I'm spending my first thousand dollars, which I already have, on wireless sets for the Desert Squadrons in the Middle East. That's apparently what they need and want most.

Here life goes on much as usual. The work still pours in, and my evenings are often pretty full up with official stuff. Last Thursday I had to make a speech to 500 people at the annual dinner of the American Legion. Fortified by a number of whiskeys I managed to get through it without making too much of a bloody fool of myself.

Two days before that I had to inaugurate (with the American Minister for Education) their equivalent of our Air Training Corps (for children) and inspected, with considerable embarrassment rows and rows of schoolboys and girls lined up in an enormous field. They all wore peculiar hats on their heads showing that they were now members of the Corps, and there was a lot of flag waving and news photographers. I hope no photograph ever gets home of me inspecting a row of schoolgirls. – The things we do for England.

Many thanks for letters from Alf and Else. I'd answer them separately but there's not much point if they read this. But go on writing because I don't get many letters from England – except masses from Air Ministry!

My head is still fairly active, but I think it's improving a little. Lots of love to all

Roald

 November 27th 1942

Dear Mama

Well, I've been to Hollywood and come back; and had the most amazing time.

I think I told you in my last letter 2 weeks ago that I had a frantic telegram from Walt Disney, saying that he was all set to start work on the Gremlins – so with everyone's permission in an official capacity I boarded an American Airlines plane Wednesday evening, the 11th Nov. at 8.30 p.m. in the evening. It's the hell of a way across America – about the same as across the Atlantic only a bit further, and I kept having to put my watch back one hour in every five. At dawn on Thursday we were over Arizona on the Mexican border, and finally got into Los Angeles at about midday Thursday (about 14 hours' trip). I was met by Jimmy Bodrero, Walt's number one artist, and taken to the Beverly Hills Hotel, and after a bath and a shave was driven out to the studio and ushered up to Walt's room. He has two secretaries outside – one called Dolores who has been with him for 20 years – and his room itself is very magnificent with sofas, armchairs, a grand piano and Dolores serving coffee or drinks the whole time.

He said he wanted to get an illustrated book out right away, based on my story, and would I sit down and write it. He would give me all his best artists to work with, and anything else I wanted. And, oh, by the way, I've put a car at your disposal the whole time that you're here.

I said thank you very much and followed Jimmy down to an enormous room where a half a dozen of his best artists were waiting with pencils poised to be told what a Gremlin looked like. I'd already told them that the ones they drew in Cosmopolitan Magazine to go with my article were lousy.

So we set to work. I wrote and they drew. As soon as I'd finished a page, it was typed out in the pattern they wanted, sometimes with the type going slantwise across the page and sometimes squiggly. Then they drew pictures all around it, and now and again a full colour picture for the opposite page.

And could they draw. I've never seen anything like it in my life. Walt has gathered together there about 80 artists, any one of whom could be placed amongst the first 6 drawers of pure line pictures in the world – Jimmy Bodrero, Freddie Moore, Bill Justice and a whole flock of others. When they choose to do a picture out of hours for a client, they sell it for about 1000 dollars.

So all the first day we worked. Then there was a party for me which Walt had arranged at which I think I met most of Hollywood in one evening.

Charlie Chaplin came in and pretended to be a Widget all around the room, and all the rest of them arrived trying to be some sort of a Gremlin or other. Greer Garson, Dorothy Lamour, Spencer Tracy, Bill Powell etc. etc. And I must say they were all very nice. There weren't many English – Basil Rathbone and Reggie Gardiner were the only ones I can remember. There was a very beautiful dame called Phyllis Brooks (who is at present co-starring with Ginger Rogers in some new film) who I thought was a great deal better than the rest, and made it my business to organise for the rest of my stay.

Well that was a good party, but next morning, and every one after that, I was up at six, then 1/2 an hour's drive out to the studio at Burbank, and work on the book until 6 in the evening, with probably a couple of hours each day in conference with Walt on the actual film script. He plans to make it the biggest film he has yet made – with real actors and actresses – in Technicolor, with the Gremlins, Fifinellas and Widgets actually drawn on to the photographs. It's a new experiment.

He's the most amazing type. He doesn't draw at all, and can't very well anyhow; but he runs everything and the people in the studio worship him. He's quite an erk and when he gets excited always gets his grammar wrong with 'E don't do this', or 'E don't do that.' When Mary Blair, the only woman artist there, and incidentally one of the finest exponents of colour in the world, brought him her picture for the outside cover of the book he didn't like it.

'Goddammit, Mary, I have to buy the stories, direct the pictures, produce them, but son of a bitch I'm buggered if I'm going to draw the illustrations as well.' At which Mary said, 'Don't be a bloody fool, Walt; I'll do you another.' And she did.

By Sunday we all thought we needed a bit of a rest, so Jimmy took me up north to stay the day with his family in Santa Barbara – or rather I took him in the car Walt had lent me.

233

Santa Barbara is a lovely place. Blue skies, and blue seas, and we lounged around drinking with the local citizens, and talking to Jimmy's two children. Then we bathed in the Pacific, because I said it was about the only ocean I haven't bathed in, and drove back to Hollywood and so back at 7.30 next morning . . .

Finally we got the book finished in a week, and it is being published in late January, which is apparently quick work. I'll send you one as soon as it comes out. And I had to go back to Washington. I held a party in Phyllis Brooks' house to which all the types came, and a fellow called Hoagy Carmichael (who composed Stardust and many others, and has the biggest house I've ever seen) played rude R.A.F. songs on the piano which were sung with great gusto by all concerned. This was Monday – 23rd Nov. and at 11.30 pm we drove out to the aerodrome where I just caught my aeroplane back to Washington.

Walt gave me four books, Snow White, Pinocchio, Bambi and Fantasia, all signed and with best wishes, and I got some of the artists who created the original characters in them to draw inside the covers.

Jim Bodrero gave me one of the best large watercolours he has ever done, which is really something, considering he is the best artist in the Studio. It's of two galloping mules with two wonderful Mexicans on their backs, and it really is a lovely picture.

Anyway now I'm back – and that was Hollywood. The most exciting thing about it was working for Walt (who calls me Stalky because he can't pronounce Roald). I believe the whole thing is going to do quite a bit of good over here in furthering the ever-present question of Anglo American Relations . . .

Lots of love to all
Roald

I'm enclosing a sketch of a young Widget drawn by Jim Bodrero, who is drawing them for Walt. Even that is well drawn. They are going to be floppy creatures who manoeuvre around the plane like little bags filled with water.

© Disney

Roald Dahl and Walt Disney with cuddly toys inspired by Roald's creations, the gremlins. He described them as 'little types with horns and a long tail, who walk about on the wings of your aircraft boring holes in the fuselage and urinating in your fuse-box'

December 28th 1942

Dear Mama

I'm afraid I haven't written for rather a long time, but some rather curious things have been happening which have taken up practically all my time.

I don't know whether you've ever heard of a film director called Gabriel Pascal – he's a great Bernard Shaw man and produced Pygmalion, Major Barbara, etc. Well, the other day this Gabriel Pascal walked into the Embassy and asked to see me. I saw him and said Hallo and he sat down and talked a bit then said, 'Come out to lunch.' So I went. Then he said he wanted me to write a script for an enormous film he was thinking of doing about the world and good and evil, etc. etc. and in which Henry Wallace the Vice President of America was very interested. I said – 'Well . . .' And the next day I found myself having lunch with the Vice Pres. of the United States and talking to him from one o'clock until 6 p.m. He said he wanted me to give up my job for 3 months, retire into the mountains somewhere and write the script! I said no, I wouldn't – but if he liked I would try to do it in my spare time. He said O.K. and then rang up Lord Halifax and I had a lot of long talks with him about it. He said, 'Go ahead.' So I suppose I'm going ahead. No-one knows, least of all myself, why they should pick on me. Money is apparently no object, because the Vice-Pres. is arranging all that with the U.S. Treasury.

We had a good party on Christmas Eve – we acted two silly plays I wrote and a good time was had by all. The mail is going on return. The bag is closing in 5 mins so must stop. Will write a longer letter soon.

Love to all
Roald

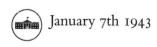 January 7th 1943

Air Attaché
British Embassy
Washington, D.C.

Dear Mama

I'm so busy these days that there's hardly any time for anything, what with the Air Attaché down in Central America, and one thing and another. I turn down nearly all my evening dinner invitations, and try to stay at home and write. I leave off work at perhaps 6.30 or 7 in the evening, then probably go along and have a short drink with someone. Then off home, stopping at my grocer on the way to buy my supper, which I proceed to cook (very well!). Then I get comfortable, may be with a glass of Californian (or if I'm rich) French Brandy and begin to write. After an hour I get fed up and play a symphony or something on the gramophone, and then start writing again.

Tomorrow I've got another long conference with the Vice President of the United States on this script he has asked me to do, and on Saturday I'm seeing the President, old Roosevelt; so we move in very high circles – so bloody high that sometimes it is difficult to see the ground . . .

As usual, I'm scribbling along as fast as I can to try to catch the air bag before it closes – so I must apologise for this scrawly letter. I always say I'm going to write you a better one, but never do – Next time I will. Will also send you a photo of self by next mail, which I had to have taken over here. As usual it's a rather exaggerated semblance of Primo Carnera.*

Lots of love to all
Roald

---

* Primo Carnera was an Italian boxer and movie star. Ten years older than Roald, he shared Roald's rangy build and stature.

January 12th 1943

Dear Mama

We've had an awful lot of snow lately and it's been very cold, but today there's a lovely blue sky and the sun is shining. But still freezing hard and driving about the streets – and even walking – has become very dangerous. Talking about driving – they've suddenly realised over here that there's a war on, and have forbidden people to use their cars for pleasure purposes, which is just about the most sensible thing yet. Now police cars patrol the streets and one is liable to be stopped and asked where one is going. If you can't think up a better excuse than that you're just going to drive down to the park and pick your nose then they reach an enormous hand inside your window and demand your ration book there and then. A very American way of doing things, but quite effective. And the people groan and grouse until one might almost think that they'd spent the whole of the war in the front line . . .

I'm getting a little tired these days – so as soon as Air Commodore Thornton comes back I think I'll take a little leave somewhere. All this is not very good for the head . . .

Lots of love to all
Roald

 April 17th 1943   Washington

Dear Mama

I'm afraid it's the hell of a time since I wrote to you, but I thought it better to wait till I came back from the West Coast – Things were so hectic out there, and there was so much to do in such a short time.

I flew out on Wednesday evening 31st March, leaving here at 6.30 pm. It's a very tiring trip, you sit up all night and try to go to sleep, but it doesn't work. By 5.30 am the next morning we'd arrived at El Paso in South Texas, just on the Mexican border, and it was fun to go out of the plane and find yourself in desert country once more.

Got to Los Angeles at 10.30 that morning and was met by Jim Bodrero and Ted Sears from Walt Disney's studio. They handed me over a very smart Packard car which was to be mine for my stay. Unshaven and feeling pretty shagged I went straight to the studio for a conference with Walt which lasted over lunch and well into the afternoon.

He told me he'd booked a palatial suite for me at the Beverly Hills Hotel, and that I was to pay for nothing. All drinks, cigarettes, meals and parties I wished to throw would be on him. I thought that was a good show and he said, 'Not at all; you're not costing us anything, whereas we should normally have to pay $400 or $500 a week for a writer.'

Anyway it was a very fine apartment, and when I arrived the manager came sidling in rubbing his hands saying that I had only to ring the bell and everything would be taken care of – it was Mr. Disney's orders.

That evening I had a bath and a shave and drove out to have dinner with Ginger Rogers. She's got a marvellous house right up on top of the hills overlooking the sea. Bars, swimming pool, tennis courts, private cinema, etc., it was all there including Ginger, who was by far the best part of the house. A very nice girl.

From then on I was at the studio at 7.30 a.m. every morning, having conferences with Walt, going off and writing, looking at storyboards, having more conferences, more writing, more story boards and so on all day till we left at about 7 p.m.

The second night I went to Dorothy Lamour's wedding reception. There we saw all the types. A milling throng of people, stars, directors, producers, etc. Half of them were very nice indeed, and the other half were pretty bogus. Spent most of the time with Marlene Dietrich with whom I was most impressed. At first she kept saying, 'I wish my daughter were here – you'd like her,' until I remembered the right American retort which was, 'Honey, forget her and don't give me that stuff about your daughter – get your hat.'

Gary Cooper is a decent type and so is Spencer Tracy.

The next day I told the studio that I was fed up, and that I wanted some sun. If they wanted to work that afternoon they'd have to come along to the edge of Hoagy Carmichael's swimming pool and do it there, because that was where I was going. So they all packed their easels and pencils and pads and we had a good afternoon's work and sunbathing.

When anyone got persistent about a foolish idea he was just rolled off into the pool to cool off.

Hoagy Carmichael plus wife and two terrific small boys called Hoagy Bix and Randy Bub are the nicest family I met there. He's the composer of Lazy Bones, Stardust, Little Old Lady etc. but apart from that he's as nice as his wife. He asked me to write a poem for his children who are mad on flying, which I did, although I can't write poetry.

TO HOAGY BIX AND RANDY BUB

> When I am old and bent and crinkly-faced
> When you are big and strong and muscle-meat
> I know you'll learn to fly; you'll like the taste
> Of freezing clouds at thirty thousand feet.
> You'll like the taste of hail and ice and sleet.

II

When you come down to earth, you'll have to pay.
You'll hear the people talk of little things;
You'll hear them laugh, and some of them will say:
'It isn't only angels that have wings.'

III

If they do this, you mustn't ever yield.
Walk away slowly, never start to run.
Stand in the middle of a poppy field
Stand on your toes and try to reach the sun.

IV

If someone hits you where it really hurts,
Then say 'I'll see you in the afternoon'
Just throw away your most expensive shirts.
Stretch out your hand and gently touch the moon.

I had a busy time also visiting aircraft factories, talking to the workers, and exhorting them to greater efforts.

My last night I threw a party in Hoagy Carmichael's house and charged it to Walt. I hired a large projector, and put on a preview of the film 'Desert Victory' which I expect you've seen, and which I think is marvellous. It created a terrific impression. I asked a lot of the types, including, let me see, Ginger Rogers, Carole Landis, Jimmy Cagney, Bob Montgomery, Bert Marshall, Joan Blondell, etc. and all the boys from Walt's studio including Duckie Marsh (the man who makes the Donald duck noises!).

Now I'm back here working very hard . . .
Lots of love to all
Roald

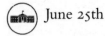 June 25th   Washington

Dear Mama

I missed the last mail, but it couldn't be helped – there was so much to do. But this evening at any rate, I can write in comparative comfort because they have just installed an air conditioner in my office. The bloody thing sits in the window and makes a noise like a four-engined bomber taking off, disgorging the while a certain amount of cold air. It makes the temperature more reasonable, but I still wouldn't like to wear a jacket in here.

It's now 7 p.m. and hot as hell outside. I'm writing this whilst waiting for my girl to finish typing some notes on a rather high powered speech I've got to make in New York on Sunday. It's to the Aviation Writers Association of America, who are holding a Convention, and I can tell you that there are a large number of Aviation writers in this country right now. Some are congenial others are cantankerous, but they are rather an important bunch of types – otherwise I wouldn't be taking all this trouble. I wish they'd go and stuff themselves, each one separately and individually . . .

Next weekend, Saturday and Sunday I'm going to run away, because I'm going (as I think I told you) to stay with President Roosevelt. I'll let you know all about it in due course. I'll tell you whether he blows his nose in his fingers, or whether he eats with his mouth open, or whether (and this will be interesting to find out) he laughs at my dirty jokes. I don't think he will, but he might as well hear them just the same.

Lots of love to all
Roald

CHAPTER 7

'A good time was had by all'

1943–1945

In July 1943 Roald was invited to join Secretary to the Treasury Henry Morgenthau and Crown Princess Martha of Norway for a weekend at Hyde Park, President Roosevelt's home on the Hudson River. Roald penned a memorable account of his time there – written both for his family and for the staff at the embassy. His observations teem with details about the President's life there: the small baths in the guest rooms, the sulphurous smell that permeated the water supply, or the eccentric behaviour of the Roosevelts' Aberdeen terrier Fala. Yet, under the mask of 'clown', like a fool at a medieval court, Roald was also uniquely able to ask innocent and uninhibited questions of senior American politicians.[64]

Roosevelt was aware that his comments to Roald would be reported back to British strategists and probably to Churchill himself, but there was clearly a connection between the two men and also one between Roald and Eleanor Roosevelt. Roald revelled in the President 'regaling his guests with rather crude stories about dead men',[65] and in Roosevelt's attempts to outrun his bodyguards in his invalid car. But the Assistant Air Attaché's flippant manner and the perception that he was acting above his station riled his superiors. And in October, he was told his work in the USA had finished. He was sent back to England. He had been sacked.

His homecoming however was a short one. Roald's society contacts and his access to the highest echelons of American government had been recognised in Whitehall – possibly even by Churchill himself – as being immensely useful to the British war

effort. So he was almost immediately re-recruited by the unortho-
dox Canadian spymaster William Stephenson to work for British
Security Co-ordination in New York.

Stephenson had established British Security Co-ordination to
go 'beyond the legal, the ethical, and the proper' to achieve its
ends, which were essentially the propagation of British wartime
interests within America.[66] Ernest Cuneo, who acted as a liaison
between BSC, OSS (the American Secret Service) and the
Roosevelt administration, claimed that, among its many activities,
BSC 'ran espionage agents, tampered with the mails, tapped telephones, smuggled propaganda into the country, disrupted public
gatherings, covertly subsidized newspapers, radios, and organiza-
tions, perpetrated forgeries – even palming one off on the President
of the United States – violated the aliens registration act, shang-
haied sailors numerous times, and possibly murdered one or more
persons in this country'.[67]

Stephenson recognised that an outspoken young maverick like
Roald could go places and say things that more circumspect career
government officials, mindful of status and discretion, would find
impossible. And Roald was instantly fascinated by Stephenson and
BSC. But its top-secret business naturally found no place in his
letters to Sofie Magdalene, which became blander – at least in
terms of political gossip – as a consequence. It is probably the
reason why Wallace's demotion from the vice-presidency following the election at the end of 1944 and Roosevelt's own death
shortly afterwards get such brief attention. But by then Roald too
was unwell.

Throughout 1944 and 1945 Roald suffered terribly from back
pain, as a result of his flying injuries. So his friend Charles Marsh
eventually arranged – and paid – for him to be operated on by a
top American surgeon called Arthur Scott, who ran a very modern
clinic in Temple, Texas. Roald was fascinated by the novelty and
innovation he encountered there, but his surgery required two

lengthy visits and, as he was recuperating, he got acute appendicitis. He ended the war in Canada, part of a small team charged with writing the history of BSC. Unsurprisingly, this task did not inspire him.

After winding up his work in Canada, he returned to England briefly in October 1945, but he flew back to New York again for the publication of his first book, a collection of flying stories entitled *Over to You*. At the age of twenty-nine, he was now clear that his vocation was to be a writer and, as the war ended, he had little trouble taking the decision to leave the RAF and attempt a career as a novelist.

On the jacket of *Over to You* he penned a short biographical blurb. It's an entertaining summary of his life to date, his priorities and an unequivocal statement of how much writing now meant to him.

My mother and father were Norwegians. The first language I ever spoke was Norwegian. The best-looking girl I have seen was Greek. After that I was sent to East Africa and learned to speak Swahili and drink whisky. Out there I had a dog and two cats. The dog was called Dog Samka. One of the cats was called Mrs. Taubsypuss and the other Oscar. When the war broke out I joined the RAF and learned still another language. We flew quite a lot in the Mediterranean and I was shot down. I got a cracked skull which seemed to qualify me for being sent to Washington. There I began to write some stories in the evenings. Now I have become quite excited about it and writing stories is the only other thing that I want to do.[68]

July 8th 1943   Washington

Dear Mama

I have dictated a brief summary of my short visit to Hyde Park
for the Ambassador and others, and I am going to send you a
copy with this letter, which is going to save me an awful lot of
writing. There is nothing secret in it at all because any
conversations which I have recorded were made quite informally
to a group of people.

I saw a great deal of Kronprinsesse Martha and her children,
and I thought they were all charming. I am going up to stay a
night with her on Long Island if I have to go to New York
sometime and can manage to get away. The children were great
fun, particularly Prince Harald, who spends his time throwing
himself into the swimming pool from the diving board. I think
he will make a good King one day . . .

Lots of love to all

Roald

A WEEKEND AT HYDE PARK

I went into the bathroom and turned on the water. There was a
smell of rotten eggs. It was a very strong smell indeed. I shouted
through the door to Richard, 'This bathroom smells of rotten
eggs.' He said, 'they [the Roosevelts] are on the porch just below
us and can hear every word you are saying.' I said, 'oh,' and we
left it at that . . .

As a matter of fact the water in the house was full of sulphur
and it took a bit of getting used to, but I believe it was very good
for the complexion . . .

The next morning I had a bath. The bathtub was so small that
I couldn't get my knees under the water, but that didn't matter.

Later I was putting on my shirt and the phone on my bed rang, I took it.

'This is Henry Morgenthau, is Mrs. Roosevelt there?'

I said, 'No, she's not in this bedroom.' He said, 'oh well, do you think you can find her?' I said, 'yes,' and put on my trousers and padded downstairs to tell her. She was making toast.

Back in the bedroom the voices of Mrs. R. and Henry Morgenthau were coming through loudly on the receiver, which I had left lying on the table, and reverberating around the room like a couple foghorns . . .

Later in the morning, we went to bathe in the swimming pool where young Prince Harald and princesses Astrid and Ragnhild of Norway were already frolicking about.

Mrs. Roosevelt said we were going to have a picnic lunch in the garden with Franklin. At one o'clock an old Ford car came bouncing over the grass, driving furiously with two other cars full of the toughest looking thugs I've ever seen in hot pursuit. The president was driving the old Ford, which is especially built so that the throttle and the clutch and everything else can be operated with his hands. In it also was Crown Princess Martha. Henry Morgenthau turned up a little later and we had a very pleasant lunch on the grass.

Young Prince Harald had a big piece of glass chipped out of his bottle of Coca-Cola, and I told him that the president had eaten it. Didn't he know that the president ate glass? He said, 'no', and went and asked him. The president said of course he ate glass every evening. It made him sharp.

The president looked to me like the most tired man I have ever seen, but he was relaxing and seemed to be enjoying himself.

Henry Morgenthau's trousers were half unbuttoned, but no one said anything to him about it . . .

We had dinner and drove home. On the way it was interesting

to note the intricate Secret Service system which protects the estate while the president is there. Everywhere there were soldiers and at most of the corners there was a telephone box. The moment the car left the big house a man picked up the receiver and phoned down to the next box low along the line, saying that Mrs. R. was on the way, and so on down the route.

We talked a little before we went to bed . . .

[The next day] The president was looking, in my opinion, at least twice as young and half as tired as the day before. He was in fine form and sat at the head of the table regaling his guests with rather crude stories about dead men.

It started with Mrs. R saying to him that they'll open great uncle so-and-so's vault, oughtn't we, and see whether he was really inside?

The president said, I know the last time we opened the vault, the end of the coffin came off and as we went in, the dead man's head rolled out.

Amidst exclamations of horror, he went on by saying that he knew some very good stories about dead men. 'For example,' he said, 'a long time ago I was dining in the British Embassy when I met a young fellow who was assistant naval attaché. This was in 1906 and that man's name was − [I've forgotten it, but I was struck, as on many other occasions, by the president's amazing memory for names and dates] . . . I said to this young fellow,' he went on, 'are you any relation to General −−−−−, who fought in our Civil War?'

The young man said, 'Yes, he was my grandfather. And do you know that he is buried in our local churchyard in Surrey at home?' I said that was most interesting, but how did they manage to transport the body, because it gets pretty hot around here.

The young man said, 'they transported him from the field of battle where he was slain in a cask of rum. The cask was lashed to the main mast and he was taken over like that. When the cask arrived at the family seat, his relations thought they would like to have a look at the body so they opened the cask. The rum had all gone and grandfather was in a rather shocking state. As a matter of fact they found the sailors had drilled a hole in the cask and drunk the rum on the way over.'

Mrs. Roosevelt started telling a lot of funny stories about sleepwalking . . . Mrs. Roosevelt said, 'well, Franklin used always to walk in his sleep when he was younger. Once during the time when we used to own an old Ford in the early days of motoring, I wakened up and found him standing at the end of his bed turning an imaginary cranking wheel as hard as he could and saying, "The damn thing won't start."'

'I said,' she went on, 'Franklin, if you get into the car I will help you start it. Whereupon he got back into bed and held an imaginary steering wheel, whilst I had to go out in front and pretend to do the cranking. Finally he went back to sleep. In the morning he remembered nothing about it.'

After a little while he started holding forth on his position in relation to the people of the country. 'They have,' he said, 'seen so much of me and had me for so long that they will now do anything for a change. They're restless because they have nothing against me, but they have, as I said, seen so much of me that they want someone else. They just want a change. But mark my words, after two years they will be shouting and yelling to get back to what they had before . . .'

The president, on Sunday at any rate, gave me the impression of being fairly happy about things in general and he did not seem over-worried. Mrs. R had said earlier in the day that the troubles on the home front were not worrying him unduly; he was too much of an old hand for that. His policy was to sit back and let everyone talk themselves to a standstill. It certainly seemed, however, this weekend that that was what he was doing . . .

*Eleanor and Franklin Roosevelt at Hyde Park, 1943. Photo taken
by Roald Dahl. Roald acted like a clown when he stayed with
the President. 'I was able to ask pointed questions and get equally
pointed replies because, theoretically, I was a nobody,' he recalled*

 July 17th 1943   Washington D.C.

Dear Mama

I must say your garden sounds wonderful. I am particularly
pleased about the raspberries. Tell me whether ours are better
than Alf's or not. If they are not I shall lose faith in scientific
gardening, because I'm sure I put much more manure on ours
and dug the trenches much deeper . . .

Last Saturday afternoon I took time off at 5 p.m. for a game of
tennis with Halifax and Vice Pres. Wallace and another American
from the State Dept. called Finlater. Finlater and I beat Halifax
and Wallace 6-0, 6-0, 6-0.

There's been a lot of rumpus over here lately with Wallace and Roosevelt. I was with Wallace the night before last when he got the news that he'd been turned out of the Bureau of Economic Warfare by the President. Things really began to hum and I spent the evening answering telephone calls from 8 p.m. till 1 a.m.; it has not all blown over yet. Wallace has temporarily lost prestige, but I think he's on the way up the ladder – not down it, as so many people seem to think.

Last Sunday afternoon we played baseball against the Americans and beat them easily. I hit a home run! If you know what that means; the only one of the afternoon, and it was very pleasant to be sure.

I got kicked out of my house yesterday by the owners, who said that they wanted to go back and live in it. That was bad because houses are impossible to find in Washington these days. But I was very lucky. My pet house agent has already rung me up and asked if I object to living in a house where there was a murder last week. I said no, I didn't object. One can't be fussy here now. I signed the lease and took the house without ever having seen it. If I had waited long enough to do that someone else would have had it. I'm going to see it this evening.

The murder was a big story in the papers last week. A man shot a girl in the living room, then shot himself through the head. He took two shots to kill the girl and two shots to kill himself, so I gathered that he wasn't a very good marksman. Anyway I'm told that the mess has been cleared up and I will move in tomorrow.

It's rather like the story of the man who was fished out of the river nearly drowned here not long ago. The man who fished him out said, 'What's your address?' The dying man just managed to whisper it before he expired and his rescuer rushed off to the address and said to the landlady – 'Mr. Rappaport has drowned, can I have his flat?' 'No,' said the landlady, 'the man who pushed him in has already taken it.'

So you see what the housing problem is like here!

It is very very hot here today, and I'm beginning to look forward to my first holiday which I hope to be able to take towards the end of August.

Here are a few photos – not very good, of our weekend.

Lots of love to all

Roald

 July 23rd   Washington

Dear Mama

I've got a bloody awful cold, but it's the first that I've had this year.

Meanwhile you may be pleased to hear that after a little deliberation I decided not to go into that house where there was a murder and a suicide. The last time I went to look at it there was still quite a bit of blood and stuff about, plus bullet holes in the ceiling, and what with one thing and another I thought I'd rather not spend my evenings alone there! I'd signed the lease, but it was a very simple matter to get rid of it again. There were hundreds of people ready to take it. So at the moment I have moved in on the Air Attaché, Air Commodore Blackford, who is an extremely nice man. I got him quite a nice house when he arrived – 3 bedrooms, and with my wireless and records in the living room it is all very pleasant until I find myself something else – but there is no hurry.

Last night he made me sniff large quantities of salt water up my nose for my cold, which doesn't seem to have done it any good.

The first night I was there I came home at 10 p.m. and found the house on fire. There was an armchair in the middle of the room completely ablaze. He had left a cigarette end on the cushion! I couldn't find anything to put it out with except a teapot and I couldn't see very much anyway, because of the smoke. But eventually after making about 75 journeys to the kitchen with the bloody teapot full of water, I got the matter under control . . .

Lots of love to all

Roald

 August 28th 1943   Washington

Dear Mama

This morning I was woken up at 7 by a peculiar tapping noise which seemed to be going on and on in the room, accompanied by squeaks. I sat up in bed and saw, sitting on the ground a very old, a very very old grey squirrel. He was bouncing up and down on his hind legs and protesting vigorously at something or other at the same time. I said, 'What do you want,' but he didn't answer. So I got up and went down to the kitchen to get him something to eat. He followed me down and sat on the top of the open door watching. I gave him some toast which he wouldn't have – then a sort of mouldy potato chip which he held in both hands and nibbled, but threw away almost at once. At last I found some walnuts and he sat down and began to eat. Now he pays regular visits, and his name, by the way, is Sigismund the Squirrel.

I am very glad to hear that the raspberries were good. I have a keen personal interest in them . . .

Lots of love to all

Roald

October 19th   Washington

Dear Mama

It's getting bloody cold here again, and I expect that it's doing the same with you. The trees are very beautiful – because the leaves turn so many more different colours in the autumn over here than they do at home. But soon they'll all be gone.

Very busy week this has been, working both in and out of the office. On Monday and Tuesday I had dinner with Thomas Mann, whose books you've probably read. I liked him very much although I didn't agree entirely with some of his views about post-war German reconstruction.

Anyway, we swapped books. He gave me three signed copies of his and I gave him The Gremlins!

Yesterday I dined at the White House with the family. Also present were Elmer Davis (their Minister of Information), General George, head of the V.S. Transport Command, and Mrs. Ernest Hemingway. We had a lot of cocktails first with Mrs. R. doing the pouring, then a good meal at which everyone was in fine form and we went down in the lift to the private cinema and saw 'For Whom The Bell Tolls'. The private cinema is quite something. After you've all got seated, great swing doors slide noiselessly together and an enormous screen descends automatically from the roof. Everything is done very efficiently and with great comfort.

Martha Hemingway is a good type. She uses as much bad language in her talk as her husband does in his books.

I was offered a Staff College Course the other day, but I said I would rather not, because I may possibly be given a more interesting (from my point of view) job, about which I'm afraid I can tell you nothing . . .

Lots of love to all
Roald

Wing Commander Roald Dahl and his literary hero, Ernest
Hemingway, in London, 1944. Roald got to meet many
of the great and good in the literary world while he was in
Washington. He thought Hemingway 'a strange and secret
man' for whom he felt 'overwhelming love and respect'

 December 16th   Washington

Dear Mama

It's time I wrote you another letter.

Our warm spell broke suddenly last week and ever since it has
been as 'cold as a frog in an icebound pool – cold as the tip of an
Eskimo's tool, cold as buggery and that's bloody chilly, but not as

257

cold as our little Willie – 'cause he's dead poor sod.' It has been very cold, and serious flu epidemics are raging throughout Washington and New York. Something like 25% of all employees everywhere have been absent, blowing their noses in bed. So far I seem to have escaped.

Had to go up to New York again last week. Stayed in Helen Ogden Reid's house and met a lot of people. Had a meal with Paul Robeson who is a fantastic type. Brilliant scholar, speaks 4 languages including Russian, is a barrister and one of the best read men I've met. In addition he's quite a good singer!

Noel Coward has just this moment phoned up from New York. He is coming down tonight and we will eat together, not especially because I know him, but because he wants an air passage somewhere!

You ought to get this just about Christmas time, so happy Christmas to everyone including the dogs . . .

Lots of love to all

Roald

For Alf: 'What'll you 'ave?' said the butler standing there picking his nose.

''Ard boiled eggs you bastard. You can't put your fingers in there.'

 January 13th 1944 Washington

Dear Mama

Had dinner last Sunday with a fabulous and rather tipsy dame called Mrs. Evalyn Walsh McLean. Her only claim to fame is that she owns the Hope Diamond and wears it constantly and is still alive. Everyone else who has owned it has either died quickly or been killed. It's a hell of a diamond; bright blue colour of an aquamarine and about this shape and size, and she walks around in her enormous house with this bloody thing around her neck and a small vicious dog under her arm. 'A monkey dog,' she says. 'Only six  in the world,' to which a man called Frank Waldrop replied after it bit him on the finger, 'Six too bloody many.'* Dinner of course was eaten off gold plate, but it tasted just the same and the butler who served me farted twice; at least I think it was him, unless it was Mr. John L. Lewis who was sitting on my right.

It's really a pretty bogus setup, but on the other hand is good value because it's like going to the circus and getting a free meal served into the bargain . . .

Love

Roald

 February 8th 1944   Washington

Dear Mama

I just got a cold; the first one that I've had for many months, since last spring, I think. There's not much point in telling you because by the time you get this, it will be gone – or I hope so anyway.

Last week a friend of mine in the embassy called Paul Scott Rankin went on leave. He left behind him for me to take care of, his enormous brown bulldog, called Winston. I said I didn't mind; he looked all right. But Winston is no ordinary old dog.

---

* Frank Waldrop was managing editor, and later editor-in-chief, of *The Washington Times-Herald*

He is stupid and lecherous and cantankerous and all the time he grunts and snorts and slobbers. Paul said, let him sleep in your bedroom and he will be all right. He snorts all of the time, but you will find that pleasant and soporific. So the first night Winston slept in my bedroom. He snored and grunted and made a great noise all night, and I slept very little.

In the morning I took him into the embassy and let him sit in my office. But he farted continuously and with great gusto. Once he did it whilst I was dictating to the secretary, and I had to turn him out on the spot so that she wouldn't think it was me. But he scratched on the door and I had to let him in again and open all the windows. He continued to fart regularly and contentedly for the rest of the day, and I was very cold with the windows open. Once when I went out of the room to see someone, I came back to find him sitting on top of my desk amidst piles of secret papers and red boxes which had G.R. in gold on their lids. I threw him off and he farted again.

That evening I had supper with crown prince Olav and Martha at the Norwegian embassy so while I went in I left Winston in the car. After dinner I said that I would have to go out and give Winston a walk and let him have a pee. They all said, 'Bring him in.' I said, 'He farts; he isn't any good and he has no respect for royalty.' They said, 'Bring him in.' So I brought him in and he spent the rest of the evening slinking around the room casting lustful eyes in the direction of the crown princess and belching quickly. He only farted once there, and they thought it was a Norwegian ambassador, so that was all right. The ambassador was embarrassed.

That evening I locked him in the kitchen. In the night he broke down the door, after relieving himself on the floor, and came rushing upstairs to the bathroom, where he shat hugely and decisively in the middle of my pink bathmat. I did not sleep much that night either.

The next day at the embassy was very much the same as the one before. Then in the evening I was dining with Carlos and Maria Martins, the Brazilian ambassador and wife, so I took him in. Now Carlos Martins is a great connoisseur of food and wines, but with Winston lying underneath the table during dinner, he was not able to smell either the bouquet of the wine or the aroma of the food. He smelt only the smell which this wretched dog was making below. Carlos said after dinner, 'Winston makes much bad smell, eh?' I said yes he did, he was constipated. Then the next morning, completely exasperated, I took him to a luxurious and expensive dog's home and told them to keep him until Paul came back. Never get a bulldog . . .

Much hard work here.

Lots of love to all

Roald

 March 29th 1944   Washington

Dear Mama

Not much news here except that spring is on the way, and the Japanese cherry blossom will soon be out along the streets of Washington. The weather is warmer, and people are beginning to dread the summer once more.

Went to have dinner with Mrs. Bloody Hope Diamond, as Alf calls her, again last Sunday. This time everything was gold. All the plates, all the knives, forks, spoons and salt cellars etc. etc. Somehow I didn't notice it at first, and just picked up my knife and started cutting my meat. I said – 'Good God, this knife's blunt as hell.' 'Of course it is, you bloody fool,' said Mrs. McLean, from the other end of the table, 'it's gold.' By then I'd bent it almost double, because it was so soft, and I caused considerable surprise by asking the Butler to get me a steel one which would cut. I've seen some foolish things in my time but never anything more foolish than a bunch of dopes trying to cut up their pieces of rather tough beef with blunt soft golden knives. And I couldn't put one in my pocket because there was a detective hanging around the room with one hand in his pocket . . .

Lots of love to all
Roald

August 25th   Transcontinental and Western Air Inc
                               Kansas City
                               Missouri

OFFICE OF THE PRESIDENT

Dear Mama

I'm not the president of TWA, but I'm sitting beside the swimming pool of the president Jack Frye, and it is very fine here in the sun, but difficult to write lying on my back. Every now and then I will gently slide into the pool and cruise around a bit to cool down then come back and lie on my back again.

Went to New York last week to see the doctors who took lots of pictures of my back and who didn't seem to know very much about it at all. No results really, but I think it's getting better slowly. Then popped out to Long Island for a day staying at Millicent Rogers house. Fantastic business. There also were Cecil Beaton, Schiaparelli (I call her shocking) and many other equally strange and rustic types. Women with ruby necklaces and sapphire necklaces, and God knows what else sauntered in and

out and down below amidst miles of corridors. There were
swimming baths, Turkish baths, colonic lavages, heat treatment
rooms and everything else which is calculated to make the
prematurely aging playboys and play women age a little less
quickly. I didn't like it much.

Must drive into town right away to get this letter to the man.

Lots of love to all

Roald

 September 30th

Dear Mama

I found my old pen so now it'll be a hippopotamus walking
across the page instead of an underfed spider.

That was terrific news about Louis and Meriel, but I think
someone might have told me a bit earlier, when it happened (one
day after my birthday, wasn't it?). I've never been an uncle before,
and I think that all in all it's a pretty fine show. I would like to see
Louis handling the baby. Tell him that he better lay off and leave
it to Meriel because I do not wish to have any of my nieces or
godchildren dropped upon the floor. Tell them also that if he
wanted to, he could make a drawing of her and send it to me.
My christening present will have to wait until I can bring it
home, but that'll be sooner or later. I am much honoured at
being a godfather and an uncle.

Furthermore the child has Norwegian, French and English
blood and should therefore be a whizzer. Tell Louis that I will
write to my niece in a few days' time. As a matter of fact the
telegram came last Thursday when I was in New York, and my
secretary phoned it through to me. I gave her the reply and told
her to send it off. Who are the other godparents, with whom I

shall have to grapple in regard to the sexual and religious life of Policarp? All, I hope, well-qualified and broad-minded persons . . .

I'm trying to write another story, but there's not much time and it's pretty distracting here. Did you get the last one *They Shall Not Grow Old*. They seem to like it up in New York, and keep telling me to write a novel. I tell them in five years perhaps . . .

Lots of love to all

Roald

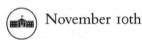 November 10th   Washington

Dear Mama

There is a large bridge near my house, which was designed by Theodore Roosevelt, and on each corner there is an enormous bronze statue of a bison. Now someone has painted the prominent personal organs of these bison bright red, so that everyone who crosses the bridge stops and roars with laughter. It is a very fine sight and I don't know who's going to take the paint off. You can't really have a fireman or someone leaning a ladder against the animal, ascending it and solemnly scraping the paint off the penises. A crowd would gather and laugh at him, and photographers from a bawdy newspaper would get a wonderful photograph.

I don't know why I tell you this, except that I've just driven over the bridge and arrived here at my office, and it really was a very fine sight.

Well, thank goodness election is over, with the expected and correct result. I've seen a lot of Henry Wallace recently, and everyone is wondering what his next job will be. Something in the cabinet, I think. He's in fine form, and going very strong. On election night I went to Evalyn McLean's. There were about 60 people to dinner – 'just a small party' she said. I saw that she

wasn't wearing the Hope diamond. She had another stone about
the size of a garden roller around her neck. 'Where is the Hope?'
I said. 'Tonight,' she answered, 'I put it down here,' and she
pointed down into her strange and padded bosom. 'Why?' I said.
'Well, because it's safer there. Twenty years ago it could've been
the least safe place of all!' And she roared with laughter and
turned round and repeated the story to a couple of Supreme
Court judges and an ambassador. She's a very peculiar woman . . .
  Lots of love to all
  Roald

 November 23rd   Washington

Dear Mama

  Today is Thanksgiving Day, and no one is doing any work
except us. The streets are quite empty, but it is lovely weather,
warmish with the yellow sun.
  Last Saturday I dined with President Roosevelt and Mrs. R.
Lots of fun. There were only about six people there. The Pres.
was wheeled in while we were knocking back a cocktail in the
Red Room, and with him, in front of him bounced his famous
Aberdeen terrier Fala. He looked fit and very hearty and was
obviously feeling good after his election success.
  At dinner I sat next but one to him, and talked a lot to him.
Dinner is his great time of relaxation, when he tells jokes and
reminisces about his ancestors, and once when he told quite a
good one he looked at me and said − 'I told that one to the
King.' I said, 'Oh.'
  Anyway, we all told jokes, and everyone laughed and a good
time was had by all. But the president is dieting. He had a little
clear soup. And just a tiny piece of roast duck, and a spoonful of

water ice. That was all. He said to me – 'You are looking very well today.' I said, 'I'm feeling lousy.'

. . .

Lots of love to all
Roald

 January 8th 1945 Temple
Texas

Dear Mama

Deep in the heart of Texas. Where the deer and the antelope roam. Cowpunchers and cattle ranchers and hillbillies and steers and bulls and cows and cowpunchers with piles because they've lived too long on a horse and miles and bloody miles of prairie and cowpunchers and cattle ranchers and hillbillies and steers and bulls and cows. And nice warm weather like April in England.

By the time you get this you'll either have a telegram telling that I've had the operation, or I won't have had it. I'm certainly being well looked after. Dr. Scott, who is a great friend of mine, is head of this huge Scott White clinic, and the town is more or less built around it. People come from all over America to go there. At the moment I'm staying in his house with his wife and two children, a very fine house with everything one wants everywhere. Yesterday and the day before, I went to the clinic for examinations and X-rays and as Arthur Scott was with me, there was no waiting anywhere, just one thing after another and with great speed and efficiency. Tomorrow I go in for final X-ray and it rather looks as though I'll have to have an operation, on the base of the spine which will keep me in bed for about four weeks. It's just something pressing on a nerve somewhere. But they are going to make absolutely sure before they do it.

I flew down here about four days ago. At least I flew to Fort Worth Texas, which takes about eight or nine hours from Washington, then Arthur S. fetched me in the car and we drove to Temple, about 150 miles. 150 miles is nothing in Texas. People drive that far just to go out to dinner in the evening.

The animals around here are deer, antelope, coyotes and rattlesnakes. That's about all. The men go out and hunt deer; and there is much venison eaten; but it isn't as good as Norwegian venison. They don't hang it up at all before eating – so it doesn't have that marvellous high taste . . .

Lots of love to all,

Roald

As I said if you haven't had a telegram before you get this I shan't have had my operation.

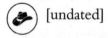 [undated] Temple
Texas

Dear Mama

I'm sitting up now, so I can write you a letter. I've been in bed now altogether two weeks and three days. I went in on a Monday and had a Lipiodol injection into my spine so that they could take some X-rays. That took a little getting over and gave me pain in my bottom and down the legs, but they operated on the following Thursday, at eight in the morning. It took them about two hours. I had a marvellous surgeon called Charles Simpson, who does brain operations as well – also there were about four other doctors in the room, one a bone grafting specialist, because they thought that they might have to take a bit of bone out of my hip and graft it to the spine; but luckily they got it done without that. The operation is called an intervertebral disc – it's where a piece of the cartilage which separates the vertebrae in your spine gets squashed inwards and presses on the nerves in the spinal column. I have had marvellous attention, because I am a great personal friend of Arthur Scott. (The Scott of Scott and White.) This is a hospital with about 300 beds, and specializing in every kind of work. It's for poor people as well as rich, and you pay according to your income. All the doctors, including the surgeons, have a fixed salary, so they treat everyone equally well – rich or poor. The only thing is that you can hire and pay for a good private room if you can afford it. I've got the best room in the place, with private bathroom and lavatory, and wireless and telephone, and a special 8 foot long bed! The nurses are very fine and always at your service.

My wound has almost stopped hurting now. It took some time because it was pretty deep; and they cut through a lot of muscles. This morning I stood up and walked a few paces, and everything was fine except for considerable pain in the nerves in my bottom, which they say is the Lipiodol, which they injected into my spine, which they will draw out again soon . . .

This is Texas ranch country round here, and there are a lot of cowboys in the hospital who have piles from sitting all their lives on a horse. I thought it was only radiators, but it seems as though it's horses as well . . .

Haven't had any letters from you since I've been here, but I expect my secretary is being slow about forwarding them from Washington. By the way, my boss was knighted in the New Year's honours – Sir William Stephenson. He works in New York.

The war news sounds marvellous. Hope it ends soon.

Lots of love to all

Roald

March 26th 1945   Scott and White Clinic Temple
                                      Texas

Dear Mama

At last they've found the trouble and I think I'm cured once and for all. I've been down here in bed now about 18 days, and have had quite a time. The business with the weights on the legs didn't help much, so as a last resort they took the Lipiodol out of my spine – and that did the trick.

It was quite a job doing it. It had to be done in the X-ray room under the fluoroscope, so they can watch what they were doing. The first time they tried under local anaesthetic they failed to get the needle in – they had to use very thick ones, because the oil is thick. Three doctors tried for 1½ hours but without success, and I personally did not enjoy it at all. Then the day before yesterday they took me up again, and gave me Pentathol – an intravenous anaesthetic, and kept me under two hours while they did the job.

Anyway they got it all out, and then I had a fairly rough night of it. My breathing when I came back to my room was apparently six to the minute. But I was given lots of glucose intravenously and also penicillin shots all through the night. The next morning – yesterday, I more or less came to and tested my legs and back and found everything cured – so in a day or two I'll be getting up and probably will be back in Washington quite fit and well in about 10 days. It was the first time that they had removed the Lipiodol in this hospital. They said that it's very rare for people to get such a reaction from having it in the spine as I had.

Anyway now I feel fine, and I've had a very pleasant time reading while I've been here. Reading Dickens, Shakespeare, the Brontes and a lot of that old stuff which I'd never read before . . .

The war news keeps sounding marvellous, but the war keeps going on. I suppose at some time or other it will just have to stop because there won't be any more of Germany to invade.

It takes a bit of time for me to get your letters down here, so I haven't had one recently. I'll probably send you a telegram tomorrow because this will probably take a bit of time to reach you.

I'm sending my book up to New York tomorrow, it is all ready, and The Gremlins is now 90 pages – a small book in itself.

Lots of love to all

Roald

 April 18th 1945   Georgetown University Hospital
Washington

Dear Mama

Today I leave this place, so you can see it has been very quick. I came in in the early hours of Saturday morning and today is Wednesday.

Well, how it happened. I had dinner Friday night with Drew Pearson and his wife (he's a famous newspaper writer) and we had for supper a piece of one of his own cows, which was called Cordell Hull.* I had two helpings also a dessert, a sort of strawberry tart so that when I got a tummy ache once afterwards I just thought that I had made a pig of myself, especially as the pain was high up in the solar plexus. Well, I played one game of backgammon with Mrs. Pearson then the tummy ache was pretty uncomfortable so I went home. I went to bed and was sick and lost Cordell Hull down the lavatory, then I was sick again and again and many times more all through the night and when bismuth didn't make it any better I thought oh hell this is some tummy ache and I said this may be an appendix so I will be careful and not take any Epsom salts, but it doesn't seem like an appendix because the pain is high up in the solar plexus.

Well at 4 AM I hadn't slept and it was worse, really quite bad, so I got up and dressed and got into my car and drove round the corner to this huge hospital – it is just around the corner – and I staggered into the main entrance and there was a nun. (A nun has just sharpened my pencil for me.) There was a nun with a large white hat like a marquee tent and I said I have a tummy ache such a terrible tummy ache and she called the nurse and I went to the emergency room and a young intern doctor came along very sleepy and took a blood count and said, 'Good God,' because it was very high, 18,000 or 20,000 or something like that, and the pulse was 120. So they wheeled me up to a ward on a stretcher, to a four bed ward where there was one other man, and I went to bed with ice on my stomach. Soon a surgeon came along and said, 'I'm

---

* Hull (1871–1955) was an American politician. The longest serving Secretary of State, he held the post for eleven years under Roosevelt between 1933 and 1944.

going to operate,' and I said, 'the quicker the better', so they operated. In the afternoon I felt all right and they told me that they just got it in time and it was a very inflamed thing, which was going to burst . . .

Today is Wednesday, and I'm going out. I'm going to Charles's Washington house where there are servants and things and I can take it easy for a bit.* But it is all very quick, quick partly because I don't want to stay here. There are two other old men in the room, one a hernia, and the other an abscess and they fart all day and have enemas and talk bull shit and then they fart some more quite openly and unashamedly just as though it was like saying good morning. It's a very good hospital, but I do prefer the Scott and White. There's no comparison. No comparison at all.

Sad news about Roosevelt, but good news about the war.†
Lots of love to all
Roald

 May 21st 1945   Palm Springs

Dear Mama

I just sent you a telegram saying I'm back in Washington after fine holiday, which is all quite true. I stayed on for a few days with Howard and Slim Hawks in Palm Springs and got fine and brown and fit and then got the US army air corps to fly me into Los Angeles. There I went and stayed in a fine house owned by Mike Romanoff, the bogus Russian prince who has the largest

---

* Charles Marsh,' Roald's friend and mentor.
† President Roosevelt died on April 12th 1945, less than a month before the war in Europe ended.

and smartest restaurant in Hollywood. It was all very comfortable with Mike's house rigged up just as he thought a Russian prince's house should be rigged up, and every kind of drink behind the bar and every kind of food in the fridge and every kind of everything everywhere else. Also his famous bulldog called Confucius who is listed in the Los Angeles telephone directory, with whom Mike holds long and serious conversations in his bedroom every morning.

'You have no idea,' said Mike, emerging from his bedroom the first day, 'of the terribly rude things that Confucius has just said to me.'

'No,' I said. 'I haven't.'

'He said I was a shitty old Russian prince.' And Mike went back to his room mumbling to himself. But it was fine staying there.

Well, that's sad news about Bestemama, but somehow I almost guessed it. I was certain that she was not alive. Anyway I expect that it made it a lot easier for the Tantes to live through the occupation . . .

I'll try to get lipsticks stockings etc. for Asta and the others.
Lots of love to all
Roald

July 7th 1945   Box 55 Terminal A, Toronto

Dear Mama

Seeing Niagara Falls made me want to pee. This job will take 2–3 months after which hope to make trip home.
Love to all
Roald

273

○ August 1st 1945   Box 55 Terminal A, Toronto

Dear Mama

Have a letter from you and two from Asta. One is very long
and interesting, the other telling me that there is a vacancy as
Assistant Air Attaché in Oslo for someone with a Permanent
Commission. Well, I couldn't face that, being in uniform all my
life, so I won't apply – not that I could get away right now
anyway. This job is more important.

No news here as usual. Lovely weather. I'm browner than I've
ever been before, really nut brown, and the back slowly but
surely getting better . . .

Lots of love to all – and Nicholas*
Roald

 December 20th 1945   BSC Room 3553
630 5th Avenue
NY

Dear Mama

Christmas is coming and the weather is getting cold. Indeed,
it is as cold as buggery in New York right now, many degrees
below freezing and yesterday we had 8 inches of snow. But I still
managed to drive around in my fine car.

Now the news is that I'm coming home again – this time for
good. My work finishes here at the end of the year, then I'm
going off for two or three weeks in January to try and rewrite the
Gremlins and get that finished. I'll be sailing home I should say
about the end of January.

---

* Roald's nephew, Nicholas Logsdail.

274

Now as this is positively the last chance you have of my bringing stuff over, you had all better make out an enormous list of everything that you want. One can buy almost anything and I'll be able to bring it with me in trunks or packing cases, although there may be some duty. And for any large items you can pay me at home. Better make it a full list, including clothes with complete details as to size (does John or Leslie for example want a jacket or flannel trousers, does anyone want shoes). You want things like mixmasters. Does anyone want saucepans etc. etc.?

So let's have a full list, with nothing left out . . . I've got plenty of money to buy the stuff.

Otherwise no news, I think.

Lots of love to all

Roald

EPILOGUE

―――

'I won't write often'

1946–1965

Roald returned from the USA early in 1946, aged twenty-nine. He moved in with his mother and his youngest sister, Asta, at Grange Farm, a remote homestead near Great Missenden. It was later owned by the British Prime Minister, Harold Wilson. Then, when Asta married and Sofie Magdalene's arthritis deteriorated, mother and son together moved to Wistaria Cottage, a large house on the High Street of nearby Old Amersham.

There, Roald bred racing greyhounds, poached pheasants in the local woods and listened obsessively to classical music. In 1947 a press release described his main hobby as, 'listening for hours to his favourite symphonies, played on an elaborate built-in recording machine'.[69] The following year he completed his first novel *Some Time Never*, a fantastical Swiftian satire depicting the destruction of the human race following a nuclear holocaust. Its main human protagonist was a thinly disguised portrait of the book's author: a demobbed pilot turned music critic. The other main characters were gremlins. It was not well reviewed. Roald's second novel, *Fifty Thousand Frogskins*, completed in 1951, was a dystopian vision of post-war rural Britain, set against a backdrop of illegal greyhound racing and populated with a cast of small-time crooks and chancers. When his publishers refused to publish the book, Roald lost his nerve. He took to his heels, flying to New York, where his friend Charles Marsh secured him a job working for his charity, the Public Welfare Foundation.

So, after a five-year absence, Roald found himself once again regularly writing to his mother. But the tone of his letters had changed. His correspondence was calmer and more matter-of-fact. In New York, he reinvented himself as a writer of grand guignol short stories with strange twisted plots. The breathless energy that had once animated his letters home now found its natural outlet in his fiction. Alfred Hitchcock started to dramatise them for television and soon the American press had dubbed Roald, the Master of the Macabre. In his letters home he enthusiastically reported back to his mother how well his books were now selling and how he had begun to make proper money from them, while also gossiping about mutual friends, enquiring about the health of his greyhounds, offering advice on the purchase of stocks and shares and lamenting the extortionate cost of dog food.

He remained reticent about anything too personal. He barely mentioned his engagement to the Hungarian divorcee, Suzanne Horvath, or the subsequent break-up of that relationship. Nor did he say much about the romance with his future wife, the actress Patricia Neal, which began when he went to see rehearsals of a revival of his friend Lillian Hellman's play *The Children's Hour*. His announcement of their marriage, for example, was characteristically bluff.

 May 23rd 1953   from 9 E 62nd St

Dear Mama

Thanks for the letter. I'll get the stockings for you and the mineral water gadgets, although I may give them to someone else to take as we are going to Italy and France first.

Here's a couple of pictures of Pat I had in my drawer. I'll get hold of some better ones soon and let you have. We think it might be a good idea if we got married before we leave, so we'll probably do that. She insists on a church, so if I can find one

Roald Dahl and Patricia Neal on honeymoon in Rome, 1953.
'I hope she will like the Dahl family, which is a bit out of the
ordinary,' Sofie Magdalene wrote to Claudia Marsh. 'I am sure
Roald wants a family,' she added, 'as he is unusually fond of and
good with children, but that is their business and not mine'

small enough and far enough away from the reporters etc., it'll be
okay with me. Except for Charles and Claudia [Marsh] (who are
very keen on this thing) I don't expect we'll have more than four
or five people. Pat's mother and sister may come up from Tennessee,
but it's a long way. Don't know any date, but as we're flying to
Rome on 3 July it'll probably be a day or so before.

. . . Charles has insisted on donating a huge yellow sapphire
ring, about 20 carats, which is very decent of him.

Give my love to Tante Astrid and Ellen if they are there.

Love

Roald

Pat, Olivia, Roald and Tessa on holiday in Norway,
1958. There he started to work on his first children's
book, James and the Giant Peach

Roald and Pat got married in New York in the summer of 1953. They honeymooned in Europe, eventually arriving in England where they stayed with Sofie Magdalene in Wistaria Cottage for several weeks, before returning to America in the autumn. The following year, Roald decided to come back to England and bought a cottage near his mother, which he later renamed Gipsy House. Sofie Magdalene helped fund its purchase. It would become her son's home for the rest of his life.

Roald's first child Olivia was born in 1955 and that year he embarked on a peripatetic existence between Buckinghamshire and the USA. Normally the family spent spring and summer in Great Missenden, returning to New York in the autumn, as Pat was often working there. Their second daughter Tessa was born in 1957 and a son Theo in 1960. Becoming a parent acted as a catalyst on Roald's desire to write for young people and in 1959 his first children's book, *James and the Giant Peach*, was published in the USA.

While in America, Roald was always in regular correspondence with his mother, who, in his absence, continued to supervise the maintenance of the Gipsy House garden, as well as any domestic repairs and renovations that were needed. Even after a severe fall, which resulted in her being confined to a wheelchair and moving in with her daughter Else's family, Sofie Magdalene was always on hand to advise and offer guidance.

In December 1960 disaster struck. The pram carrying Roald's four-month-old son was hit by a New York cab and crushed against the side of a bus. Theo suffered terrible head injuries and almost died. For three years Roald and Pat were in a constant state of anxiety, because the tube that drained excess fluid from their son's cranial cavity kept blocking. When that happened his head would swell dramatically, leading to blindness, fitting and potential brain damage. These blockages happened seven times over the first nine months after the accident and each of these alarming episodes resulted in major surgery under a general anaesthetic.

Roald decided he would devise a more efficient valve that did not block so often, and so he approached his son's neurosurgeon, Kenneth Till, and a model aeroplane engineer called Stanley Wade to help him. The resulting Dahl–Wade–Till valve transformed that aspect of paediatric head injuries. It was used on more than 3,000 children around the world, before it was eventually superseded. Sofie Magdalene too played her part in the early stages of its development.

February 16th 1961   New York

Dear Mama

Theo's tube blocked up again and we took him to the hospital at eight o'clock this morning. His sight was failing, but hadn't quite gone.

They're just finished operating, and the valve at the end of the tube in his heart was faulty and had allowed blood to get in – therefore to block it. They have now put in a new tube, but this time into the pleura, the lung, not the heart.

Pat and I going out again soon. Very distressing, the whole thing.

Love

Roald

Sofie Magdalene in the conservatory of her annexe at Roald's sister, Else's house near Great Missenden, 1961. In the foreground is Roald's son Theo, who was still recovering from the injuries he had received the previous year when a rogue New York taxi crushed him against the side of a bus

February 18th   New York

Dear Mama

Saw Theo at lunchtime today, and Pat, who finished work at 4 PM, has just phoned saying that she is up there now at the hospital. (It's 5:30 PM.) He's made a good recovery from this very uncomfortable operation, and the tube appears to be draining well. His sight is coming back slowly, and he can see a person at about 8 feet. He is beginning to take milk and to keep it down, and is moderately cheerful. In fact, altogether as good as can be expected.

I don't think much of the tubes that they use here for this work, particularly the valve at the lower end, which is meant to open up between 40 mm and 80 mm water column pressure. This valve is literally nothing but a slit in the plastic tube. The thing is made by a small lab in Pasadena, California, and is called the Pudenz-Heyer shunt valve. Do they have anything better in England, something less likely to block and clog? If Ellen gets a chance, could she please ask Wylie?* I don't understand how that Kyle chap has gone along with so little trouble. Everyone here has blockages all the time. What valve do the English put into a) the heart, and most important, (b) the pleura? Does Wylie have a lot of blockages?

I broke my ankle two weeks ago in the snow and forgot to tell you. I went to a place I know and got an X-ray for five dollars, and the doctor friend read it for me. They wanted to take me to hospital and put the bloody thing in plaster, but I refused. It's mending now, but it hurt like hell for twelve days, walking on it.

---

* Wylie McKissock (1906–94) was a pioneering British neurosurgeon. Theo became his patient when the Dahls returned to England.

Please thank Asta for her letter, arrived today. Everyone else
here is well.

Love

Roald

Theo's accident confirmed Roald in his view that New York
was no place to raise a family and from then on Great
Missenden became his permanent year-round base. He had
constructed a writing hut in the orchard at the bottom of his
garden as a sanctuary from his children and was just beginning
to settle into a new story there, when, in 1962, he was
stricken by the greatest misfortune of his life. His eldest
daughter Olivia died unexpectedly of complications from
measles. She was seven years old. Sofie Magdalene had of
course gone through the same experience herself forty years
earlier, yet there was little she could do to help him. From her
annexe in Else's house, ten minutes' drive away, she gave him
what solace she could. But only time could ever begin to heal
that wound.

1964 was a happier year. It saw the birth of another daughter,
Ophelia, the publication of Roald's second children's story,
Charlie and the Chocolate Factory, and Pat winning a Best Actress
Oscar for her role in *Hud*. But the following February the
family faced the third of its terrible reversals. Three months
pregnant with their fifth child, Pat suffered a major stroke in
Los Angeles, while shooting John Ford's last movie, *Seven
Women*. She was in a coma for three weeks. On February 20th
the *Los Angeles Herald Examiner* reported that there was 'little
hope' for her. Two days later *Variety* ran the headline, 'Film
Actress Patricia Neal Dies at 39'.

But Pat was a fighter. She did not die. On March 10th,

*Roald, Theo and a young friend laying flowers on the intricate
alpine garden Roald constructed around his seven-year-
old daughter Olivia's grave. On the headstone was carved
the inscription 'She stands before me as a living child'*

almost three weeks after the haemorrhage that nearly killed her,
she began to regain consciousness. Her doctors had warned
Roald that if Pat came out of the coma she was likely to be 'a
vegetable' for the rest of her life, but Roald was determined that
he would do whatever he could to restore her health. His
pioneering intensive therapy yielded amazing results and within
three years Pat was back at work and had even been nominated
for another Oscar. Her baby, Lucy, had been delivered safely in
the summer of 1965.

Throughout the early stages of her recovery, Roald wrote
regularly to Sofie Magdalene, informing his eighty-year-old

mother of Pat's progress with characteristic bluntness and lack of sentimentality. The childish need to sugar-coat adversity and protect her from bad news had given way to the understanding that she was someone on whom he could always rely for clear-headed advice and assistance. Mother and son were made of the same material and shared the same practical outlook on life. This was the final crisis they would face together.

 Saturday

13515 Romany Drive
Pacific Palisades
California

Dear Mama

It happened like this: Pat came home from the studio at around 5:30. She felt good. At six she had one martini. At six-thirty she went upstairs to bath Tessa. Five minutes later, Sheena called me up. I found her sitting on the bed. She said, 'I have a terrible pain between the eyes, and I've been having hallucinations. I think I am ill.' I at once found the home phone number of a neuro-surgeon I've been working with on our valve (a top neurosurgeon in Los Angeles), and I called him. I said, 'Come at once.' As I was speaking to him, Pat lost consciousness and was sick. Charles Carton (the neurosurgeon) said he would send an ambulance at once and he himself would go to the Emergency entrance of the U.C.L.A. Hospital. The ambulance came in 10 minutes. I rode in it with Pat. We got her to the hospital altogether within 25 minutes of her feeling the pain. Charles Carton was waiting. By then Pat had come round and could talk, but her memory had gone. Dr Carton examined her. He said he found no real evidence of cerebral haemorrhage. 'Perhaps she has had a seizure,' he said. The fact was that we had got her there so quickly that the real signs (stiff neck etc.) hadn't had time to develop. I went in to see her. While I was there, she had another haemorrhage and passed out. I called in Dr. Carton. He did a spinal tap on the spot. It showed the spinal fluid scarlet with blood. He rushed her up to X-ray. They injected contrast medium into her neck arteries and took photos. While they were taking them, she had her third and largest haemorrhage. The X-raying took 2 ½ hours. When I was called in to inspect the pictures, it was about 10.30pm. They showed a massive haemorrhage in an artery over the left frontal lobe. Dr Carton said to me, 'If we operate she will probably not survive. Her respiratory system will pack up.' I said, 'What will happen if you don't operate?' He said, 'Then she will die for certain.' So I said, 'You must operate at once.' He agreed. It took an hour to prepare her for the op., and they actually started at midnight. At seven in the morning it was finished, including a tracheotomy, and they brought her up into the 'Intensive Care Unit'. She had stood it well. Lungs still functioning etc.

This morning, ten days later, she is, as you know, still unconscious. But there are signs of her beginning to come closer to the surface. She opens an eye occasionally (though probably doesn't register anything she sees), and she squeezes one's hand, though here again, it is doubtful if this is anything more than an involuntary action.

This morning's spinal tap showed the fluid becoming far clearer and less bloody. And now all we can do is wait and see.

She has very little use of her right side, right arm and leg, but there is some response in it to stimulation. The left side is okay. The face is unaffected and looks normal. But the hemisphere where the bleeding took place is the speech control, and that may well be damaged. That, of course, is looking far ahead. The first thing is to get her back to consciousness.

Sheena, Angela, and masses of friends have all been wonderful.* There is no trouble about running the house. I am mostly at the hospital. I get there first at 6.30 a.m., see the doctors, come back for breakfast, then return. I make my last visit at 10 p.m., and stay till 11.

Tessa is very good, but obviously disturbed. We are keeping her busy. She goes out all the time to play with friends' children when she is not at school. She goes to school mornings only, and comes home for lunch. Theo also goes to nursery school mornings.

That's about all except that Pat couldn't be in a better hospital. She's getting fantastic attention, and every possible medical aid.

I won't write often. Cables and telephone are better.

I don't know what to say about the work on our house. My inclination is to let them go on with it, and if that is what they are doing, and if they are prepared to do it, I would let them go ahead.

Love to all
Roald

Roald's very last letter to his mother dates from this period. It was written just before he returned home from Pacific Palisades with Pat and the children. A British magazine had offered to redecorate Gipsy House while the family were away. Sofie Magdalene was keeping an eye on the progress of the works and wrote to him warning him that she did not think he would like what the decorators were doing. They were stripping out old floorboards and antique tiles, installing

* Sheena Burt was at the time the family nanny. Angela Kirwan was helping her.

bookcases with fake books, and painting the walls brown. Roald assured her that everything would be okay. But it wasn't. When he returned home, he found that – just as his mother had warned him – he had to undo almost everything that had been changed. He later complained to the magazine that the walls had been painted 'the colour of elephant's turds'.[70]

Despite age and infirmity, Sofie Magdalene could still teach her headstrong son a thing or two. He knew that. And so did she. Roald paid a moving tribute to her in the cookbook he wrote with his second wife, Liccy, just before he died in 1990:

> She was the matriarch, the mater familias, and her children radiated around her like planets round a sun. In some families children rebel and go as far away as possible from the parents, especially after they are married, because mothers-in-law are not always popular in the household. But with Mama's children and their marriage partners there was a genuine desire to keep this remarkable old parent within reach.[71]

When Sofie Magdalene herself had died twenty-three years earlier, in 1967, Roald had been in hospital and too ill to attend her funeral. His sisters scattered her ashes near the grave in Radyr where her husband Harald and her daughter Astri were buried. Roald did not mourn her. Indeed it was twenty years before he visited the gravesite. Her redoubtable spirit surely continued within him. Yet the absence of any of her letters in Roald's archive is perplexing. For a man who kept so much correspondence, it is doubly surprising that not one letter survived and it leaves one wondering, who was this mysterious, missing correspondent?

Of course, his side of the correspondence reveals much about her. She was private. She could be obstinate. She shared his fascination with invention, his scurrilous sense of humour and delight in a dirty joke. She gave wise advice and unstinting love. She celebrated self-control and lack of sentimentality. She was calm and level-headed in a crisis. Through war and separation, right up to her own end, she was a loyal, tireless, phlegmatic and unshockable correspondent.

In all this, mother and son were very much alike. In their later correspondence there is often a confessional tone, a sense that Roald is talking to himself. His letters are honest, unvarnished, almost like entries in a diary. The famous Dahl imagination, the sense of wonder and fantasy, the madcap humour, the naughtiness – the elements, in short, that characterise his children's fiction – are almost entirely absent. By contrast, the earlier letters – which make up the bulk of this collection – are quite different. They are brimful of these qualities.

In this they reflect the fact that Sofie Magdalene was Roald's first reader. More than anyone else, it was she who encouraged him to tell stories and nourished his desire to fabricate, exaggerate and entertain. Reading these letters, one often has the impression of a writer flexing his storytelling muscles, a sense that a literary apprentice is rehearsing, practising, honing his craft. To use an analogy that Roald himself might have appreciated, we are watching a trainee pilot preparing to fly solo. In this, Sofie Magdalene was an essential and invaluable foil. Without her unique sensibility to guide him, Roald might have returned to work for Shell after the war and eventually retired as a senior executive to play golf, drink whisky and crack jokes. Such timeless tales as *The BFG*, *Matilda*, *Fantastic Mr Fox* and *The Witches* might never have seen the light of day.

Thankfully that did not happen. And Sofie Magdalene, who would probably have preferred her son to work in an oil company, instead became unwitting midwife to his development as a writer. Without her correspondence and without the vicissitudes of war, Roald might never have embraced that literary destiny his 1938 horoscope had predicted. And, for that, we all have reason to be grateful.

ACKNOWLEDGEMENTS

This book is the work of many hands. Thanks are due in particular to Rachel White, the archivist of the Roald Dahl Museum and Story Centre, and to her predecessor Jane Branfield for making the letters and so many photographs available to me over the course of the last ten years. Barney Samson and Diane Sullivan kindly helped in the transcriptions of the originals. I owe a lot to their patience, care and industry.

Over an even longer period, many members of Roald's family helped me put the letters in context, most notably Roald's three sisters Alfhild, Else and Asta, who kindly gave me long interviews before they died. I used these in my biography *Storyteller* and the information gathered from them has been invaluable to this book as well. Roald's children Tessa, Theo, Ophelia and Lucy also gave generously of their time, as did both of Roald's wives, Patricia Neal and Liccy Dahl. Ophelia, in particular, was a huge force of encouragement behind the scenes. Roald's nephew Nicholas Logsdail and his nieces Alexandra Anderson, Anna Corrie, Astrid Newman and Lou Pearl gave me invaluable assistance as well. I am grateful to all of them for their support.

I also owe thanks to others, who I consulted while researching *Storyteller* and whose interviews helped put letters in context. These include: Jonathan Cuneo, Nancy Deuchar, Tim Fisher, Deb Ford, Douglas Highton and Charles Pringle.

From the Roald Dahl Literary Estate, Amanda Conquy supported my initial proposal for a book of Roald's letters and her successor, Roald's grandson, Luke Kelly, has been the most intelligent, sensible, sensitive and perceptive of collaborators imaginable. I feel immensely lucky to have had his involvement on this intriguing and strangely daunting project.

Kate Craigie, Nick Davies and Rosie Gailer at John Murray have worked tirelessly to make the book happen as have my agent, Caroline Dawnay and her assistant Sophie Scard and Anthony Goff at David Higham. I owe them all thanks, as I do to Justin Somper and John Collins for their energy and enthusiasm in promoting it. I am grateful too to the design team at Sunshine for their clear and witty maps and icons.

I am grateful to Walt Disney for permission to reproduce photographs and images connected with *The Gremlins*.

SOURCES AND ILLUSTRATION CREDITS

Almost all the letters, photographs, and illustrations in *Love from Boy* come courtesy of the Roald Dahl Museum and Story Centre in Great Missenden (RDMSC). It is the source of many of the references as well. Other reference sources used include The Public Record Office (PRO), The Farrar, Straus and Giroux Archives in New York (FSG), The Watkins Loomis Collection in the Library of Columbia University, New York (WLC), the archives of Jonathan Cape at Reading University, and the private papers of Charles Marsh, the custody of which is currently in the hands of his great grandson, Andrew Haskell.

Photograph of Montgomery Blair High School Victory Corps, page 217, courtesy of Library of Congress Prints & Photographs Division, Washington (LC-USE6-D-006480), photograph by Howard Lieberman. Photograph of Roald Dahl and Ernest Hemingway, page 257 © Bettman/Corbis. Sketches and photographs, pages 235 and 270 © Disney Enterprises, Inc. Photograph of Pat Neal (pregnant) and Roald in the conservatory of Sofie Magdalene's house, page 277, by Leonard McCombe/Time & Life Pictures/Getty Images.

NOTES

INTRODUCTION

1. Roald Dahl, *Boy*, Jonathan Cape, 1984, pp.76–7.
2. Tessa Dahl, conversation with Donald Sturrock, 22 October 2007; Astri Newman, conversation with Donald Sturrock, 15 October 2007 and Else Logsdail, 'Casseroled Ptarmigan' in Felicity and Roald Dahl, *Memories with Food at Gipsy House*, London, Viking, 1991, reprinted as *The Roald Dahl Cookbook*, Penguin, 1996, p.61.
3. J. Harry Williams, letter to Roald Dahl, 2 October 1976 – Roald Dahl Museum and Story Centre RD 16/1/2.
4. Alfhild Hansen, conversation with Donald Sturrock, 7 August 1992.
5. Sofie Magdalene Dahl, letter to Claudia Marsh, 16 January 1955 – Andrew Haskell Collection.
6. Louise Pearl, conversation with Donald Sturrock, 9 May 2008.
7. Roald Dahl, *Boy*, p.21.
8. Ibid.
9. Asta Anderson, conversation with Donald Sturrock, 1997.
10. Roald Dahl, *Boy*, p.53.
11. Felicity and Roald Dahl, *Memories with Food at Gipsy House*, p.65.
12. Ibid.
13. Ibid.

14. Alfhild Hansen, interviewed in *A Dose of Dahl's Magic Medicine*, 28 September 1986.
15. Valerie Kettley, internal memo to Tom Maschler – Jonathan Cape archive, 'BOY' file, University of Reading.
16. Stephen Roxburgh, memo to Tom Maschleer – Jonathan Cape 'Boy' file, University of Reading.

A NOTE ON SPELLING AND PUNCTUATION

17. Roald Dahl, letter to schoolchildren, 17 April 1984 – RDMSC.

CHAPTER 1: 1925–1929
'Send me some conkers'

18. Roald Dahl, *Boy*, p.81.
19. Ibid., p.72.
20. Ibid., p.73.
21. Douglas Highton (1915–2013), interview with Donald Sturrock, 8 November 2007.
22. Roald Dahl, *Boy*, p.77.
23. Roald Dahl, *Matilda*, London, Jonathan Cape, 1988, p.106.
24. Ibid., p.109.
25. Ibid., p.117.

CHAPTER 2: 1930–1934
'Graggers on your eggs'

26. Air Marshal Sir Charles Pringle, conversation with Donald Sturrock, 5 December 2007.

27. Tim Fisher, conversation with Donald Sturrock, 17 September 2007.
28. Roald Dahl, *Boy,* p.128.
29. Roald Dahl, *Boy (First Draft)* – RDMSC RD 2/23/1/166.
30. Ibid. – RDMSC RD 2/23/1/159.
31. Sofie Magdalene Dahl, postcards to Else Dahl, 27 June 1930 – RDMSC RD 20/9/2 and RD 20/9/3.
32. Air Marshal Sir Charles Pringle, conversation with Donald Sturrock, 5 December 2007.
33. Nancy Deuchar (née Jenkyns), conversation with Donald Sturrock, 4 December 2007.
34. Roald Dahl, letter to his mother, June 1931 – RDMSC RD 13/1/6/43.
35. Alfhild Hansen, conversation with Donald Sturrock, 7 August 1992.
36. Nancy Deuchar, conversation with Donald Sturrock, 4 December 2007.
37. Roald Dahl, 'Things I Wish I'd Known when I was Eighteen', unpublished article for the *Sunday Express Magazine* – RDMSC RD 1/2/7/1.
38. Roald Dahl, letter to his mother, 4 February 1934 – RDMSC RD 13/1/9/24.

CHAPTER 3: 1935–1939
'Another iced lager'

39. Else Logsdail, conversation with Donald Sturrock, 3 January 1998.
40. Roald Dahl, letter to his mother, 14 July 1936 – RDMSC RD 14/2/2/8.
41. Dahl later relocated the story to wartime Greece and it was eventually published as 'Yesterday was Beautiful'.
42. Alexandra Anderson, conversation with Donald Sturrock, 14 November 2007.

43. Letter from Emma to Sofie Magdalene Dahl, 4 October 1938 – RDMSC RD 14/3/4/1.
44. Roald Dahl, *Going Solo*, London, Jonathan Cape, 1986, p.32.
45. Roald Dahl, speech to boys at Repton School, 21 November 1975 – RDMSC RD 6/1/1/25.
46. Roald Dahl, *Going Solo*, p.87.

CHAPTER 4: 1939–1940
'Thoroughly good for the soul'

47. Roald Dahl, *The Minpins,* London, Jonathan Cape, 1991, p.41.
48. Roald Dahl, *James and the Giant Peach*, New York, Alfred Knopf, 1961, p.95.
49. Roald Dahl, *Going Solo*, p.96.

CHAPTER 5: 1940–1941
'Don't worry'

50. PRO Air 27, 669.
51. Roald Dahl, *Going Solo*, p.105.
52. Roald Dahl, letter to his mother, 20 November 1940 – RDMSC RD 14/4/38.
53. Roald Dahl, *Going Solo*, p.105.
54. Ophelia Dahl, *Memories of My Father* (unpublished manuscript).
55. Roald Dahl, letter to Barbara McDonald, 24 April 1953, now in the possession of the Roald Dahl Museum and Story Centre.
56. Roald Dahl, letter to Stephen Roxburgh, undated – Farrar, Straus and Giroux archive, New York.
57. 'Jonah' Jones, C.O. of 84 Squadron, cited in T.H. Wisdom, *Wings over Olympus, The Story of the Royal Air Force in Libya and Greece*, London, George Allen and Unwin, 1942, p.169.

58. Roald Dahl, 'Katina' from *Collected Stories*, Everyman, pp.26–7.
59. Roald Dahl, 'Searching for Mr. Smith', Browse and Darby Catalogue, 1983

CHAPTER 6: 1942–1943
'Teeth like piano keys'

60. Roald Dahl, *The Gremlins*, New York, Walt Disney/Random House, 1943.
61. Jeremy Treglown, *Roald Dahl*, Harcourt, Brace, 1994, p.56.
62. William Stevenson, *A Man Called Intrepid*, Lyons Press, 1976, p.169.
63. Isaiah Berlin, interview with Jeremy Treglown, in Jeremy Treglown, *Roald Dahl*, p.69.

CHAPTER 7: 1943–1945
'A good time was had by all'

64. Bill Macdonald, *The True Intrepid*, Raincoast Books, p. 200.
65. Roald Dahl, *Visit to Hyde Park* – RDMSC RD 15/5/94/5.
66. Jonathan Cuneo, conversation with Donald Sturrock, 20 March 2007.

EPILOGUE:
'I won't write often'

67. Ernest Cuneo Papers Box 107, CIA file – Franklin Delano Roosevelt Library, Hyde Park. Cited in Thomas E. Mahl, *Desperate Deception – British Covert Operations in the US 1939–44*, Brassey's, 1998.

68. Roald Dahl, Draft Author Biography for Reynall and Hitchcock, 4 July 1945 – RDMSC RD 1/1/222.
69. *Saturday Evening Post*, Vol. 3, No. 39, 13 September 1947 – WLC Box 22.
70. Patricia Neal, interview with Stephen Michael Shearer, June 2005. Cited in Shearer, *Patricia Neal, An Unquiet Life*, Louisville, University Press of Kentucky, 2006, p.261.
71. Felicity and Roald Dahl, *Memories with Food at Gipsy House*, Viking, 1991, reprinted as *The Roald Dahl Cookbook*, Penguin, 1996, p.66.

From Byron, Austen and Darwin

to some of the most acclaimed and original contemporary writing, John Murray takes pride in bringing you powerful, prizewinning, absorbing and provocative books that will entertain you today and become the classics of tomorrow.

We put a lot of time and passion into what we publish and how we publish it, and we'd like to hear what you think.

Be part of John Murray – share your views with us at:

www.johnmurray.co.uk

 johnmurraybooks

 @johnmurrays

 johnmurraybooks

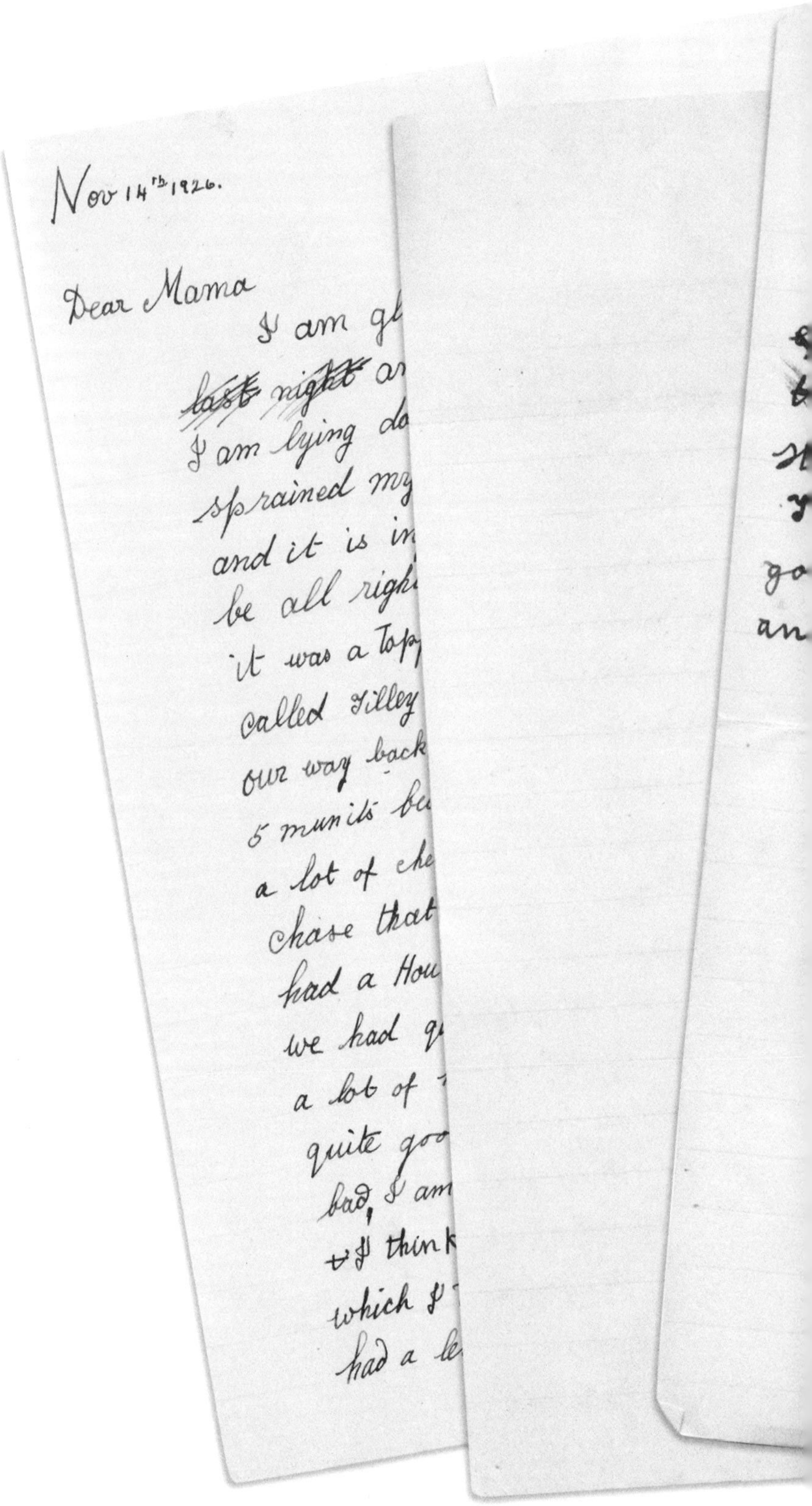

Nov 14th 1926.

Dear Mama

    I am gl

~~last night~~ ar

I am lying do

sprained my

and it is in

be all righ

it was a To

called Tilley

our way back

5 munits be

a lot of che

chase that

had a Hou

we had g

a lot of

quite goo

bad, I am

& I think

which I

had a le